Critical Studies in the History of Anthropology   Series Editors: Regna Darnell, Stephen O. Murray

Ruth Landes

Sally Cole

Ruth Landes
A Life in Anthropology

University of Nebraska Press : Lincoln & London

Permission to quote from Ruth
Benedict's and Margaret Mead's
correspondence with Ruth Landes
has been granted by the Institute for Intercultural Studies, Inc.,
New York. Permission to quote
from Melville J. Herskovits's correspondence with Ruth Landes
and Guy Johnson has been granted
by Dr. Jean Herskovits. Permission to quote from Ruth Landes's
personal correspondence has
been granted by Lambros Comitas,
Literary Executor.
Book design by Richard Eckersley.
Typeset in Enschedé Trinité

Library of Congress Cataloging-in-Publication Data
Cole, Sally Cooper, 1951–
Ruth Landes : a life in anthropology / Sally Cole.
p. cm. – (Critical studies in the history of anthropology)
Includes bibliographical references and index.
ISBN 0-8032-1522-3 (cloth : alkaline paper)
1. Landes, Ruth, 1908–1992 2. Anthropologists – United
States – Biography. 3. Women anthropologists.
I. Title. II. Series.
GN21.L36C65 2003 301'.092–dc21 [[B]] 2003040996

To My Parents
  Jean Murray Cole and Alfred Cooper Cole

Contents

List of Illustrations viii
Series Editors' Introduction ix
Acknowledgments xv
Introduction 1

Part One: Beginnings

1 Immigrant Daughter 19
2 New Woman 37
3 Student at Columbia 49

Part Two: Apprenticeship in Native American Worlds

Prologue 65
4 Maggie Wilson and Ojibwa Women's Stories 71
5 Lusty Shamans in the Midwest 109

Part Three: She-Bull in Brazil's China Closet

Prologue 149
6 Fieldwork in Brazil 155
7 Writing Afro-Brazilian Culture in New York 179
8 The Early Ethnography of Race and Gender 203
Conclusion: Life and Career 227

Notes 253
Bibliography 275
Index 293

LIST OF ILLUSTRATIONS

following page 142
1. Ruth Landes, 1912
2. Ruth's parents
3. Joseph Schlossberg, Ruth, and "Mattie"
4. Anna Grossman, Ruth, and "Mattie"
5. Brookwood School graduation, 1924
6. Ruth, summer 1929
7. Ruth Benedict
8. Ruth at Red Lake, 1933
9. Maggie Wilson
10. Will Rogers
11. In the garden, Museu Nacional de Rio de Janeiro
12. Sabina's festa de Iemanja, Bahia
13. A Festa da Lavagem do Bonfim, Bahia
14. Edison Carneiro
15. E. S. Imes
16. Ruth in London, 1951
17. Ruth in Los Angeles, 1963

Series Editors' Introduction

IF TO LIVE in interesting times is a curse, it was one that beset Ruth Landes (née Schlossberg). As an unconventional participant observer of Afro-Brazilian culture and a Jew in an increasingly Nazi-sympathizing Brazil during the 1930s, she made the times in that place still more interesting. In many ways her stay in Brazil before World War II resembled that of the Ingrid Bergman character during the war in Alfred Hitchcock's classic film *Notorious*. Landes was branded as "notorious" for nonmarital sexual relations (and for "betraying" her class and race in associating with the black "lower orders"). There were spies and wild accusations of spying (these led to Landes's expulsion from Brazil). She had a suave and romantic champion (a darker Cary Grant type), and her enemies tended to be connected to local Nazis and Nazi sympathizers.

After the very interesting time in Brazil Landes had a long afterlife as a marginal anthropologist, not securing a stable position until 1965, three full decades after earning her Ph.D. from Columbia University, and then at what she considered a Canadian backwater (McMaster University in Hamilton, Ontario). As Sally Cole's perceptive and massively researched biography shows, being a woman in a man's world was less of a problem for Landes than underestimating the will to dominance of those whom she supposed were on the same side as she, other inter–World War students of Franz Boas.

Not just Landes's field results but also her living among her subjects and doing participant observation in Afro-Brazilian Bahia challenged the patronizing Brazilian authority on "Negroes," Artur Ramos, who never got his hands dirty visiting the slums. Ramos was allied with American anthropologist Melville J. Herskovits, who was claiming for himself paramount authority for identifying what was African in the cultures of "the new World Negro" and whose genteel mixing with the local elites and gathering folklore and ideal norms in verandah interviews in West Africa, the Caribbean, and Brazil was also vulnerable to dismissal within the emerging standards for the more intensive, more participant, and more protracted fieldwork of Landes and Zora Neale Hurston, which showed divergences from idealized norms in social practice and in lived experiences in various cultures. Whether or not Herskovits was personally shocked that a fellow anthropologist of New York Jewish background had a sexual relationship with an Afro-Brazilian (and, earlier, an African American professor at the black Fisk University), he and Ramos knew how to leak the information and innuendo to discredit Landes to those who would be appalled.

Without ever seeming to recognize the underlying motivations of Herskovits, Landes was aware that he was maligning her. Less visibly — and therefore more insidiously — another of the postwar cohort of Boasians, Margaret Mead, was also systematically undercutting Landes and blocking a potential rival with better claims than hers to have done real participant observation. Whereas Landes worked within the (vast) territory Herskovits claimed, she did not work in the geographical area (Oceania) Mead did. Hindering a professional career for Landes maintained Herskovits's empire and Mead's position as the public woman anthropologist and, in particular, as authoritative explicator of sex and gender to Americans. (At least when they were in graduate school, Herskovits and Mead were close friends, and to some extent she may have been aiding him in keeping Landes scrambling and peripheral. One gets the impression that Mead was also vying for the easily scattered attentions of Ruth Benedict, mentor to them both: gossip was one means of getting Benedict's attention.)

After her adventures and misadventures in Brazil and her besmirchment by Ramos, Herskovits, and Mead, Landes worked with Gunnar Myrdal on the Carnegie Institute's project that became *An American Dilemma* and wrote what seems in retrospect to have been a premature reflexive ethnography (as well as one that looked directly at class in the purported "racial democracy" of Brazil). Both before and after her Brazilian work, Landes made important contributions to the study of contemporary Native American/First Nations peoples on both sides of the U.S.-Canadian border, pioneering in telling the stories of women of aboriginal North American societies, as well as those of candomblé "mothers and fathers of the spirits" in her vividly experience-near *City of Women*, which Cole has introduced to a new generation that is better able to understand description of the power and class dimensions in ongoing societies.

As in the earlier case of Edward Sapir (see Darnell 1976, 1990; Murray 1981), Landes bemoaned isolation in Canada but produced more research publications in "exile" than in the bustle of large American cities (metropolitan New York and Chicago for Sapir, New York and Los Angeles for Landes). Five of the eight books Landes authored or edited were published during her first six years at McMaster (along with her M.A. thesis, "Negro Jews in Harlem"). As Cole shows, Landes's professional career may not have started in earnest until she was 56 years old, but before then she had all-too-interesting relationships with other famous social analysts.

Regna Darnell and Stephen O. Murray

It is not by the direct method of a scrupulous narration that the explorer of the past can hope to depict that singular epoch. If he is wise, he will adopt a subtler strategy. He will attack his subject in unexpected places; he will fall upon the flank, or the rear; he will shoot a sudden, revealing searchlight into obscure recesses, hitherto undivined. He will row out over that great ocean of material, and lower down into it, here and there, a little bucket, which will bring up to the light of day some characteristic specimen, from those far depths, to be examined with a careful curiosity. Guided by these considerations, I have written the ensuing studies. . . . I have sought to examine and elucidate certain fragments of the truth which took my fancy and lay to my hand.

Lytton Strachey, preface to *Eminent Victorians*, 1988

Acknowledgments

MANY PEOPLE helped launch this study of the life and work of Ruth Landes and have encouraged me along the way. Especially, I thank Marianne Ainley, Ruth Behar, Victoria Burbank, Jim Conley, Susan Hoecker-Drysdale, Michael Huberman, Ellen Jacobs, Lynne Phillips, and Krisha Starker.

For our conversations about the Schlossberg family I thank Ruth Landes's paternal cousin Emily Sosnow and niece Lois Karatz. Emily Sosnow has supported the project from the beginning and kindly granted permission to publish Schlossberg family photographs. I would like to thank Lambros Comitas and the Research Institute for the Study of Man (RISM) for an initial seed grant that supported my first trip in 1992 to the National Anthropological Archives (NAA) at the Smithsonian Institution to see what the Ruth Landes Papers contained and for continuing interest in the work. The Faculty Research and Development Program at Concordia University and the Social Sciences and Humanities Research Council of Canada provided subsequent funding. James Glenn, former chief archivist at the NAA who indexed the Ruth Landes Papers, was an invaluable guide. I thank the NAA for permission to publish photographs and to quote from Landes's unpublished papers and correspondence. Nancy McKeachnie, director of special collections at the Vassar College Library, offered wonderful support when I was there working with the Ruth Fulton Benedict Papers, as did the Library of Congress staff when I worked with Margaret Mead's papers. I would like to thank Mary Catherine Bateson and the Institute for Intercultural Studies, Inc., for permission to quote from the unpublished correspondence of both Mead and Benedict. I would also like to thank Jean Herskovits for permission to quote from the unpublished correspondence of her father, Melville Herskovits, held in the Northwestern University library.

I would like to thank students, staff, and Ruth Landes's former colleagues at McMaster University, especially Cookie Brymer, William Noble, Richard Slobodin, the late Lynne Teskey-Denton, and Ellen Wall. At Concordia University, the Autobiography and Biography Fellows Seminar at the Simone de Beauvoir Institute offered an early platform to present some of the work, and students Jessica Cattaneo, Anne-Catherine Kennedy, Silvia Richli, and Valerie Shamash provided remarkable research assistance.

Ruth Landes's former students in California, social workers Lucille Lorenz and Jan Covell, were instrumental in solidifying my commitment to the project. Their regard for Ruth Landes and their recognition of her special influence on their lives continue to impress me. At Manitou Rapids, I thank descendants of Maggie Wilson for our discussions of Ruth Landes's Ojibwa work. In Britain, I thank Raymond Firth and Sally Chilver for inspiring interviews. Elsewhere, Mariza Corrêa, Kevin Yelvington, and Virginia Kerns have assisted the progress of the work at important moments by sharing their interest in the intersections of lives and theory making in anthropology. Regna Darnell and Stephen Murray, editors of the Critical Studies in the History of Anthropology series, provided detailed comments and suggestions that were an invaluable guide to me in revising the manuscript. Krisha Starker read and commented on the entire manuscript several times. I hope she knows how much I will always treasure our discussions about immigrant experiences, women's lives, and anthropology.

To my children, Sam and Bella, who do not remember a time when I was not "working on Ruth Landes," thank you for your patience and for being smart enough not to listen to me when I urged that we "wait until the book is finished" to get a dog, a black Labrador named Max, now four years old. My partner, Michael Huberman, has always been encouraging and, most importantly, has understood the importance of the work to me — if not the idea of a woman's pilgrim soul. For Friday night suppers I thank Ruth and Leon Huberman. I dedicate the book to my parents, Alf and Jean Cole, who gave me a love for history and writing that enriches my life every day.

Finally, I thank Ruth Landes, whose work has guided mine to Brazil, where I am now conducting fieldwork, and for living her own life.

Ruth Landes

Introduction

A Fleeting Glimpse

IN THE INDIAN summer warmth of a southern Ontario October afternoon in 1990, I was getting off the elevator on the sixth floor of Chester Hall to enter the Department of Anthropology at McMaster University. Passing me to get onto the elevator was a small woman with bent shoulders and shortish silver-gray hair. She was wearing a gray cardigan and gray tweed trousers. She carried white plastic grocery bags in both hands; the bags were not lumpy with groceries but were smooth and heavy, containing, it would appear, papers and files. As soon as the elevator door closed, I realized the woman must have been Ruth Landes. I thought of running after her to introduce myself, but I refrained. I was self-conscious and lacked confidence at the time. I was acutely aware of my impermanent status at the university as a new postdoctoral fellow, a commuting part-time instructor, and a mother of two preschool-age children. My life was structured around the domestic routines of child rearing: I would be commuting and spending one night each week in Hamilton, a mid-sized town, one hour west of Toronto and 300 kilometers from my home in the smaller town where my partner taught at the local university. I had taught part-time there the year before but had been turned down for another appointment. What little I knew about Ruth Landes I had learned just in the preceding few weeks as I met and introduced myself to the faculty and students in the McMaster Department of Anthropology. Mainly, graduate students had brought her to my attention. There were no women sociocultural anthropologists in the department. The students, knowing that my research was in the area of gender and development and that I was "a feminist," volunteered stories about Ruth Landes as the "feminist" who had once taught in the department and who was now professor emerita. The stories were all anecdotal and told with varying degrees of awe, dismissal, fascination, and intrigue.

The character who had so far emerged from these tales was one who had consistently refused to do any administrative work in the department; whom graduate students either loved or hated but whose often caustic tongue and rigorous academic standards all feared; who lived in a time warp where her primary referents were the people she had worked with in the 1930s, anthropologists Franz Boas and Ruth Benedict—both long dead—and the candomblé specialists of Bahia, Brazil, and the indigenous shamans of Ontario, Minnesota, and Kansas; a grande dame who, long after her retirement from teaching, continued to treat the department's office staff as her personal secretaries and who relied on a few former students to drive her on her errands to do banking and grocery shopping and to take her out to lunch; who still enjoyed flirting with handsome men and who disdained men who did not combine, for her, the necessary attributes of both keen intelligence and good looks; a woman who took pride in her body and could be found several days each week swimming lengths in the McMaster University pool or holding forth in the women's locker room where, standing nude, feet firmly planted, she would ensnare an unsuspecting student in her conversational web (the student more often than not frantically trying to cover her own body with a towel as a shield from the authority that registered from Landes's unclothed body); a woman who still delighted in saying and doing the outrageous; who advised female students against marriage and childbearing, reminding them that she had had three abortions (and no children) herself and that her two short-lived marriages had only interfered with her career.

I hesitated to run after Dr. Landes as the elevator closed because I feared her dismissal of me as a mother and housewife who did not put career first. My identity at that time in my life was, even for myself, conflicted between maternal and professional. In time, I thought, I would tell her of my travels and travails and my own unconventional lifestyle prior to having children at the age of 35. But I had been told she reached quick and harsh assessments of people. You only received one chance with her. I thought there would be another opportunity: I would bank my one chance.

Teaching ended in December. The next term I was conducting field research with Portuguese emigrant fishing families in the town of Leamington on nearby Lake Erie and was only infrequently in the department. I heard that Ruth Landes had died on February 11: her friend and former student, Ellen Wall, had found her lying beside her bed where she had been doing her morning sit-ups, with a photograph of her parents prominently displayed on the night table. Ellen said she died lonely and discouraged by her failure to publish her two remaining manuscripts. There was no apparent cause of death. She was 82. She died, Ellen said, of "a broken heart."

McMaster University held a memorial service at the faculty club on April 25, 1991. Colleagues and former students spoke about Landes as a "pioneer." I began to wonder why I had never heard of her during my 14 years of training in anthropology at three different Canadian universities, especially given my own interests in gender and women's lives. I wanted to find out more about her career and her work. Given the challenges I was finding in placing myself in the discipline, I approached learning about Ruth Landes's life and career as an opportunity to learn how a predecessor — a foremother — had combined "Life" and anthropology. As it turned out, I could not have been more misguided in imagining Ruth Landes as a role model, but the process of discovering this has itself helped me to structure and discover my own anthropological career during the past decade. In unexpected ways she has proven herself a steadfast companion. She has greatly shaped the architecture of my life, perhaps as much or more than I have shaped hers in the pages that follow.

Later in the fall of 1991 while conducting fieldwork in Leamington, I visited my friend and colleague, Lynne Phillips, at the University of Windsor. She and I were collaborating on an edited volume of essays by Canadian feminist anthropologists (Cole and Phillips 1995). My own contribution was an essay that explored the then-current frustration of many feminist anthropologists at postmodernist claims to a new experimental ethnographic practice, one that profiled the politics of textual construction and the use of strategic narrative devices such as multivocality, personal narrative, intersubjectivity, and reflexivity. These same practices were, I argued, also the foundation of efforts by feminist anthropologists to democratize ethnography and anthropology.

During that visit, Ruth Behar came to the University of Windsor to talk about *Translated Woman: Crossing the Border with Esperanza's Story* (1993). Behar had been an enthusiastic reviewer of my book *Women of the Praia: Work and Lives in a Portuguese Coastal Community* (1991), but we had never met. She took that opportunity to ask me if I considered *Women of the Praia* to be a "feminist ethnography." I mumbled not much by way of reply, embarrassed that I did not know what she was talking about. Because *Women of the Praia* had started out as a doctoral dissertation in a nonfeminist anthropology department, I had tried to write about gender in a way that would convince my thesis committee that "anthropology that takes gender into account is not only good anthropology but better anthropology" (Abu-Lughod 1990:16–17). In the book I had recorded women's life stories, which I had presented in the first-person voice, in each woman's own words. I had placed these stories in different chapters and hoped they served to offer local voices and nuances on the book's analysis of changes in women's work and household structure over three generations in a rural community that was increasingly integrated into a global economy. I had also intentionally written the book in a direct and accessible language because I wanted to draw undergraduate students into the large issues of gender, economic development, and social change. As a student I had found feminist scholarship often dauntingly theoretical and thus somewhat exclusionary. This, in my view, defeated feminist goals to reduce hierarchy and increase participation in working for social transformation. When Ruth Behar asked if I thought of my book as "feminist ethnography," I had never heard the term. I thought of my research and writing as feminist practice in anthropology in the sense that I had political goals for social (and disciplinary) change. I had tried to conduct fieldwork employing non-elitist and nonhierarchical research methods, and I had tried to write a democratic and open text that would help make women's lives visible and their voices heard on both local and global terrains.

But the conversation moved on. Ruth Behar talked of her plans with Debbie Gordon to bring together a collection of essays on women's writing in anthropology (Behar and Gordon 1995). I mentioned that I had begun to reread the work of Ruth Landes and had been astonished to discover that in the 1930s she had undertaken fieldwork with Ojibwa women in Canada and Afro-Brazilian women in Bahia that had resulted in books—The Ojibwa Woman (1938) and The City of Women (1947)—that not only profiled women's lives but also experimented with textual strategies that anticipated late-20th-century postmodernist and feminist ethnography. Her writing was reflexive, and she used dialogue, life histories, and personal narrative in multivocal texts that create a sense of the dynamic complexity, contradictions, and constraints that compose the experience of living in culture. It was, I said, curious to me that there seemed to have been little interest in Landes's work in her own time and that she had died relatively unknown and forgotten. I wanted to find out more about how Ruth Landes's work had both mirrored and debarked from the anthropology of her day and how, in fact, it had been received in its time. It seemed to me that this would lead me to a greater understanding of the roles and experiences of women in my chosen discipline—one in which I was myself somewhat tenuously positioned—and, given Landes's explicit focus on women, would also help me to develop a historical perspective on the history of theorizing gender in anthropology. I wanted to find out the extent to which the study of gender—fundamental, one would think, to anthropology's goals to study human "nature" and the diversity of human experience—was tied to political and social movements within which anthropology is practiced. Ruth Behar asked me to contribute an essay about Ruth Landes to the Women Writing Culture volume (Cole 1995a). Thus it was that my personal interest in Ruth Landes's life and work joined forces with the then-emerging project of writing "a critical feminist history of anthropology."

Toward a Critical Feminist History of Anthropology

In Barbara Babcock's words, "'woman' is anthropology's unspeakable savage, the irony of the tribe" (1993:61). Like other feminist historians of anthropology (Behar and Gordon 1995; Di Leonardo 1998; Parezo 1993), Babcock urges that to begin to practice a critical feminist anthropology, we need to "think back through our mothers" as well as our fathers. We need to build a theoretical gene-alogy of women, an anthropological matrilineage. As there are few founding mothers in anthropology, this means revisiting the work of often little-known or forgotten practitioners. A feminist criti-cal history of anthropology would "rethink theory" and recover silenced theoretical positions through rereading women's writing in the discipline (Babcock 1993, 1995; Deacon 1997; Lamphere 1995). As Babcock writes, "the problem of 'women' as well as 'woman' in/and 'the science of man' entails the recovery and revaluation of . . . previously marginalized and underestimated work, demands theories and perspectives that are compensatory as well as critical" (1993:62). This study of Ruth Landes's life and work is a contribu-tion to that project.

A critical feminist history of anthropology is consistent with the critical history of anthropology Joan Vincent envisions. Vincent has called for rehistoricizing the discipline, which, she says, re-quires that anthropology be attuned to the politics of its history and reflexive (1991:45). Vincent's critical historicist anthropology delineates context and understands ethnography not as aesthet-ics or "poetics"—as a postmodernist "ethnography-as-text" ap-proach would have it (Clifford and Marcus 1986)—but as a commu-nal process conditioned by social forces, "a historical phenomenon that must be associated with social, political and material circum-stances" (Vincent 1991:47). This contextual approach places eth-nographers and their writing within social processes such as colo-nialism or capitalist expansion or professionalization or civil rights movements or postcolonialism.

A critical historical practice delineates the hegemonic processes by which some works are anointed as "classics" and others are not. It recognizes that classics are not designated "classics" solely because of the "value of their ideas or the truth of their representations" but because they are "the victors in struggles for past and present recog-nition" (49). According to Vincent, some texts are more vulnerable than others to selective reading and misrepresentation, especially those of ethnographers who, like Landes, were not securely placed within the academy and who did not exclusively locate their work within an accepted convention or paradigm. The social position of texts and authors—which includes the relative prestige of the publisher, the gender of the author, and so on—affects the way they are read.

Landes tried to work within the conventions of Boasian particularism and Benedictine pattern, and her ethnography and career were firmly located on the periphery of mainstream anthropology during the 20th century. This study seeks to understand why this was the case. I argue for a complex intersection of a number of factors, the first of which is the fact that Landes never fully articulated her theory of culture, which remained implicit in her work. Rather than proclaiming general laws and offering explanations, she worked with an intuitive understanding of cultural processes as dynamic, contradictory, and contested. As a result she produced multivocal, unruly texts abounding in rich descriptions. Other factors are her own individualism and insistence—in life and work—on challenging orthodoxies and blurring boundaries that others kept firm, and the fact that she did not find a useful patron among the more senior and better placed scholars in the discipline.

My goal in this book is to situate Ruth Landes—her life, work, and career—in the history of anthropology. I treat her life and career as a case study that provides a lens onto the larger processes of canon building and disciplinary professionalization that placed her on the margins. From one point of view the book is "biography as historical anthropology" (Laslett 1991). Historians of anthropology such as George Stocking and Sydel Silverman consider that biographical or individual case studies of anthropological careers are necessary data to develop a full understanding of the history of theory in anthropology. Silverman writes:

That the development of theory is a social process, a product of life histories embedded in time and place, is a principle that most anthropologists take as axiomatic. Yet the rapid expansion of anthropology . . . and the necessity of simplifying ideas for teaching purposes have produced a standardized treatment of the history of anthropological theory—as seriated "isms," concepts, and names of notables divorced from the social and personal contexts out of which they have emerged. As anthropological theory becomes codified in this manner, and as each generation of anthropologists and students becomes further removed from the seminal figures of the field, an understanding of their work as part of a life, a career, a personality, and a social and cultural setting, becomes more and more elusive. (1981:ix)

Ruth Landes is not a leading figure in the history of American anthropology. She is not known for a distinctive theoretical approach. She did not train and influence a cadre of students, and her books and articles were, until recently, rarely cited. Those who knew of her work usually knew of only one aspect of it: those working in Native American anthropology were often unaware of her Brazilian work as much as Brazilianists were unfamiliar with her contributions to Americanist anthropology. In this book I try to bring together these two fields of scholarship. Most students who complete graduate degrees in anthropology do so as I did — without reading any of her work. Invariably when students have heard of Ruth Landes, they have heard not about her work but about her personality, that she was blackballed from the discipline because she was somehow a "problem." I attempt to get behind the folklore by returning to her work. This book is, then, a study in the life and work of a marginalized practitioner, not a biography of a seminal figure in the discipline. From this point of view, writing about the life, work, and career of Ruth Landes is "backstairs" or "pantry-door" history of anthropology (Marcus 1988).

I link my project to feminist life writing. Feminist theorists argue that writing women's lives is different from writing biography (Caine 1994; Heilbrun 1988; Laslett 1991). Conventional biography characteristically tells the story of a successful quest. It privileges public achievement and extraordinary individuals. Where biography seeks to legitimate a "great man" status for an individual, feminist life writing seeks to reveal the significance of the "everyday," the embeddedness of women's lives in relationships of intimacy and power and in contexts of time and place. Unlike the lives of "great men," women's lives are "much more likely to be tangled than purposeful" (Cameron and Dickin 1997:9) and to be characterized by fragmentation, marginality, and "improvisation" (Bateson 1989).

In contrast to the resources available to biographers who work in the "great man" genre, those of us writing lives of little-known women are often working with a relatively small corpus of published works, fragmented diaries, and interrupted correspondences. Ruth Landes's archival remains include diaries for only a few years of her life during the 1950s, her letters to and from Ruth Benedict and Margaret Mead during the 1930s and 1940s, preserved only because Mead's and Benedict's papers are preserved, and other correspondence mainly for the years after she was settled with tenure (1965) and was able to keep her papers in one place. A few early drafts of some of her published work as well as a number of unpublished papers and lectures also exist. Field notes survive from her Brazil fieldwork but not her notes from the Native American research, which she had deposited with Benedict at Columbia University during the 1930s and which were subsequently lost. In the last decade of her life, Ruth Landes herself organized her papers for deposition in the National Anthropological Archives and tried unsuccessfully to relocate the missing field notes.

The scattered and impoverished resources available for writing a life of Ruth Landes are probably typical of women in mid-20th-century anthropology and in academia more generally. Unlike male scholars whose wives often typed their manuscripts, organized and filed their correspondence and papers, and kept their names alive after their deaths by publishing their remaining unpublished works, female scholars of Landes's generation were typically unmarried and childless and left behind no one to nurture their legacies. As in the case of Landes, female scholars often had unstable careers, moving from institution to institution on short-term contracts and shedding their papers each time they moved. The abundant resources available to scholars of Mead's and Benedict's stature are the exception. Mead was extraordinarily prolific and also has an anthropologist daughter; Mead herself served as Benedict's literary executor. That established male scholars usually also had wives and children means that wives and descendants are often available for the biographer to interview. Ruth Landes left no descendants. Her two ex-husbands and one brother are dead.

During the years I have worked on Ruth Landes's work and life I was often asked, "But is there enough for a biography? After all, she wasn't a very important person. She didn't make a brilliant contribution to anthropology." The paucity of resources were discouraging at times, but as biographer Elspeth Cameron notes: "[To] give up, to let the inviting array of materials on male writers dictate who will be canonized by biographers is to confirm a skewed, male-centred . . . tradition and further silence the women who were their equals. . . . The choice . . . is between an academically self-righteous silence, which imprisons [a forgotten or little-known woman] in unfair anonymity, or a no doubt flawed attempt to interpret the incomplete assemblage of documents, interviews, fictions and nonfiction in order to release at least the echo of her voice" (1997:147). The primary resources I have relied on are Ruth Landes's own writings — especially her six ethnographies based on her 1930s fieldwork — not only because other resources are scarce but because my intention in this book is to return Ruth Landes to anthropology through her own work.

My research reveals that Ruth Landes was drawn to anthropology because she thought it offered her new possibilities to live a life outside the immigrant world of her childhood and outside the gendered constraints she experienced in her youthful marriage. She self-consciously sought to live an original life as a woman in 20th-century America. It is her life and career that lead me to situate this study of a woman's career in anthropology within feminist storytelling of women's lives.

In 1929, the year Ruth Schlossberg married at the age of 20, Virginia Woolf declared, "very little is known about women's lives." Woolf's entire literary opus — her essays, diaries, fiction, readings of history, feminism, politics — can be understood as being motivated by her desire to find new forms for "women's as yet unnarrated lives" (Lee 1997:13). Much more, of course, has since been written about women's lives, but at the end of the 20th century such feminist literary critics as Carolyn Heilbrun maintained that the "scripts" for women had changed little. In *The Education of a Woman: The Life of Gloria Steinem* published in 1995, four years after Ruth Schlossberg Landes died, Heilbrun portrays the life of one of the 20th century's most powerful feminists as riddled with contradictions, as ruled by the "romantic script," and, finally, as culminating in marriage at the age of 60.[1] Heilbrun urges that there is a need for new and alternative narrative forms for women's lives, especially "ambiguous women" like Landes. Unambiguous women are those whose lives have followed the age-old "female plot," the "romantic script." Telling stories of the lives of ambiguous women is difficult: the lives "are painful, the price is high, the anxiety is intense, because there is no script to follow, no story portraying how one is to act, let alone any alternative stories" (Heilbrun 1988:39). Telling stories of such lives is, Heilbrun says, necessary to the creation of new scripts for women. The lives may not be lives to emulate, but they are lives to learn from. Certainly, this life of Ruth Landes is a cautionary tale.

That storytelling is a resource for women is a lesson that her Ojibwa informant Maggie Wilson taught Ruth Landes in northern Ontario in 1932. For me, one of the most exciting finds in writing this book on Ruth Landes's life was to discover her as a storyteller of other women's lives. Returning to her life discloses to us these other women in other times and places. A life of Ruth Landes not only explores the challenges she faced in the creative construction of her own life but also takes us to the lives of Native American and Brazilian women who charted unconventional life courses in *their* worlds. While recognizing the particular parameters and constraints of women's lives in these different cultural and historical contexts, Ruth Landes nonetheless boldly wrote about Brazilian and Native American women and men also as members of the world she herself inhabited. Landes profoundly believed that there were some aspects of women's experiences — of the institutions of conjugal relations, for example — that crossed cultural boundaries. Landes had married and divorced before she began field research as an anthropologist. She sought cross-cultural knowledge of women's experiences of marriage and divorce as a resource for herself in coming to terms with her own sense of loss and loneliness. The women she met and introduced to us in her ethnographies are, as her McMaster colleague Richard Slobodin once remarked, "women who strangely resembled herself: individualistic, energetic, strong-minded, stubborn."[2]

For Ruth Landes, the hazards and hurdles along the way were many. First and foremost they were ideological: despite her best attempts the romantic script of courtship, marriage, and family continually interfered with her efforts to establish professional goals for herself. She wavered between convention and individualism, between compliance and confrontation, and between a desire for marriage and family and the goal of a professional career in anthropology. Second, there were institutional constraints: the economic depression of the 1930s; the increasing professionalization of universities, which hired few women during the decades after Landes received her Ph.D. in 1935; and the discipline of anthropology itself, which, in the mid-20th century, welcomed some research topics — such as cultural evolution, ecology, materialism, semiotics — more than others, such as gender, sexuality, race, power, the topics that concerned Ruth Landes. The third obstacle was Landes's own individualism, her rejection of orthodoxies, her refusal to compromise.

The story that follows is laden with contradictions. Ruth Landes was the daughter of Jewish immigrants, but she lived her adult life firmly outside Jewish contexts. She sought integration, taking on the attitudes and mores of modern, middle-class American girls of the 1920s and 1930s. But after a short-lived marriage to her sweetheart, the son of friends of her parents, she experimented in a series of interracial relationships — something most middle-class American girls did *not* do. Landes admired her mentor, Ruth Benedict, more than any other person (including her father, whom she had adored as a child), but she was not, like Benedict, a woman-identified woman. Her open sexuality was firmly directed toward heterosexual relationships.

As it was for many immigrants, a university education for Ruth Landes offered a route into mainstream America. Once in the academy, however, she did not conform to the patron-client relations required in the intellectual lineage system — although she tried in her compliance with Ruth Benedict. She knew the prevailing theoretical conventions in American anthropology, and because of her desires for acceptance, her work always maintained one foot firmly in Boasianism. But she chose unconventional research questions and methods. In Bahia, for example, she observed the Afro-Brazilian spirit possession religion, *candomblé,* in terms of bodies and sexuality, and she described the rituals and temples as women-centered, offering members economic support and social solace from poverty, discrimination, and abuse. Her contemporaries, by contrast, either catalogued the symbolism of the African spirits and speculated on the intensity of surviving African traits or measured the heartbeat, pupil dilation, and other physiological responses during trance and possession. Bronislaw Malinowski's *The Sexual Life of Savages* became foundational in anthropology, but Ruth Landes's ethnographic focus on sexuality was regarded not as science but as symptomatic of "disorderly conduct" (Smith-

Rosenberg 1985), as a sign that she was not a dutiful anthropological daughter (Landes 1970b). Among the Canadian Ojibwa, where her anthropological contemporaries described male shamans as the cultural apotheosis and marriage as an economic partnership, Ruth Landes heard and recounted story upon story of women's struggles both in marriage and for economic survival. Critics, however, labeled her focus on women's experience "idiosyncratic." Although Landes was interested in gender, race, and sexuality—and, in the pages that follow, I argue this was so precisely because she was *not* a dutiful, middle-class American daughter—she also sought a place in American society as a professional person, in this case as an anthropologist. Her efforts to establish the legitimacy of her work using mainstream Boasian anthropology contradicted and hindered her ability to theorize the original questions presented by her research among Afro-Brazilian and Native American women and men. Seeking both to be accepted in the discipline and to challenge orthodoxies, her ethnography is, as a result, often contradictory or ambiguous. Her great strength was that she had an acute eye and the audacity to record what she saw.

Landes sought professional recognition as an anthropologist but found herself unable to play by the rules. She did not compromise in the ways women must in order to occupy the tenuous spaces available to them in the academy. She had a quick mind and tongue, always ready to engage in intellectual banter, and she did not defer to either men or women in academic debates. On the contrary, she passed rigorous judgment on peoples' intellects—both men's and women's. In letters to Benedict and Mead she would often describe male colleagues in terms of their physical presence ("that little man," etc.), for she linked physical appearance to both intellectual stature and virility. Her insistence, through her comportment, on absolute equality with men sabotaged her efforts to secure a place for herself within professional anthropology. Her personal comportment was problematic not only for men but also for some women in the discipline, notably Margaret Mead, who once wrote to Benedict that she wished that Ruth Landes would behave either "like a lady" or in a more "routine way" in academic situations (October 2, 1939, MMP, box B1).

Ruth Landes is a lonely figure in the history of anthropology.

She seems to have been happiest and to have found a sense of belonging, of shared experience, among the (extra)ordinary women and men she met in other cultures. Through her conversations in Bahia and Manitou Rapids, Red Lake, and Kansas, she developed and began to articulate her cross-cultural perspective on collective experiences of race, class, gender, and sexuality. Ruth Landes represents one of the first critical voices in anthropology to argue for a radically new mode of understanding gendered subjects' relations to social-historical realities. In the 1930s Benedict had written about gendered "others" in the guise of writing about cultural "others" (Babcock 1995). Mead had projected American bohemian ideals onto other cultural contexts such as Samoa (Di Leonardo 1998). Gladys Reichard had found an idealized communal "earth mother" among the Navaho (Gordon 1993). Others, such as Phyllis Kaberry, found women's worlds that paralleled and complemented men's in aboriginal Australia and the Cameroon grasslands (Kaberry 1939, 1952). Only Landes wrote about gender conflict, contradiction, and ambiguity cross-culturally. Hers is a new critical analytical voice — the trickster of 1930s anthropology.

The book is organized in three parts. Discussion centers on Landes's field research during the 1930s and on my rereading of her ethnographic writing based on this work. This was the period of her training under Franz Boas and Ruth Benedict. It was her formative and most productive time, during which she incubated her theory of culture, honed her ethnographic writing style, and developed her philosophy of fieldwork, which I argue place her in the center, not the margins, of the discipline.

Part 1, "Beginnings," traces the roots of her anthropological interests in her experiences as the daughter of Jewish immigrants, her childhood in a liberal trade unionist family, and her coming of age as a New Woman in the interwar years and leads to her discovery of anthropology as her route to integration in individualist America. In part 2, "Apprenticeship in Native American Worlds," I describe her initiation in anthropology through fieldwork with the Canadian Ojibwa and her extraordinary collaboration with shamaness and storyteller Maggie Wilson, which resulted in the pioneering text Ojibwa Woman. In this part I also discuss her subsequent fieldwork in different Native American contexts with the Minnesota Chippewa, the Santee Sioux, and the Prairie Potawatomi. Through this work she fine-tuned her ethnographic observation skills by recording the marginal and subaltern voices of transgressing women, lusty shamans, and gender variants. Her ability to see marginality as a site of culture making, her focus on the interstices of culture — the cracks in cultural hegemonies — is, I argue, a product of her own gendered experiences of acculturation and provides the basis for her theoretical understanding of culture as dynamic and internally diversified. In part 3, "She-Bull in Brazil's China Closet," Landes, having received her Ph.D. in 1935, is now a professional anthropologist and is sent by Columbia University to study race relations in Brazil. The fieldwork results in her most original work, *The City of Women*, but also in her ultimate marginalization from the mainstream of the discipline for her ethnographic focus on gender, race, and sexuality, her theoretical interpretation of candomblé as a New World cultural creation and not a holdover from life in Africa, her personal comportment in the field, and her reflexive, multivocal, "unscientific" writing style. In the final chapter, "Conclusion: Life and Career," I summarize the events in her life after her professional marginalization, her years on the road as a gypsy scholar, and during what she considered to be her eventual exile in Canada. In the process we rediscover her work and find that, far from being marginal, Ruth Landes and her writing lie at the very heart of the discipline of American anthropology.

PART ONE

Beginnings

It was an extraordinary gift for hope, a romantic readiness such as I have never found in any other person and which it is not likely I shall ever find again. – F. Scott Fitzgerald, *The Great Gatsby*

CHAPTER ONE

Immigrant Daughter

*Relatives and friends filled my mother, Anna, with feeling for Old Testament
events that might touch her life. Especially there was the Book of Ruth, the young
Moabite who clung to her Jewish mother-in-law. Anna "knew" she carried a girl-
child and felt inspired to visit the Museum of Art on Fifth Avenue where she
seated herself near Millet's reverent painting of "Ruth Gleaning in the Fields of
Boas." By Jewish law, Boas was obliged to marry the widow of a near kinsman,
as Ruth's late husband was, in order to raise children for the deceased (who had
died without issue). The grave Bible story was echoed in Anna. And 20 years later
this Ruth would join some six others of the name, varied in age and origins, to
work in the American field governed by Boas.*[1]

R UTH LANDES enjoyed telling this story that related her
choice of a career in anthropology to the choice made by
the biblical Ruth after whom she was named. As she tells
it, she was predestined for anthropology by events that took place
when she was carried in her mother's womb.

In the biblical story Ruth, after the death of her husband, attached herself to her mother-in-law, Naomi, saying: "Whither thou
goest, I will go; and where thou lodgest, I will lodge: thy people
shall be my people, and thy God my God" (Book of Ruth, 1:16).
Naomi brought Ruth with her to the land of her elder kinsman,
Boaz, who allowed Ruth, the Moabite stranger, to glean a living in
his fields until he eventually married her, making her kin and no
longer a stranger. Through this personal origin myth Ruth Landes
claimed that she was predestined to meet the paternal Franz Boas
— known to his women students as "Papa Franz" — and to become
his anthropological daughter.[2] And, in Ruth's story, Naomi, the
adoptive mother, may be understood as Ruth Benedict, to whom
Ruth Landes attached herself in anthropology. The story tells of
Ruth's experiences of marginality, her desires for integration, and

her inclination toward spirituality and suggests that these led her to anthropology.

Immigrant Mother

In telling her personal origin story, Ruth gave her mother, Anna, an important role in naming her and in anticipating her career in Boasian anthropology. Did Anna also know that Ruth Landes would always be a stranger, like the biblical Moabite Ruth? Did Anna know that Ruth, the child of immigrants, would be an outsider, not owning but only gleaning a place for herself in anthropology and in the wider American society? If so, this is a deep and critical understanding of Ruth, who would always be seeking acceptance, who would always feel on the outside looking in, and who would spend the last 25 years of her life in what she called "exile" in Canada. The story, told after Anna's death, suggests that Anna "knew" and understood Ruth in ways she did not directly express when she was alive. During their lifetimes there was little understanding and much conflict between mother and daughter.

Anna Grossman had had her own experiences of displacement, and she lived her life torn between dreams and practicalities. She was born in Russia in August 1881 to well-educated and comfortably well-off Bundist parents.[3] Her mother died when she was young, and Anna and her sister Miriam were separated, Miriam going to live with the paternal grandparents and Anna to live with her maternal grandmother and her mother's two younger sisters. One of these aunts, Adele, married the poet David Pinski. The son of a tea merchant, David Pinski was born in 1872 in the Belorussian town of Mohilev. His family's wealth and their non-Jewish business connections had enabled him to circumvent many of the legal and social restrictions on Jews and permitted him to study at Moscow University. David and Adele moved to Berlin in 1896 for David to continue his university studies, and they took the teenaged Anna with them.

Anna would remember David as a dreamer who had charmed and inspired her during an otherwise sad and lonely adolescence. Late in her life, after receiving news of the well-known Yiddish writer's death in 1959 in Israel, where he had emigrated ten years earlier, Anna wrote to Ruth:

Uncle David's passing brought back to me my sad adolescent years with him as the central figure in my life. He was a brother, an impatient teacher, and, according to his own judgment, a practical advisor. He erred in many of the things he advised me but he and his home environment were definitely different and it made an inroad in my life. In that home I met Pa and that too changed my entire outlook on life. I cannot say that uncle David was a great thinker but he was a great dreamer. He built castles in the air which, of course, would enchant adolescents. In his youth, uncle David was a lover of people. He helped many people find themselves. I was one of them. At the age of fourteen I did not believe there was another person living to match David. (August 1959, RISM)

In Berlin Adele took paramedical training in massage therapy. Anna studied bookkeeping at a commercial school and lived at a boardinghouse with other girls who were studying at the school. Although many of the girls enjoyed a lively social life, Anna remembered being a cautious and lonely adolescent:

In my loneliness I had two good friends in the house. They lived at the boarding house and studied at the [school]. They were Lieschen Höning and Vera Farber, close friends but very different in appearance and character. Lieschen, the younger one, was pretty and temperamental; Vera, the older one, was eventempered and plain and had a heart of gold. The three of us went to picnics and to the famous Berlin Tiergarten (Zoo). Lieschen liked the boys and they liked her. She was always asked to dance and had a wonderful time. Vera's reserve, and mine, was strange to her. Marriage to a military man was an unrealizable dream. Girls without a substantial dowry could never reach such height. A military officer was expected to marry in his own social status. The result: illicit relations. Many babies were born out of wedlock. That happened to Lieschen. She was compelled to leave the school and the boarding house. The baby was placed in a foundling home. Lieschen never showed up again. Vera and I graduated. . . . She went back to her home in Hamburg. I lost track of both girls. (AG to RL, December 2, 1964, RISM)

After graduating, Anna found her first job as a secretary to a medical specialist. She was a serious and practical girl but was soon unhappy with the constraints this work imposed on her: "I learned Russian stenography and took dictation in Russian and German. I lived with the doctor's family, his wife and four children in Charlottenburg, a section of Berlin. . . . I had a room, board and a small salary. The Doctor and his wife went out evenings and I did babysitting. I endured that for a year. I became restless. When the Spectors [family friends] asked me to come to them in Warsaw, I lost no time and went. In Warsaw I took up medical massage which was very popular at that time" (December 2, 1964, RISM).

Anna, who had wanted to study medicine, retrained in medical massage, a profession that women turned to because medical schools then were closed to women. When the Pinskis moved to New York in 1900 they invited Anna to join them, and she did. David attended Columbia University, and Anna went to work in Adele's medical massage practice. The Pinskis moved in a social circle of writers and socialist intellectuals, and Anna enjoyed the world they introduced to her. As her daughter Ruth would later describe it, the Pinskis were "beautiful, ambitious and rebel 'secularists.' . . . Flourishing on wifely earnings and David's reputation, they kept lavish open-house for artists and political radicals; inevitably my father was a guest, then an intimate" (RL to George Park, May 20, 1985, box 1, RLP).

Thus it was through David Pinski that Anna met Joe Schlossberg, the man she would marry in 1905. Joe Schlossberg was six years Anna's senior. He was then working as a floorwalker in a department store earning a paltry income and devoting his energy to unionizing garment workers and writing for the Yiddish presses. Joe was handsome and a passionate idealist—a man very much a dreamer like her uncle David. Anna "admired him and his bond with the Pinskis" and proposed the marriage, offering to support them through medical massage, which she did for several years. In their marriage, which would last almost 60 years, there would be room for only one dreamer, and it was Anna who would have to become the practical one.

Trade Union Father

Born in 1875 in Koidanov (now Dzerzhinzk), Belorussia, near Minsk, Joseph was the eldest child of Bessie Feldman and Matthias Schlossberg.[4] Bessie's mother had died when she was only seven years old, and when her father quickly remarried and started a second family, Bessie was sent out to work as a domestic servant. Recalling his mother, Joe once wrote to Ruth: "In the tiny Russian town motherlessness was a tragedy. A stepmother came into the family. She tyrannized the young orphan. At a very tender age, before her teens, she became a servant girl with another family. She was not taught how to read and write, but all her half brothers and sisters received, for that time and place, a good education. Their mother saw to it and their father could afford it. My mother was always conscious of her inability to read or write, and suffered bitterly" (JS to RL, December 22, 1964, RISM). Bessie married Matthias, a tailor and Talmudic scholar, in 1870, and in quick succession they had four children, Joseph, Dora, Mary, and Isaac. The violent pogroms and laws that restricted Jewish settlement, employment, and education made conditions unbearable for Jews, and Matthias, like hundreds of thousands of others, made the decision to immigrate to America. He went alone, planning to send for Bessie and the children once he was settled. Matthias arrived at Castle Gardens, New York, in 1886 and attempted to establish a tailoring business on the Lower East Side. His wife and children joined him in 1888.

The family lived in desperate poverty. Bessie took in boarders to help pay the $12.00 a month rent for their crowded tenement rooms. Four more children, Anna, Harriet, Julia, and Abraham, were born. Thirteen-year-old Joseph was forced to go to work in a sweatshop to help support the family. Joe left school after only one year; angry with his parents, he also rejected Orthodox traditions and refused to be bar mitzvahed. Instead, embittered by the conditions that made the lives of immigrant families like his own so difficult, Joseph joined the movement to unionize the garment sweatshops and fight for better wages and working conditions. In 1890, at the age of 15, he was involved in his first strike and was soon recognized as a leader and orator. He avidly pursued his own self-education through extensive reading and that year organized the Cloak Makers Citizens Educational Club. For the next 50 years, from 1890 to 1940, he was a moving force in the American labor movement, and education for the working poor would always be one of his deepest concerns.

By the time Ruth was born in 1908, Joe was 33 years old and an active public figure and forceful speaker in the Yiddish labor socialist community. A self-taught writer and thinker, he had served as editor of *Abendblatt*, a Yiddish labor daily newspaper, from 1899 to 1902 and of *Der Arbeyter*, the socialist labor party's weekly, from 1904 to 1911. In 1914 Joe was working as secretary-treasurer of the New York Joint Cloak Board of the United Brotherhood of Tailors when a group of Jewish labor socialists led by Chicago unionist Sidney Hillman (1887–1946) recruited him to help found the Amalgamated Clothing Workers of America (ACW). Joe was elected first general secretary-treasurer of the ACW, an office he held for more than a quarter of a century until he retired at the age of 65.

As secretary-treasurer, Joe Schlossberg edited the ACW's weekly, *Advance*, for many years and regularly contributed to both the English and Yiddish labor presses for 40 years. In 1935 the American Labor Party published a collection of his essays entitled *Workers and Their World: Selected Essays by Joseph Schlossberg*. The same year he was appointed to the Board of Higher Education by New York's Mayor Fiorello La Guardia, a position he held until 1963 and described as "twenty-eight years of joy, close association with the colleges and gifted students."[5] In 1938 he ran for the U.S. Congress on the American Labor Party ticket but was defeated.

Labor Zionism was also an important part of the context within which Ruth grew up. Her father was an organizer of the first Congress for Labor Palestine held in New York in 1918. During World War I he helped organize the massive relief efforts sponsored by the American Jewish Committee to send aid to Jews suffering in Eastern Europe. In 1923 he was a charter member of the National Labor Committee for Palestine and was elected its president in 1934. He worked with the leading socialist Zionists of the day, including David Ben-Gurion and Albert Einstein.[6] He traveled to Palestine in 1930 and 1937 and accompanied Ben-Gurion on an overland trip from Palestine to Europe in 1930. When he retired from the ACW in 1940, Schlossberg devoted the next 30 years of his life to Zionist affairs. Following the establishment of the state of Israel in 1948, he worked in the New York office of Histadrut, the Israel General Labor Federation, and became chairman of the American National Committee for Labor Israel. Histadrut established a cultural center in his honor at Ashkelon, Israel, in 1955.

Ruth was six years old when her father became secretary-treasurer of the Amalgamated Clothing Workers, and the "Amalgamated" had a direct impact on her life and career. The world of her family was governed by labor politics, and even as a child she knew this was not the world of mainstream America. She recalled that on her school forms her father always signed his occupation simply as "bookkeeper" and did not identify his work with the union movement (RL to George Park, May 20, 1985, RLP, box 1). She intimately experienced her marginality and fiercely longed to belong. The Schlossberg family, however, critiqued dominant practices of exclusion and discrimination, and Ruth also grew up not only with a deep sense of her own entitlement to equality but also with a deep concern for the rights of minorities.

Ruth adored her father and frequently accompanied him to union meetings, where she listened to his speeches and met activists, writers, and intellectuals in the labor socialist movement. She was bright, precocious, and a lively observer. Her parents and their friends encouraged her dramatic retellings of events in the union halls, and early on she developed confidence in her own intuition. One of the most heated topics in union circles of the time was the "woman question." Immigrant women workers had predominated in the wave of strikes that had paralyzed the clothing industry in major cities across the country between 1909 and 1920. Women had emerged as passionate spokespersons for the garment workers and had played instrumental roles in the founding of the ACW (Glenn 1990:169; Hyman 1998:320). By 1920 the "Amalgamated" had enrolled nearly 170,000 members, one third of whom were women.

Unlike traditional American unions that were geared almost exclusively to male workers and that conducted their business in taverns, the ACW faced the challenge of accommodating the large numbers of women members in its ranks. The ACW introduced educational and recreational programs aimed to meet the specific needs of its immigrant female membership and maintain their allegiance. Drawing on models from the late-19th-century German socialist movement and the Jewish Labor Bund in Russia and Poland, the ACW established an array of cultural programs including gymnastic competitions, choral and drama societies, reading circles, schools, and clubs (Glenn 1990:220). These educational and recreational programs offered young people social alternatives to the urban consumer activities, dance halls, clubs, and commercial amusement parks that attracted young working women and men.

The Amalgamated's educational program, established in 1917 when Ruth was nine years old, included cultural field trips, concerts, and movies for members and their families. Lectures by Columbia University professors in history, economics, anthropology, English, and art education were especially popular. Participation in these programs had a special meaning for women, many of whom would not have had educational opportunities in the shtetls of Russia and Poland, where education was typically religious and the prerogative of men. Union-sponsored courses and programs provided acceptable contexts within which women could obtain education. They offered women opportunities for intellectual growth and personal self-improvement and embodied their broader ambitions to integrate in American society.

The Amalgamated also developed summer holiday programs at resort centers in the mountains of New York and Pennsylvania. For years the Schlossbergs holidayed at Tamiment and later at Woodridge and other summer colonies of Jewish labor socialists. Here the young Ruth escaped the August heat of crowded city living, swam, picnicked, and continued her education in labor politics. Here she and her brother, David, also met their future spouses, children of like-minded family friends.

At union meetings Ruth listened to militant women organizers as they expressed the concerns of women workers about piece rates, working conditions, sexual harassment, and women's representation on the male-dominated union executive (Hyman 1998:321). These women offered the young Ruth dynamic public female role models.

The women labor activists were divided on the question of what kind of strategy would best advance women's interests — whether to try to integrate into male-dominated union organizations or to form semi-autonomous women's institutions. The question plagued both the union and the socialist movements in this period and was much discussed at ACW meetings. Most women wanted to participate in the labor movement on the same terms as men; they spoke in terms of their shared experiences with men as wage earners and providers. But increasingly frustrated with the men's lack of concern for women's working conditions, some women organizers tried to organize women's locals within the ACW. The educational director of the ACW in Chicago, Raissa Lomonossoff, explained in a letter to Joseph Schlossberg in the fall of 1919 why she thought a woman's local was "abnormal" but necessary: "Being a Russian, I [am] inclined to believe that if men and women work together, they can meet together also, and respect each other's opinions. [In the union] men are very 'nice' to women, but when it comes to business matters the women are being pushed aside." This is not "normal," she continued, in labor organizations "on which we all build our hopes for a better world to live in" (as quoted in Glenn 1990:232). The viability of the women's locals in the Amalgamated was continually challenged, however, by the women's own dilemmas about how to advance their position without undermining class solidarity. They were torn between ethnic loyalties, class interests, and their specific concerns as women.

For Ruth Landes, women labor activists were a potent symbol of the possibilities of a modern life for a young Jewish woman in America. Union-related activities had created new opportunities for women and men to come together in a mass movement based in class and community interest and legitimated women's participation in the public affairs of their communities. Union activism was clearly a forum for women's political participation, for claiming citizenship, and, for some, a route to integration in the broader society. The movement provided the young Ruth Schlossberg with a broad vision of roles and responsibilities for women, one that moved them out of the household and neighborhood into the wider political sphere of communal life and toward the mainstream of American society.

The labor politics of working-class immigrant women that inspired Ruth also provided inspiration to American-born middle- and upper-class militant suffragists and radical feminists. Viewed by an earlier generation of American reformers as "victims to be pitied," immigrant women wage earners and union activists emerged in early-20th-century America as "a vanguard to be imitated" (Cott 1987). And in their leisure activities working-class men and women pioneered new styles of mixed-sex public behavior:

"Well before the appearance of the flapper of the 1920s, immigrant daughters engaged in leisure habits that defied both the norms of the shtetl and the standards of respectable middle-class American morality. Seeking pleasure and male companionship, young female wage earners who went to dancehalls, amusement parks, and theaters and participated in other forms of mixed-sex leisure, anticipated—even paved the way for—the new feminine styles of the Jazz Age" (Glenn 1990:209).

Gender Politics of Family Life

The Schlossberg household was firmly secular. Both son and daughter attended ethnically diverse public schools in New York and embraced the 1920s youth culture of the wider American society. The Schlossbergs strongly supported higher education for both children. Ruth graduated from Brookwood High School in May 1924, received a bachelor's degree in sociology in 1928 from New York University and a master's degree from the New York School of Social Work (now Columbia University) in 1929, and received a Ph.D. in anthropology from Columbia in 1935. Her brother, David Matthias, graduated from Harvard Law School and became a practicing lawyer.

In important ways the Schlossbergs also retained immigrant sensibilities and aspirations for their daughter. They hoped that her higher education would secure her social mobility in America, and for a young woman mobility was signified by marriage to a man whose single income could provide them both with the security of a middle-class standard of living.[7] Joe and Anna also expected Ruth to marry within their social and ethnic milieu—and she did: on June 14, 1929, following her graduation with a master of social work, she married Victor Landes, a medical student and the son of family friends, fellow socialists. Joe and Anna had encouraged Ruth to pursue higher education, but they had not anticipated that she would pursue a career after marriage. Ruth had assumed she would marry, but she also hoped for a different kind of marriage than that of her parents.

The pattern of the contradiction between ideals and aspirations for equality and the reality of constraint in everyday life that Ruth observed in the ACW also dominated her own life. Although the Schlossbergs' public life expressed their progressive politics and labor activism, gender roles and relations within the family remained conservative. Joe was like other men in the union and socialist movements who "contrary to their 'liberated' or 'revolutionary' attitudes towards marriage and the family . . . lived very conventional married lives which, in fact, provided them with certain comforts and allowed them certain freedoms" (Baum et al. 1976:160–161). A small man (5 feet 5 inches tall) with thick, bushy hair that turned a startling white as he aged, Joe was intense and preoccupied with social philosophical questions and political issues rather than with the practical concerns of family life. Ruth idolized her father and from him learned to argue and defend intellectual ideas and principles. She did not, however, learn how to bend or accommodate the imperfections and messiness of emotional relationships in everyday life. Both father and daughter would argue to the end for the correctness of their principles and were unable to compromise.

Ruth described the Schlossberg home as emotionally cold and comfortless, as a place where "one let down one's hair and dedicated oneself to aches and pains" (1950, Notebook 1, RLP; see also Bordo 1997). Joe, who was fondly thought of by his comrades in the labor movement and by nieces and nephews as a warm and loving uncle, was uninvolved in the daily life of the Schlossberg home, whose management he left to Anna. Anna took little pleasure in the tasks involved in running a household. In contrast to Joe, she is remembered by extended family members as "shrewish" and incessantly critical. She made domestic tasks as joyless and labor intensive as possible. A frugal housekeeper, she insisted on walking great distances for bargains and on struggling home alone with the loaded shopping cart. Although she did not enjoy it and was a poor cook, she also insisted on entertaining. She prepared the food herself for extended family gatherings and for the numerous occasions when Joe would invite local and visiting dignitaries for dinner. Nor did Anna take pleasure in mothering. She apparently rejected Ruth as a newborn and would later tell family members that she had not wanted to have any more children. Twenty-two months later, however, David Matthias (1910–84) was born. Anna apparently limited further intimacy with her husband in order to ensure that there were no more pregnancies.[8]

If family members remember Anna as a cold and angry person, we can only guess at the reasons. Was she unhappy in the marriage? She admired Joe and had herself proposed the marriage. A photo taken of Joe and Anna shortly after their marriage shows them as a handsome couple and suggests a physical attraction between them (see figure 2). But she had also married an older, less educated man in part because of the endogamous marriage practices of the immigrant Jewish world in which she found herself on her arrival in New York in the first decade of the 20th century. She had been attracted to the dreamer Joe who was like her uncle David, but marriage to a political idealist who showed little concern for earning money meant that she had had to give up her own dreams and assume the practical responsibilities of managing the household. Had she imagined herself living in the style and comfort of her childhood in her grandparents' home in Russia or as the hostess of a Berlin-style salon like her aunt Adele for poets like her uncle David? Was she frustrated trying to create that social life with few resources? Did she resent the routine of the domestic work of wifehood and motherhood? She had lived independently as an adolescent in Berlin and Warsaw, and she had had a career and income for several years both before and after her marriage. Did she begrudge the time Joe gave to his political work in the labor and Zionist movements? She was proud of his work, but was she also often lonely in the marriage?

Whatever the roots of Anna's anger, frustration, or disappointment, she communicated ambivalence to her daughter, and their relationship was always fraught with tension. Anna recognized Ruth's quick intelligence and early precociousness and was proud of her academic achievements. But her pride was tinged with jealousy as Ruth energetically sought a life that was both grounded in intellectual work and also sexually and emotionally fulfilling. In one breath Anna would praise Ruth's academic accomplishments and in the next would criticize her hair, her dress, her comportment. Anna could not justly attack Ruth's intellectual achievements. Instead, she focused on her sexuality. Especially after the failure of Ruth's first marriage, Anna would relentlessly criticize Ruth's lifestyle, sexual freedom, and choices in male partners.

Reflecting on her unmarried and childless status at midlife, Ruth Landes would write in her diary in 1951:

I unconsciously regarded "husband-material" as similar to my family and my brother, and so avoided it because I had enough of family; and so I chose lovers who were exotic and distinctly outside the family-constellation which was so fraught with unappealing qualities. . . . I have loved and even wanted to be the brilliant, irresponsible, charming weak man — beginning with Peter Pan (played by Maude Adams!) which Aunt Hattie took me to see when I was seven. . . . My fear of marriage and childbirth is all tied up with my rejection of my mother — she was so cold, cruel and small, filled my young life so with terror that I rejected anything that would put me in her role — and there lay all my "destructiveness." . . . No wonder I hated to be a wife and have that usual household. Better a Peter Pan who flies away. (Notebook 7, RLP)

Ruth was claustrophobic in the role of immigrant daughter. She chose integration and embraced American individualism as the path to creating a modern autonomous self. And she would embrace anthropology closely following upon her rejection of feminine roles in immigrant Jewish households and her choice for integration. Her engagement with anthropology and her writing about women's lives in other cultures can be understood as an "act of defiance" against the script for immigrant daughters in America (Antler 1998:3).

Ruth's rejection of her mother as a role model was accompanied by a strong admiration for her father and dependence upon him and his social network for her escape from the gendered conventions of the immigrant world. In rejecting constraints within the immigrant world she fully exposed herself to new vulnerabilities in the male-dominant social structures and institutions of mainstream society. This dependence was at the root of the deeply contradictory sense of self she developed. Although she refused dominant social constructions of women, she would always seek male recognition both professionally and personally. Literary critic Janet Burstein has described a similar conflicted sense of self for other bright, creative, and ambitious Jewish immigrant daughters—writers like Mary Antin, Anzia Yezierska, Emma Goldman, and Kate Simon—who, like Landes, rejected "the subordinated mother" and found the father was the "way into the world" they needed and longed to enter. Burstein speaks of the "not always heroic" "manifold self" of immigrant daughters like Ruth Landes who were, on the one hand, driven, assertive, and vividly self-expressive and, on the other, "emotionally dependent on the confirming gaze of a powerful man" (1998:17–18).

Reflections on the Eastern European Jewish Family

As an anthropologist, Ruth Landes would later write about family relationships in immigrant Jewish households in a 1950 article she coauthored with Mark Zborowski entitled "Hypotheses concerning the Eastern European Jewish Family." In 1948, unable to find employment in anthropology, she had moved home again to live with her parents in their apartment in the Bronx and was working as a contract researcher for the American Jewish Congress, a job her father had obtained for her. Margaret Mead, who had succeeded Ruth Benedict as director of the Columbia University Research in Contemporary Cultures Project (RCC), recruited Landes to conduct interviews for the RCC with 128 immigrants from the Russian shtetls and 10 immigrants who had been born in New York. These informants included 74 women and 64 men of different social classes and degrees of education and ranging in age from 20 to 90. The article is written in the distinctive voice of Ruth Landes, and she said she had been the principal author (1950, Notebook 1, RLP). In Margaret Mead's words, Ruth Landes contributed "her broad and rich anthropological experience and her second generation acquaintance with the culture" (1952:17).

In the article Landes and Zborowski describe how the Eastern European Jewish family supported gender hierarchy. In the idealized gendered division of labor, men worked outside the home in scholarly or business activity, and women were located firmly in the home, where they were responsible for the daily maintenance and overall well-being of the home and family members: "Tradition views the differentiation as complementary, but in actuality there are frequent implications of male status-superiority and of

female status-inferiority.... There is ... a complete dichotomy between the intellectual burdens and opportunities charged to men,
and the earthy ones charged to women (462)."

Landes and Zborowski reported: "It came as a surprise to all of
the researchers to realize the seemingly considerable perseverance
of traditional European modes in American surroundings, even in
the third generation, despite some evidence of important changes
or, at least, of shifts of emphasis" (448). They note that these patterns of gendered relationships persisted alongside certain significant changes such as the change from arranged marriages to marriages based on romantic love and the changing basis of paternal
authority from religious and scholarly expertise to financial success.

The article describes husband-wife, father-son, mother-son,
father-daughter, and mother-daughter relationships and portrays
all as carrying considerable tension. The portrait resonates life in
the Schlossberg home and is consistent with the now-extensive
writings on the Russian Jewish immigrant family (Prell 1999; Weinberg 1988). The focus is on the mother-daughter and father-daughter relationships and strongly echoes Landes's personal experiences:
"A girl's place in the family is a reflection of her mother's, but her
truly affectionate tie is with her father. She is peculiarly his; when
she is little, her father calls her his 'queen' and 'princess.' At all
ages she is the one family member in whose company he can relax"
(Landes and Zborowski 1952:455). "The mother observes all this and
complains that the father spoils his daughter ... she herself nags
her daughter, especially before marriage, but conveys none of the
overtones of affection and play that temper her nagging of husband and son" (456). "With his daughter, the father is indulgent
and undemanding.... Real intimacy is not expected of a Jewish
father ... but he shows his daughter a unique affection and comradeship" (456). "The daughter may utilize her father's indulgence
to advance herself beyond the limitations of her status" (456).

Ruth Landes was an avid filmgoer all her life, and here she reflected on the film *God, Flesh and the Devil*, which she had recently
seen. Based on a Yiddish play, the film told the story of a childless couple who raised the orphaned daughters of the wife's sister.
When the eldest girl reached marriageable age, her foster father

proposed marriage, saying he could legally divorce his wife because their 20-year marriage had not yielded any children (as he phrased it, "she is barren"). The foster daughter accepted the proposal, and her foster mother resigned herself to the situation. Ruth interpreted the plot as indicating "the powerful emotional current that possibly underlies relations between father and daughter, threatening to draw them together and to displace the mother from her wifely status" (456). She continued in a passage that described her own troubled relationship with her mother:

Since her status is defined in terms of her domestic roles, [the mother] expresses her anxieties in this area. . . . The mother-daughter relationship contains more rivalry and even hostility than do the other family couplings. . . . Though she nags at all members of the family, in her special woman's idiom of communication, she nags at her daughter in a consistently hostile manner . . . she is determined to keep the daughter in her place as a junior female as long as the latter lives in the parental home . . . the mother does not really wish to teach the daughter cooking or any other skill that might replace her own services, and so she rails, for example, "Keep out of my kitchen! This is my kitchen! You don't know how to cook! You just waste time and food." . . . When the daughter makes a household suggestion or any other suggestion touching on the mother's sphere of influence, the mother may react as to a challenge and strive to confine her. This can be interpreted as the mother's jealous protection of the adult status she acquired by marriage. (456–457).

A shift "from authoritarian to egalitarian" in the relationship between mother and daughter would occur only upon marriage when the daughter leaves her parents' home.

* * *

Ruth's relations with her parents were never resolved in part because she never fulfilled the ideal adult roles of an immigrant daughter: she never did establish her own household with husband and children. Instead, she married twice, briefly both times, and divorced. Rather than become a mother, she terminated three pregnancies in abortions. In midlife, she told her mother that "my trouble re marriage and other things was that this family—unlike other Jewish families, doted on its daughter instead of its son, and reared her in confusion as to whether she was a boy or a girl" (December 3, 1950, Notebook 4, RLP). Because Ruth lived many years working without secure employment, she often called on her father for financial help or even returned home to live with her parents when she was between jobs and looking for work. As late as 1959 when she was still working on short-term teaching contracts and hoping for a permanent academic appointment, her parents were writing to her, as they had when she was a student, to say that they were "happy with her progress."[9] She was over 50 years old, but because she was an unmarried woman without children she did not have adult status in her parents' eyes. When her father died in 1971 at the age of 95, he left Ruth's inheritance in trust with her brother. She was 62 years old. Anna died in 1976, also at the age of 95. Ruth did not attend either of her parents' funerals.

CHAPTER TWO

New Woman

*In anticipation I can say that my gender was never an argument by my parents
against schooling, graduate study, association with Blacks, Africans, people of
other revealed religions.* – RL to George Park, May 20, 1985, RLP, box 1

COMING OF AGE in New York during the 1920s and 1930s,
Ruth was caught in the furor of flappers, the gendered
images in advertising, films, and plays, the arguments for
companionate marriage, and the public debates surrounding the
working girl. Popular images of women were changing from self-
sacrificing and maternal to sexually provocative and glamorous. Ex-
pressions of feminism moved away from the political and economic
reforms advocated by the turn-of-the-century women's movement
and toward a more individualized focus on equality with men and
freedom of (hetero)sexual expression. This was the period between
the two World Wars and encompassed the Great Depression (1929–
33) and a further economic downturn during 1937–38.

The time was one of massive social and economic transformation
in the United States. Over one-half of the population now lived in
urban areas. Most lived in apartments, but by the end of the 1920s
people were flocking to newly built suburbs. By 1928 one in six
Americans owned a car. Economic growth measured by manufac-
turing production, per capita income, and consumer spending was
at an all-time high. Advertising emerged as a major industry in the
1920s, becoming a new means of both socialization and representation of women, who purchased 80 percent of all consumer goods
(Cott 1987:172). Wage earnings of industrial workers, advertiser-
promoted consumer behavior, and new forms of communication
and leisure (especially radio and movies) combined — despite continuing rural-urban and South-North differences and increasing
immigration and ethnic diversity — to give birth to American mass

culture in the 1920s. During that decade, 40 percent of households acquired radios, and by 1929 weekly attendance at movie theaters numbered 100 million to 115 million (142).

When Ruth Schlossberg entered New York University in the 1920s, daughters of immigrants, second-generation Jewish women, were enrolling in coeducational high schools and colleges in disproportionately higher numbers than women of other ethnic groups. At the turn of the century, most women who went to college were daughters of elite families and attended the private women's colleges. In the early decades of the 20th century, public postsecondary education expanded and became more accessible for an increasingly ethnically diverse population. By 1930 nearly 20 percent of Americans between the ages of 18 and 22 were enrolled full-time in college or graduate school, quadruple the proportion of young people who were receiving higher education at the turn of the century. Women's attendance advanced faster than men's: in 1890 only 35 percent of college students were women, but by the 1920s women constituted almost half of the college population (Cott 1987:219). By 1934, 52.1 percent of female college students in New York were Jewish (Weinberg 1988:175).

When upon her graduation in 1929 at age 21 Ruth Schlossberg married, she followed the course of most women graduates of the time. The average age at marriage for women was 22.5 in the 1920s. Historians Charlotte Baum, Paula Hyman, and Sonya Michel note: "For women of all classes and all educational levels, marriage was the prevailing social expectation of the twenties and thirties. It was the unusual woman who went against the tide" (1976:233). Although the divorce rate also increased in the 1920s, the proportion of women who never married was reduced by almost one-third. "People were marrying younger and more of them were marrying. . . . The same cohorts of women who were flowing into secondary and higher education and into the job market in the 1920s, in other words, were those who were marrying younger and making more certain to marry" (Cott 1987:147–148, 332). Women's increased labor force participation also encouraged younger marriage since the earnings of both husband and wife could contribute to the savings of the household.

Most women quit their jobs once children were born, and this was especially true of college graduates in the 1920s. The consumer-housewife symbolized a husband's and household's material success and also became intimately tied to dominant notions of masculinity, so that a working wife symbolically emasculated a husband by publicizing his inability to provide for the family. Immigrants aspired to these middle-class notions of respectability that stressed that married women remain in the home. Immigrant daughters were expected to work before marriage, but the question of women working after marriage was unresolved for this generation. Economic necessity might require that women return to wage work at some points during the marriage, but aspirations for social mobility and for integration in American society made married women's wage work undesirable.

Premarital sexual experimentation was widely assumed and accepted in the 1920s, and such feminist historians as Nancy Cott suggest that the increased rate of marriage for college women was a product of greater public discussion and acceptance of women's sexuality. Like other young college women, Ruth Schlossberg flaunted a new image of femininity whose trademarks were smoking, drinking, sex, and staying out at night. She linked free expression of sexuality with a modern American identity — not with feminism. In this she was also typical of modern young women of her generation. According to Cott: "Young women in the 1920s connected female heterosexual expression with bravado, pleasure, and knowledge, with a modern, and realistic approach to life — perhaps even with a more egalitarian ideal of relations between the sexes — but they did not (by and large) connect it with feminism" (151). At the turn of the century the term *New Woman* referred to ambitious, career-oriented, middle-class reformist and unmarried women who had been educated at the women's colleges. The New Woman in the 1920s referred to women like Ruth who located their identity in individualism, consumerism, experimental heterosexual relationships, and "companionate marriage" based on notions of romantic love.[1]

Overt critique of the institution of marriage all but disappeared in the 1920s (Cott 1987:160). In its place a modern discourse on companionate marriage seduced the young Ruth Schlossberg into thinking that in a modern marriage she could avoid the pitfalls that

she observed and feared in her mother's married life. She was also
attracted to American idealization of romantic marriage. Romantic marriage, as Riv-Ellen Prell writes: "created a new household
through freely chosen love that simultaneously rejected traditional
Jewish authority relations and espoused the national values of
freedom, equality and pleasure" (1999:60). Romantic marriage
appeared as a desirable alternative to traditional Jewish marriage
arrangements, and because it was based on love and attraction, it
appeared to translate modern notions of comradeship and partnership into the domestic setting.

The idea of companionate marriage was constructed in the context of a public debate on the nature of female sexuality in the 1920s
and 1930s. Experts—social scientists, physicians, sexologists, and
ethicists—produced "scientific evidence" to argue the heterosexuality of "normal" female sexual drives and the "abnormality" of
homosexuality.[2] New social sites for heterosexual mixing—public
high schools and universities, factories, movie halls, amusement
parks—promoted women's sexual expression within these contexts and reinforced heterosexuality as the norm. As Cott observes:
"Just when individual wage-earning made it more possible than
ever before for women to escape the economic necessity to marry,
the model of companionate marriage with its emphasis on female
heterosexual desires made marriage a sexual necessity, for 'normal'
satisfaction" (1987:158). The experts described companionate marriage as a new site for "emotional intimacy, personal and sexual expression, and nurture among husband, wife, and a small number
of children" even though married women did not have economic
equality with men, and the gendered division of labor within marriage remained unchanged in that women, as wives, were responsible for domestic tasks and child rearing (156). As Riv-Ellen Prell
notes: "Companionate marriage and love implied a very specific
set of social relationships built on men as providers and women
as consumers and managers" (1999:85). Marital advice books described "an ideal of intimate sexual partnership in which female
sexuality is presumed and marriage was for eliciting the partners'
individuality as well as for uniting them" (Cott 1987:157). The ideal
of companionate marriage in the 1920s made sex the ostensible
centerpiece of marriage, firmly established heterosexuality as the

norm for female sexual expression, and simultaneously confirmed conventional marriage as women's destination.

Women who did not marry were now suspect, and relationships between women — once so prevalent as to go unnoticed — were re-assessed. As a majority of the women who publicly identified as feminists in the late 19th century and the first decades of the 20th century were also unmarried, feminism now became linked in the public mind with "maladjustment" and "abnormality." By the 1920s, charges of lesbianism had become a common way to discredit women professionals, reformers, and educators (Smith-Rosenberg 1989:115). Although small groups of lesbians, especially writers and artists, did continue to flourish in the 1920s, these groups withdrew from the kind of collective public defense of women's political, economic or professional rights that had concerned earlier generations of feminists.[3]

According to historian Carroll Smith-Rosenberg, two symbolic constructions now stigmatized the feminist New Woman: the "Mannish Lesbian" (who was linked to transvestism and women's assumptions of male roles) and the aging "Lady in Lavender" college professor who was said to "prey . . . on the innocence of young girls, teaching them to fear men and their own [i.e., heterosexual] sexual impulses" (1989:113–116). Sexologists linked lesbianism — which they referred to as "sexual inversion" — to a rejection of conventional female roles and saw it as a sign of disorder, a threat to social order. Male sex reformers, psychologists, and physicians effectively removed the question of women's autonomy from political and economic contexts and redefined it in sexual terms. In Smith-Rosenberg's view, the subjectivity of the younger generation of New Women of Ruth Schlossberg's cohort in the 1920s is "de-centered" and "incoherent" — the result of "investing male images with feminist political intent" (117).

The "flapper," not the "feminist," emerged as the symbol of female emancipation, and the dominant image of the modern young woman as "the culture of modernity and urbanity absorbed the messages of feminism and re-presented them" (Cott 1987:174). Not interested in political activism, this new single woman sought physical freedom, lack of parental interference, sexual awareness, and escape from routine. The educated middle-class woman-identified suffragette whose self-presentation was asexual and morally superior seemed to have disappeared, buried under the new images of carefree smoking, drinking, and sexually adventurous flappers, of exceptional public role models such as Amelia Earhart, of glamorous Hollywood stars, and of happy consumer-housewives.[4]

Ruth Landes saw herself as progressive in her free expression and pleasure in sexuality, but she never identified with feminism as a political movement. That she did not can partly be explained by the public conflation of feminism with "sexual maladjustment" during the interwar years of her young adulthood. Unlike her father, who dedicated his life to collective political organizing for communal well-being, Ruth was driven by individualistic goals for self-actualization. It would be through anthropology, not feminism, that she would launch her critique of gender relations in American society.

Black Jews of Harlem

As Ruth Landes dramatically told it years later, a chance encounter "stirred [her anthropological] imagination" in the fall of 1928 when she was still a student at the New York School of Social Work before she met Boas and before she studied anthropology.

I myself heard of them purely by chance, from a stranger, one afternoon at a Broadway theatre when attending a new George Gershwin musical with my father. Near us sat a blond young rabbi turned lawyer, named Harold Roland Shapiro. Was it Gershwin's genius for Negro themes that led him to tell us that he had been attending Black Jewish services? This accident, more than the rising and brilliant 'Negro Renaissance' of the intellectuals, stirred my imagination. (Landes 1967b:175)

Landes suggests she was *by nature* an anthropologist because she recognized the phenomenon of the Black Jews as a creative cultural process and because she appreciated the cultural agency of the marginal and dispossessed. Her storytelling highlights how acculturation challenged stereotypes and how the mixing attracted the iconoclast Ruth Landes: the blond rabbi turned secular lawyer; the Jewish composer writing in the black mediums of jazz and spiritual; the Black Jewish services in Harlem. Among these hybrids she inserted herself and her own project of composing a new life course for an immigrant daughter.

Following this afternoon encounter she and the former rabbi, Harold Shapiro, attended a service of the Black Jewish congregation, Beth B'nai Abraham, in Harlem. She found a group of poor recent Caribbean migrants, mostly women, struggling against racial discrimination and poverty and following the charismatic leadership of Barbadian choirmaster Arnold J. Ford. Ford asserted hereditary rights to the office of rabbi and had adopted the wearing of the skullcap and the shield of David emblem for his "synagogue." He argued that Judaism originated in Africa, and through a convoluted history of past migrations, intermarriages, and cultural contacts he identified his congregation as descendants of the first Hebrews. Ford planned to lead a group of "pioneers" back to Africa to reclaim their rights and homeland. Landes decided to study this social and cultural phenomenon as the subject of her master's thesis.

The School of Social Work was one of the channels of higher education open to Jewish women in the 1920s, and for Ruth social work neatly combined the Schlossberg family's goals for higher education, images of gender-appropriate work, and socialist ideas about the social responsibility of intellectuals. Studying the Black Jews in Harlem allowed Ruth to build on values of her family and at the same time to move out from the Jewish milieu as she so wanted to do. Ruth passed through both Jewish and black neighborhoods of Harlem as she traveled each day to and from the Bronx to the School of Social Work.

Significantly, as she tells it, she was with her father at this portentous moment, and it would be through him that she would discover anthropology as the intellectual forum that would give her license to observe, record, discuss, and analyze the cultural worlds on the margins of mainstream society that intrigued her and with which she identified. It would be with her father's friend, "Goldy," the "brilliant and thoroughly unreliable" Alexander Goldenweiser, that she would first discuss the Black Jews, and it would be Goldenweiser, Franz Boas's favorite student, who would lead her to Boas and anthropology (Deacon 1997:99).

After her graduation and marriage in June 1929, Ruth worked as a social worker in Harlem and continued to visit the Beth B'nai

Abraham synagogue. During this time she met with Boas to discuss the beliefs and practices of the Harlem Black Jews. He encouraged her to publish the results of her research and to consider doctoral studies in anthropology.[5]

Ruth's anthropological sensibility was rooted in her intimate personal experiences of acculturation. As she recorded her observations of cultural mixing in Harlem in the 1920s, she began to hone the ethnographic skills she had intuitively begun to develop as a child in the union halls. Here she also began to develop the comparative perspective that is so central in anthropology. It was the height of the Harlem Renaissance, the explosion of African American artistic production in theater, poetry, literature, and music known as the New Negro Movement (Baker 1998; Franklin 1974; Huggins 1971; Johnson 1968). Ruth, like her father, admired the work of the Harlem intellectual elite: the poetic writing of the cosmopolitan Langston Hughes, the social critique of Walter White, James Weldon Johnson, and Alain Locke, and the spiritual voice of Paul Robeson. As a social worker, however, she worked with the poor and illiterate recent migrants from the southern states and various Caribbean islands who had moved north by the tens of thousands during the Great Migration after World War I and whose lives were far removed from the artistic world of the intellectuals of the Harlem Renaissance. Class and cultural differences divided Harlem's 350,000 blacks, and Ruth's sympathies and intellectual curiosity led her to explore the less well known communal life and cultural production of the poor. And so in Harlem in the 1920s she began her career of observing the social worlds of the nonliterate and non-elite, of those who were excluded in modernist nation building. Of the Harlem black community, she observed:

Although the group as a whole has the same fundamental problem to face — the winning of status in the American community — the different classes within it are not equally equipped to handle the problem. A very small minority possesses real advantages, such as higher education, physical traits of the white group, friends among the upper-class whites, wealth, opportunities for demonstrating ability; while the majority lacking these assets are quite disabled ... find practically no support from the white world and its social system and are driven to test their own slight, untutored, resources. They encourage the emergence of certain restless personalities, men born of them who most eloquently symbolize their strivings. The Jamaican Marcus Garvey and the American Father Divine are the two such leaders best known to the white world. Besides these there are a number of minor leaders, supported by small and usually short-lived followings.[6] (1967b:177)

There were more than 100 African American churches in Harlem in 1930. Intellectuals of the Harlem Renaissance such as James Weldon Johnson and activist organizations such as the National Association for the Advancement of Colored People (NAACP) criticized the churches as "ephemeral," "nomadic," and "belonging to no established denomination." According to Johnson: "Many of their leaders are parasitical fakers, even downright scoundrels, who count themselves successful when they have under the guise of religion got enough hard-working women together to ensure them an easy living" (1968:163–164).

Arnold Ford was one of these minor leaders. He was the former choirmaster of Marcus Garvey's Universal Negro Improvement Association (UNIA) and had founded the Beth B'nai Abraham congregation in 1924 as a breakaway group from the UNIA. Like Garvey, Ford's religious philosophy was a political nationalist program advocating a "return to Africa." For ritual and scripture, Ford had turned to Judaism because, Landes said, he had observed "the prominence of philanthropic Jews in the American Negro world and more immediately in Harlem" and had noted how successful other churches were in fund-raising from Jewish sympathizers (1967b:180). According to Landes, he secured patronage for the congregation from many of their Jewish neighbors in Harlem (175). The Black Jews, Landes noted, through their adoption of Jewish religious ritual, hoped to reproduce the material success of immigrant Jews. Some members of the congregation sent their children to a white high school in Jewish Harlem for Hebrew instruction. As one practitioner bluntly explained to her: "We think the Jews are a great people! They have gone far in spite of their persecution! They own all the money in the country. Their religion did that for them, and may be it will do the same for us" (186).[7]

The Beth B'nai Abraham congregation dissolved after six years due to internal disputes. Arnold Ford, criticized for unscrupulous handling of money and for his relations with women congregationists, abandoned the group and reportedly sailed for Africa. Landes concluded her thesis by observing that, although the group disbanded, the conditions of social and economic insecurity that spawned it continued and "provid[ed] fertile soil for the growth of all mushroom organizations. The Negro masses drift among religious sects, among healing cults, among lodges, among political clubs seeking stimulation and substance" (187).[8] An article based on her thesis was rejected by the *American Journal of Sociology* because, the editor explained, the movement was not endorsed by the NAACP and therefore was "unimportant" (RB to RL, August 2, 1933, RFBP).

Ruth Landes's master's degree study of the Black Jews presaged her lifelong interest in new religious movements, one of the threads that runs through her ethnographic research in different cultural contexts: the Ojibwa Midéwiwin society and shamanism in Ontario and Minnesota; the Potawatomi Drum Dance, Peyote religious movement, and medicine bundle religions in Kansas; the Afro-Brazilian candomblé spirit possession practices and healing rituals in Bahia. Her original interests in anthropology also presaged the studies of acculturation and cultural change and messianic and nativistic revitalization movements that soon became important subjects of study in the discipline.[9] Building on the Harlem experience, in her Brazilian fieldwork Landes would also be a pioneer in adapting anthropological methods to urban settings. Urban research was atypical in the anthropology of her day, which focused on isolated and small-scale societies.

Seeking Independence

Ruth's work in Harlem aggravated tensions in her already fragile marriage. In an unpublished "lightly fictionalized" autobiographical memoir,[10] she described her sense of loss in the romantic ideals of companionate marriage:

What did the whole situation mean? The confusion was terrifying. The only comprehensible period had been the courtship, an impassioned playtime when they had visited each other at their respective colleges and gone to dances and weekend parties. The marriage ritual, which should have opened stately corridors, seemed instead to drop curtains over young glamor. She had become bored. The handsome young man she married was metamorphosed into a sulky, fatigued, penniless doctoral student, averse to her conversation but intent on her presence at home. She would ask herself aghast, Must I endure this for decades to come, my God, for fifty years more? There isn't even any passion. Does marriage destroy sex, at the age of twenty? What happened to love? What happened to our dreams? What happened? (N.d., "Athens":77)

As the protagonist "Adele," she presented herself as daring and different from her "set" — from the group of friends she shared with her husband — because she was choosing separation and divorce and because she was moving outside their social circle to friendship and intimacy with blacks: "Their intellectual friends (still unmarried) discussed free love, companionate marriage, divorce, and even partying with Negroes. Free love and companionate marriage were not altogether mysterious. . . . Divorce and Negroes were something else. No one in their set had first-hand acquaintance with either. But discussion approached these rising phenomena bravely, in a noble spirit of daring and so-called 'frankness.' . . . But thus was talk; who of them had actually sought divorce!" (78–79).

Although she dared to be different, she also experienced the dissipation of her marriage as humiliation and failure:

The humiliation that the law added to the private torment decided Adele to choose, for future use, an alternate word to divorce. Could she say she was widowed, even at her early age? People died of heart attacks in childhood. As widowhood meant being left alone, then that was the word. It had been some time coming, if she'd but understood portents. For her husband had broken his hostile silence to denounce her graduate studies, though . . . was he not studying? Had they not met through college circles? But it was "different" for her; she was to stay in. Oh-h-h! Weren't they intellectual equals? Especially while they couldn't afford a family? Oh-h-h! "Stay home and quit school — or I leave!" "Well! Leave then!" she had declared. He had sprung up, snatched his hat (to think she'd married a chap called "the best-dressed in his class yearbook"!) and departed for good to his mother. All was over. At age twenty-three.

Over! Nothing had even begun! There had been no pattern, no purpose — nothing to test themselves by. There had been her illusions, probably attached to his presence and to the words reflecting their married status. For at his be-hatted exit, these pillars of her universe trembled, thundered,

and crashed. Bruised and stunned, she slept, wakened to weep, slept fur-
ther. Sleeping and waking, her mind circled the debris of old assumptions.
What did they mean: love, marriage, partnership, ideals? How could she
continue without faith in illusions? What was she to do? Who was she?
When they married, she and her husband had talked of life as fulfilling
themselves and adding to society by fine deeds and thoughts, expedited by
professional skills. In the end, this was not his dream. (N.d., "Athens":79)

In 1931, within two years of their marriage, Ruth and her husband had separated.[11] She was 23 years old. Taking with her "a less
Jewish sounding name" but with the stigma of divorce and a sense
of loss and disillusionment, she returned to live with her parents in
their Bronx apartment. In the fall of 1931 she entered the doctoral
program in anthropology at Columbia.

CHAPTER THREE

Student at Columbia

How many loved your moments of glad grace,
And loved your beauty with love false or true,
But one . . . loved the pilgrim soul in you . . .
– W. B. Yeats, "When You are Old and Full of Sleep"

"MRS. LANDES meet Mrs. Benedict. Mrs. Benedict, this is Mrs. Landes" was Franz Boas's introduction when, one September day in 1931, he took the new student, 23-year-old Ruth Schlossberg Landes, down the hall to meet Ruth Benedict, who was his "right-hand" (Mead 1959) and was to be Landes's main supervisor. "I never had the courage," Ruth Landes later recalled, "to inform him that the marriage was dissolved when I joined his Department. For it was still considered disgraceful when a woman lived unmarried" (n.d., "Ruth Benedict":4). Although neither woman in fact lived with either Mr. Landes or Mr. Benedict, Boas allowed himself to think of them as financially provided for by husbands, as not requiring secure paid employment, and as pursuing anthropology as a vocation motivated purely by intellectual curiosity.[1] While Boas was incorrect in assuming that the two women were economically protected by husbands, it was true that they were pursuing anthropology not only for career purposes but also as part of their creative efforts to improvise lives as New Women in early-20th-century America. In this project of self-realization that Richard Handler calls a "hallmark of modernism" (1990:164), they quickly recognized one another as "pilgrim souls."

Landes later recalled the moment of meeting Benedict: "Boas had taken me, a bewildered young creature, into her office to explain that he had invited me to study with them. He had in fact invited me a whole year before, when I had ventured to consult him about Negro movements that were bursting out all over the United States, in all social groups. I had taken the year to ponder this very re-condite discipline, to consider spending time on the luxury of it during the profound economic depression when I actually had a social work job (paying about $2,500 a year), to appraise my inten-tion against the threat of my young husband to depart if I adopted graduate study. My final decision promised a very difficult if inter-esting life" (Landes n.d., "Ruth Benedict":1).

* * *

If Landes's domestic life was undergoing irreversible changes, her first year of study during the winter of 1931–32 also marked the beginning of a decade of change in Columbia's Department of An-thropology. Franz Boas suffered a heart attack in December 1931. Already emotionally debilitated by the sudden death of his wife in a car accident in 1929, Boas began to withdraw from the admin-istration of the department he had founded in 1899 and in which he had trained the first generation of professional anthropologists, several of whom were now directing new anthropology programs in universities across the country.[2] Ruth Benedict (1887–1948) had entered the graduate program in 1921 and received her Ph.D. in 1923. After his heart attack in 1931, Boas increasingly left the responsi-bility of managing the day-to-day affairs of the graduate program to Benedict. Although he continued to supervise doctoral students until he retired in 1936, during this prewar decade he also began to devote his energies to anti-Nazi activities in the United States.[3]

The impetus for Franz Boas's anthropology was his critique of the speculative generalizations of 19th-century unilinear schemes of social evolution. In these schemes small-scale foraging societies were the least "evolved" — the most "primitive" — and Western so-cieties were at the pinnacle of this presumed universal process. Ar-guing against evolutionary thinking that supported the political subordination and economic marginalization of small-scale soci-eties through racism and colonial processes, Franz Boas argued in-stead that each society, no matter how simple or complex its social organization, was the product of its own history. He established it as anthropology's mandate to place individual cultures within the contexts of their own particular histories and environmental settings and to endeavor to appreciate the meaning of behavior and customs within these specific contexts. The first step in this program for cultural relativism was to employ rigorous descriptive methods to record the distribution of culture traits and trait complexes and to establish local and regional histories and relationships among groups. The doctoral dissertations of Boas's students were such trait distribution studies as "Decorative Symbolism of the Arapaho" (Kroeber in 1901), "The Concept of the Guardian Spirit in North America" (Benedict in 1923), or "The Cattle Complex in East Africa" (Herskovits in 1923).

If the ultimate goal was to understand what was called "the native point of view," Boas saw this as a later stage possible only after a large number of descriptive studies using empirical methods had cumulatively illustrated that a unilinear sequence did not exist. These detailed empirical studies of the distribution and clustering of traits revealed culture patterns that are the result of social processes of integration produced through local cultural dynamics. In the 1920s some of his students, notably Edward Sapir (1924) and Ruth Benedict (1930), had begun to theorize the integration of culture patterns and the individual's experience of enculturation and membership.[4] Boas identified 1910 as the date that he himself had begun to stress "the problems of cultural dynamics, of integration of culture and of the interaction between the individual and culture" (1940:311). These questions gave direction to culture and personality studies in the late 1920s and 1930s.

The early trait distribution studies were library theses based on published sources. It was only in the 1920s following the pioneering field studies of Bronislaw Malinowski (*Argonauts of the South Pacific,* 1922) and Margaret Mead (*Coming of Age in Samoa,* 1928) that professional anthropology became clearly identified with long-term intensive fieldwork and with the production of scientific monographs that recorded data collected through firsthand observation. And it was only through such intensive fieldwork that anthropology could make the transition from trait distribution as a critique of evolution to a psychologically oriented examination of the integration of cultural wholes that would begin to understand cultures in their own terms. It would be Ruth Benedict who would train students, including Ruth Landes, to identify and study the patterning of values and meaning that integrated and provided the "psychology" of a culture: "Benedict was the key figure in moving the Boasian program from the study of cultural traits to their articulation into cultural wholes" (Darnell 2001:195).

If Boas held a unifying vision for the discipline, by the 1930s it was increasingly apparent that his students did not. With the growth and expansion of the discipline to universities across the United States, the discipline diversified. Each of Boas's students had a slightly different theoretical focus: Benedict and Mead on personality; Sapir on language; Kroeber on cultural configuration and culture areas (from which his student Julian Steward would develop cultural ecology); Paul Radin on religion and philosophical thought; Robert Lowie and others on social organization; and many working on material culture and in archaeology and physical anthropology. Ruth Landes allied herself to Benedict and the culture-and-personality approach.

The anthropology program at Columbia under Boas and Benedict in the 1930s embodied Ruth Landes's ideal intellectual world, one in which individuality could be openly expressed in a climate of debate and controversy. Franz Boas has been described as an "iconoclast," and there is no doubt that Ruth Landes, having these characteristics herself, was attracted to the intellectual environment Boas had created in the anthropology department at Columbia (McMillan 1986). Many of the students in anthropology at Columbia in the 1930s were also mature students who, like Landes, brought diverse life experiences into the classroom. And unlike the Midwestern or New England Anglo-American student bodies of other anthropology departments, a large proportion of the students in anthropology at Columbia were Jewish. Like Ruth Landes, they were propelled by personal and romantic optimisms and motivated by the social urgencies of the time: race relations, poverty, fascism, communism, and the imminence of war.

The program was unstructured: students registered for two years of graduate work and spent the first year in residence taking courses. There were few required courses, and often no exams and no grades were given. In a 1932 letter Boas described the program to his former student Alfred Kroeber, who had established the Department of Anthropology at Berkeley: "Our general method of

administration has been such that we set aside a very general allocation of work that has to be done and we leave everybody free to
do what he considers himself best fit to do. . . . I am of the opinion that the principal thing students have to learn is how to tackle
problems, while the subject matter has to be learned by them by
experience" (February 27, 1931, FBP Papers).

Boas and Benedict possessed an enormous capacity for hard work;
they were in their offices seven days a week and expected the same
intense commitment from their students. Boas set high standards
for students and assumed a breadth of knowledge that few possessed. Students were expected to develop a "general knowledge"
in the four subfields of anthropology (linguistics, physical anthropology, archaeology, and cultural anthropology) and to special-
ize in one. Boas also encouraged students to take courses "across
the hall" in the psychology department, with which anthropology
shared a student reading room in Skermerhorn Extension. Sociology, however, was clearly separated from anthropology at Columbia, and students rarely took courses in both disciplines.[5] Key to
student learning was the weekly Wednesday afternoon graduate
seminar where students who had recently returned from the field
presented their preliminary research and discussed their experiences. Students also gathered daily at "Al's place," a stationery store
and luncheonette just off campus, to discuss and debate their readings. Both community and factionalism ruled. Anthropology at
Columbia in the 1930s was "more in the nature of a debating society" than a "school of thought" (McMillan 1986:56). This learning
environment socially and intellectually suited Ruth Landes.

Ruth Landes entered anthropology at this transitional time in
its history, and she can be understood as a transitional figure in the
discipline. She would retain elements of Boas's trait distribution
approach and implement Benedict's theory of the psychological
integration of culture, but building on her own gendered experiences of acculturation, she would also innovate an intuitive analysis
contextualizing culture within relations of gender, class, and race,
an analytical approach that anticipates the studies of power and
cultural dynamics that were to become so important in late-20th-
century anthropology.

Women in the Discipline in the 1930s

I recall the decade of my studies at Columbia University, when "women's lib" was as yet uncoined but, under Boas, there was professorial acceptance of women as equally people... it was heady for us and obnoxious to certain men. Its singularity still arrests the mind. (Landes 1976a:348–349)

The same urge to see aboriginal mentality in all its phases has made Boas encourage work by trained women. Since primitive peoples often draw a sharp line between the sexes socially, a male observer is automatically shut out from the native wife's or mother's activities. A woman anthropologist, on the other hand, may naturally share in feminine occupations that would expose a man to ridicule. Women have made important contributions independently of Boas, but probably nowhere have they achieved so much work as under the stimulation of the Columbia atmosphere. (Lowie 1937:134)

During the interwar years under Boas and Benedict, Columbia was unique among American universities in its openness to women, and the number of women who obtained degrees in anthropology nearly equaled the number of men.[6] Contrary to Lowie's essentialist construction of the "woman anthropologist," women have adopted different personas and produced a wide diversity of scholarship and writing in the discipline. Their guises have included the 19th-century social reformist, Alice Fletcher (Lurie 1966; Mark 1988); the wealthy patroness, feminist, and New Woman, Elsie Clews Parsons (Deacon 1997); the mentor and poetess, Ruth Benedict (Babcock 1995; Modell 1983); the honorary male, Margaret Mead (Parezo 1993); the anthropological wife, Frances Herskovits or Marjorie Shostak (Tedlock 1995); the African American and Native American Boasian daughters, Zora Neale Hurston and Ella Deloria, who humanized and "voiced" colonized experience (Finn 1995; Hernandez 1995; hooks 1990); the dutiful daughter, Gladys Reichard (Lamphere 1993); and the unruly daughter/disruptive woman, Ruth Landes (S. Cole 1995a).

Despite their number and diversity, in *Hidden Scholars* (1993) Nancy Parezo refutes the view that anthropology is the "welcoming science" for women. Not only did few of the women find permanent employment, but she maintains that they were also constrained in the research they undertook.[7] According to Parezo, women's careers have followed strategies of accommodation, compartmentalization, or confrontation. These gender-specific strategies are reflected in choice of research topics, of field site, of writing style, and of career goals. Successful (or secure) women in anthropology have typically been those who accepted and accommodated the constraints. Parezo observes: "[Women] tried to work around [the barriers] — to whittle away at the edges — by working hard, ignoring the discrimination, hoping no one noticed them, demonstrating they were not bad risks" (338). This is what Margaret Rossiter has referred to as "a strategy of deliberate overqualification and personal stoicism" (1982:129). Accommodation required adopting the comportment of a dutiful daughter — of a "good girl." It meant conducting research on topics that reflected what Robert Lowie called "natural feminine occupations," topics that minimized competition with men, that, he said, would "expose a man to ridicule" if he showed interest in them, and that were "considered of minor theoretical importance" (Lowie 1937:134; Parezo 1993:337). These were topics such as culture-and-personality studies, child rearing and socialization, and health and nutrition.[8] Accommodation strategies also often included adopting a nontheoretical (and therefore "nonscientific"), descriptive style of writing; emphasizing one's role as teacher rather than researcher; and popularizing anthropology rather than maintaining an exclusive professional scientific audience for one's work.

Compartmentalization, Parezo says, characterized the anthropology of Ruth Benedict, who "compartmentalized [her] discourse, writing poetry under pseudonyms, disguising or eliminating [her] feminist writings under pressure to conform to standards of scientific, objective, and apolitical academic anthropology" (1993:339–340). Barbara Babcock, one of Benedict's biographers, has similarly interpreted Benedict's writing as "coded and double-voiced," with "issues of race and ethnicity stand[ing] in for gender," and suggests that Ruth Benedict's anthropological writing about cultural "others" was a way to write metaphorically about (her own) gendered experience as "other" (1995:122).

Least successful were women who fought against gender stereotypes and adopted an uncompromising "bad girl" confrontational style that aptly describes Ruth Landes's eventual comportment in anthropology. Parezo writes: "The confrontational style . . . was used by idealistic, stubborn, liberal/radical women who continually fought against all societal stereotypes of women and worked for the feminist goal of full equality" (1993:339). Nancy Lurie has observed that a woman anthropologist who incited controversy through confrontation "is remembered for her personality rather than for her works" (1966:65). This is certainly true in the case of Ruth Landes, whose writing was rarely cited until its rediscovery in the late 20th century, but whose personality was much talked of for years in the corridors of universities. Furthermore, according to Parezo, "Even for confrontational women, certain areas of writing and theoretical statements were too controversial and too dangerous to use. A strong feminist controversial style would have led to ostracism or blacklisting" (1993:339–340). Late in her life, reflecting back on her career, Ruth Landes herself would say that her ethnographic focus on the lives of women in Ojibwa and Afro-Brazilian cultures had hampered her from gaining "straight professional attention" and that "my personality was focussed on, not theirs . . . I was the presuming woman" (1980).

Ruth Benedict, Teacher and Mentor

You and Boas have set a tone to the Department which has unfitted many of us for effective dealing with the critters outside. On the other hand, you provoke something like religious enthusiasm among those of us who draw breath from great personal qualities rather than from the pursuit of ambition. I was never happy until I began to study with you and I owe you far more that my Ph.D. The Ph.D. was incidental to the things I was doing through your inspiration. (RL to RB, November 11, 1939, RFBP)

Ruth Landes had never known anyone like Ruth Benedict. On that September day when Boas introduced them, the two women began a relationship that was probably the most complex in Landes's life. Benedict was a woman who, like Landes, had escaped a stifling marriage and who sought productive and creative work, but she had also been born into an established Anglo-American family and was a Vassar graduate and New York professor. She represented much that Ruth Landes aspired to in her personal quest for both integration and autonomy, and Landes longed for her approval:

She was the sole woman employed in graduate anthropology at a major American university. . . . To see her was looking at a star. . . . She met her appointment with brilliance, of a special sort; and we, her students, shone in the reflection. . . . From such as she, none doubted who worked with her, were goddesses made. . . . Her physical self was important though not principal. Her face was elegantly lovely — oval and olive-skinned, graced by a dainty aquiline nose, long watching grey eyes that lipread to compensate for her partial deafness, prematurely white cropped hair that crowned her considerable height. Her dress was often dowdy, even for Academia and the Great Depression; and her strong body moved rigidly erect, awkward on turned-out feet, as if trained in ballet. . . . What mesmerized students and others were the attentive, unblinking, luminous eyes. There was her hushed voice also, hushed in volume always, as if restraining something. . . . It put restraints on the listener. Then we who came into her hospitably open office to discuss our studies — we remember that receptiveness all our lives — we would look to her still face with the wide eyes intent upon the speaker and project upon its seeming serenity the approval we longed for. (Landes n.d., "Ruth Benedict":4–6)

Benedict's open, extemporaneous style of presenting ideas during lectures captivated Landes, who usually sat in the front row "looking up her dusty length to the intense half-stricken face. I felt I was about entering that head where the furnace of concepts blazed. . . . When Ruth lectured to us, standing, unconcerned with her chalk-smeared black dress, her voice small, soft, hesitant, she sounded as if she was thinking, in sound. The sentences came slowly, incompletely; words were begun and abandoned; corrections moved back and forth; there were pauses in the parts of speech to incubate a thought. I found it wonderful, wonderful, because the style prompted myriad ideas in me" (n.d., "Ruth Benedict":12). For Landes, Benedict was "a great teacher because she was a unique personality to responsive minds. . . . She pursued anthropology to answer her own private questions about the individual's fate. Her lectures focused on the cultural designs and their sanctions that in each of the various societies mark out the scope of individual lives, bringing torment, dreary suffering, and occasionally special fulfilment. The overwhelming designs or 'patterns' must imprison the soul of each 'culture carrier', or member of society, and they accomplish this in ways that vary from place to place and from one era to another" (14).[9] Landes, in her Native American and Brazilian ethnography, would try to discover the ways in which the individual spirit — the pilgrim soul — can thrive within the constraints of culture.

Benedict's teaching was very much based on establishing personal relationships. According to another biographer, Margaret Caffrey, Benedict had "a bias . . . toward students who were somewhat out of step with the world around them, who grew up like herself as misfits in American culture . . . she seemed to take these people especially under her wing" (1989:266). At the time this seemed a blessing for Landes, who sought Benedict's approval, but in the long term this would not prove strategic. Benedict would discover in Ruth Landes a keen observer and able fieldworker and would help arrange funding for numerous field trips, but she would not help Landes find a permanent academic job in anthropology. Landes's faith in Benedict's mentoring, however, was unshakeable for years to come. "What I . . . remember is that she expected students to produce serious written works, inducing in all of us a grim sense of that responsibility. She conveyed the *attitude* that made scholars of the survivors, receiving us when we wanted to talk, reading every scrap of our manuscripts for eventual appearance in print, finding stipends to support us during the writing, editing the final drafts, and forgetting to congratulate us when the article or book appeared. . . . She paid the inspiring compliment of taking our little achievements for granted" (n.d., "Ruth Benedict":14–15).

Anthropology and the "Abnormal"

Two aspects of Ruth Benedict's theory of cultural integration appeared to address Landes's interests in acculturation and marginalization: Benedict's theorizing of the "abnormal" and her focus on the experience of the individual. Ruth Landes would see that Ruth Benedict's cultural patterns constituted patterns of dominant norms that also created the marginalization of individuals and groups of individuals — "abnormals" — who live outside the patterned norms. Landes's empathy for cultural mixing based on her own experience would lead her to blur the boundaries that Benedict maintained in her dichotomy between the "normal" and the "abnormal" and to see them instead as necessarily coexisting in cultural dynamics. But Benedict's theory of culture would initially guide Ruth Landes's fieldwork with the Canadian Ojibwa (1932) and would continue to frame her research with the Minnesota Chippewa (1933), Santee Sioux (1935), Kansas Potawatomi (1936–37) and Afro-Brazilians in Bahia, Brazil (1938–39), even as her field observations challenged its simplicity. Where Benedict was primarily a theorist, Landes would prove to be a dauntless fieldworker and an acute, intuitive observer. In her ethnography she would highlight the experiences of women, spiritualists, and gender variants and discover the social spaces they created for themselves in marginalized Native American and Afro-Brazilian cultural contexts. In her ethnographies of gender, race, and religion, Landes, basing her work on her observations in the field, ultimately would expand on Ruth Benedict's theoretical framework by showing a more explicit concern for power and cultural change.

Ruth Benedict had moved forward Franz Boas's particularist and cultural relativist program. She simultaneously engaged in an argument that cultures are psychologically integrated wholes and in a critique of American society. She theorized that each culture is integrated around a set of norms, values, and practices in a "more or less consistent pattern" that guides behavior and social interaction (1934:46–47). According to Benedict, a cultural pattern represented an arbitrary selection, through adaptive processes and "unconscious canons of choice," from an "arc" of possible norms, values, and practices (48). She described dominant norms as local cultural definitions of "normality" that are reinforced and reproduced because they are socially constructed as "morally superior." Defining "normality" as "primarily a term for the socially elaborated segment of human behavior in any culture," Benedict talked of "abnormality" as the term for "the segment that [a] particular civilization does not use" (1966:276). "The concept of the normal is properly a variant of the concept of the good. It is that which society has approved," wrote Benedict (276).[10]

Benedict taught that temperaments that are consistent with dominant behavioral norms in a particular cultural setting will also become dominant in that setting, and that other personalities and behaviors will be seen as "abnormal" and will be marginalized in this context. Observing that "most individuals are plastic to the molding force of the society into which they are born" (1966:278), Benedict noted: "Most human beings take the channel that is readymade in their culture. If they can take this channel, they are provided with adequate means of expression. If they cannot, they have all the problems of the aberrant everywhere" (1934:113). Those whose behavior lies outside the local definition of "normal" are "culturally unprovided for" (1966:277).

Rooted in her personal knowledge of marginality due to her experiences of deafness, childless marriage, homosexuality, and the conflict she found between the domesticity of middle-class marriage and her desires for creative expression, Benedict sought to show how dominant values and behaviors are local cultural products, how behavior that is devalued in one cultural context may be the source of authority or distinction in another culture: "Most of those organizations of personality that seem to us most incontrovertibly abnormal have been used by different civilizations in the very foundations of their institutional life. Conversely the most valued traits of our normal individuals have been looked on in differently organized cultures as aberrant," she wrote (1966:276).[11]

She trained her students to observe and document the ways individuals find agency in diverse cultural contexts, and she advocated the life history method for the cross-cultural study of the individual's experience of cultural norms. The life history, she argued, "tests out [an interpretation of] a culture by showing its workings in the life of a carrier of that culture" and is "the essential tool in the study of a culture" (1948:592). She urged the collection of life histories and ethnographic illustrations of cultural contexts in which behaviors deemed "abnormal" in American society (heightened psychic powers, homosexuality) — behaviors that American culture "makes no use of" — may be the foundation of honor, authority, and power. She underscored: "One of the most striking facts that emerge from a study of widely varying cultures is the ease with which our abnormals function in other cultures" (1966:263). Her motivation was her belief that awareness of diverse cultural systems (systems of normality) would create greater tolerance for individual diversity within American society.

Landes saw that by using Ruth Benedict's theoretical framework and methodological approach she could focus on her own interest: individuals whose behavior lies outside the local definition of "normal"—those Benedict called the "culturally unprovided for" (1966:277). Landes's concern was for those members of society whose experience is not reflected in the dominant pattern. She recognized that an analytical focus on the "abnormal" would both reveal dominant norms and patterns and make visible the experience of acculturation and marginality. Sidney Mintz has written of Benedict that "her anthropology was, in some basic way, her own self embodied" (1981:145). This became true for Landes as well.

Planning Fieldwork

As her thesis supervisor, Ruth Benedict advised Landes against further study of African American religious movements and instead encouraged her to conduct her Ph.D. fieldwork in a Native American community as was then the convention in the discipline. Benedict also directed Landes to study the guardian spirit concept, which had been the topic of her own doctoral thesis written almost ten years earlier.[12] Benedict suggested that Landes study the religious practices of the Canadian Ojibwa because little had been published about Ojibwa religion and because she thought they were less assimilated than the Chippewa (Ojibwa) on American reservations. The only published study of Ojibwa religion was W. J. Hoffman's "The Midéwiwin or 'Grand Medicine Society,'" published in 1891 and based on secondary written sources, not on firsthand observation.

Benedict was also concerned about her student's safety. The previous summer a Columbia graduate student, Henrietta Schmerler, had been raped and killed when conducting fieldwork in the American Southwest, and Benedict was cautious now about sending young women to the field alone. She consulted other anthropologists who had recently conducted research in the area: the British-trained New Zealander Diamond Jenness, who had succeeded Edward Sapir as director of the National Museums of Canada and who was conducting research with the Ojibwa of Parry Island, Ontario (Jenness 1935); A. Irving Hallowell of the University of Pennsylvania, who had initiated his long-term research with the Berens River

Ojibwa in Manitoba (1936, 1942, 1953, 1955, 1981, 1992); and Father John Cooper of the Catholic University in Washington DC, who had made a brief field trip to the Ojibwa of Rainy River district along the Minnesota-Ontario border in 1928. The men all recommended that Landes go to Manitou Rapids because a renowned visionary and competent interpreter, Mrs. Maggie Wilson, lived there. Benedict asked Jenness to arrange letters of introduction for Landes to the local Indian agent.[13]

After a year studying with Franz Boas and Ruth Benedict, Ruth Landes left New York by train for Fort Frances, Ontario, where she would spend the summer working with Maggie Wilson at the nearby reserve of Manitou Rapids.

PART TWO

Apprenticeship in Native American Worlds

Prologue

AUGUST 16, 1995: Driving through endless stands of birch and pine bush, we knew we had arrived on Manitou Rapids reserve lands when a police car, appearing from nowhere, signaled me over to the side of the road, and an Ojibwa officer handed me a $300 speeding ticket. The speed limit on reserves is 60 kilometers per hour, a great deal slower than the 90 kmph on provincial highways. I had been traveling 100 kmph.

I had driven almost two thousand kilometers from Montreal in a Honda Civic Wagovan with my two children, Sam, age eight, and Isabella, age six, and was beginning to think the entire expedition foolhardy. I was also nervous, wondering how I would be received. When I had presented a paper discussing Ruth Landes's Ojibwa ethnography at the annual Canadian Anthropology Society meetings the year before, a few anthropologists had accosted me afterward to tell me that some people at Manitou Rapids were unhappy with Ruth Landes's writings. I was making a pilgrimage to meet descendants of her key informant, Maggie Wilson, and to find out for myself how Ruth Landes and her work were remembered.

We continued driving, more slowly now, and arrived in the small community of Manitou Rapids. Ruth Landes's descriptions had not prepared me for the peace and beauty of the place. It was early on a hot afternoon. There was no one on the streets. The community sat on a flat, treeless piece of land that dropped in a clay bluff to the Rainy River. The river could not be seen from the houses. Stark, unadorned, and unlandscaped pastel-colored boxlike houses and trailers sat in the open meadow. Lazy, soft white cumulus clouds drifted in the blue sky; a maze of telephone and hydroelectric wires and poles dissected the horizon. This landscape contrasted sharply with the spruce and pine bush that circled the lakes just 20 kilometers to the north at the hunting-and-fishing camp where we were staying.

We went first to find the river. The water level was low at this time of year, and the river ran gently along a beautiful cracked clay shoreline. It was perhaps a kilometer wide here — Minnesota lay on the other side. A shallow set of late summer rapids slowed the river flow just below the community council office where Sam and Bella explored the shoreline, collecting rocks.

Reluctantly, I tore them away from the idyllic site to climb up the hill to the council office. There the first person we met said he was a grandson of Mrs. Wilson. He did not work for the council; he hung around the office to pass the time and to keep up on town happenings. He told me he "didn't know anything about her" and that I should speak to Jeannie (pseudonym), a granddaughter of Mrs. Wilson, sister of a former chief, and mother of a recent chief. He phoned Jeannie and asked if I could come to speak to her about "our grandmother." She graciously said I could visit her that same afternoon; our aide pointed us in the direction of her trailer, which was just visible on the horizon, and we walked to it across an open grassy field and along the gravel streets of town.

A large, pleasant woman with short gray hair, Jeannie had re-tired that year at the age of 65; she had worked for the Ministry of Education as a consultant for the Ojibwa language. In the living room adjoining an immaculate modern kitchen, we sat on the couch together. Jeannie was wearing cotton pants, a T-shirt, and new deerskin moccasins that her sister had made for her. The room was lined with books and decorated with Ojibwa crafts and art. Throughout our conversation I kept one eye on my son, who could not resist picking up and admiring the carved wood and stone fig-ures of birds and animals that rested on the coffee tables and book-shelves. The O. J. Simpson trial was on the 24-inch TV screen.

Jeannie well remembered her grandmother, Maggie Wilson, but regretted that she had been more interested in "playing" than in learning from her at that time. She said that if she'd "paid atten-tion" then she could "help" me more now. She was 10 or 11 years old when her grandmother died.

Jeannie remembered that her grandmother did beautiful work in embroidery, birch bark, buckskin, and hook rugs. "I don't even know how to hook a rag rug! The ones you see here were made by my sister. . . . My grandmother was also a wonderful cook. I remember her teaching my [future] husband's mother how to make cookies and cakes. It was during the depression and we didn't have all the ingredients, but my grandmother knew how to make wonderful cookies. They were good—really good—even without the ingredients."

Jeannie also admired Maggie Wilson's spiritual powers. She had been "blessed" with her dance and her drum, Jeannie said. Her drum had recently been repaired, she told me. Unfortunately, the neighbor who looked after it was away from Manitou for a few weeks so I would not be able to see the drum. Jeannie remembered that her grandmother "used to do naming ceremonies and received gifts."

I turned the conversation to The Ojibwa Woman, which had been reprinted in 1971, at which time many in the community became aware of it for the first time. "A lot of people were upset by that book," Jeannie told me. "I've read only a few parts. I didn't want to read the book afterwards. There's a lot that's exaggerated. It was only gossip, stories. It should not have been written down. A lot of people felt that it was gossip." Jeannie said that she had not known about it before the 1970s, and until I told her, she had not known that Landes had written two other books about the Ojibwa: Ojibwa Sociology, published in 1937, and Ojibwa Religion and the Midéwiwin, written in the 1930s but not published until 1968. People were concerned only about The Ojibwa Woman, she said. "My grandmother had turned Christian. Why would she talk like that?" she asked me, expressing the same moral outrage by which the community had disciplined Maggie Wilson three-quarters of a century earlier. She was also asserting to me, the anthropologist, that she and her people were Christian, not pagan, and were—then as now—civilized, not "primitives." I suggested that being Christian did not preclude being lots of other things as well. She immediately agreed and became animated, saying: "Like around here. Even in these small communities there's lots of prejudice. It's who you know, your influence, that matters, or people will pass you over. There's a lot of prejudice in these small Christian towns." Returning to "the book," she said, "It's not that the things she writes are untrue; it's that the book is written like gossip — it's exaggerated — and disturbing."

I had the feeling that if she and I had had the opportunity to continue our conversation over several days and weeks, we might have found ourselves collaborating in a way and on topics similar to those Maggie and Ruth had discussed 60 years earlier. We might have explored the truths between the lines of the "gossip." As it was, my children were getting restless. We had been talking for an hour and a half. Jeannie's daughter had just come into the trailer and was talking to us now from the adjoining kitchen. Jeannie told her we were talking about her grandmother and "the book the anthropologist wrote." Her daughter, a teacher in her 30s, became irate and, like Jeannie, expressed moral outrage: "There's a story in there about my grandmother that says she had seven husbands! It's not true! It makes her sound like an easy woman. There's a lot that simply isn't true, that's gossip. I had the book taken off the shelves when it showed up here. It should never have been written!"

I asked why they thought Maggie Wilson had participated in the project, why she would work with an anthropologist. Both said they did not know why she would. The daughter suggested that Maggie probably had not known that what she said would be written down in a book. When I said that she was paid for her time and to write accounts of women's lives in Manitou Rapids, Jeannie said, "I didn't know she was paid." Jeannie suggested that translation was part of the problem: "My grandmother was one of the few around here who spoke English, but she wasn't educated. Everyone spoke Ojibwa, and Ojibwa can't be translated into English." I described how Maggie and her daughter, Janet, worked together, first discussing the stories in Ojibwa and then developing an English version that Janet would write down. They would mail batches of stories to New York, and Ruth Benedict, Ruth Landes's teacher, would send money orders back to Manitou Rapids: $1.00 per fifteen pages, one side. "She [Janet] wasn't educated either," Jeannie's daughter said then.

I asked the question that stemmed from my own thoughts on why Maggie Wilson might have collaborated with the anthropologist (beyond the important cash earnings during the depression). I wondered aloud if Maggie might have been trying to tell the outside world about the difficulties of women's lives, if perhaps she was sending a message *through* the anthropologist. Neither Jeannie nor her daughter saw what I was suggesting—that women's issues can be uncomfortable to hear about, that they may not reflect cultural ideals or dominant images, and that as a result they are often silenced or dismissed as gossip. Both women were themselves well connected to the current power structures and employment opportunities in Manitou Rapids—not marginalized or ostracized as their grandmother had felt herself to be.

It was time to go. The afternoon had passed quickly. Jeannie seemed to have enjoyed the conversation—as I had. She had been gracious, relaxed, and forthcoming; she wished she could have "helped" me more, she said, as we parted.

I left with a strong sense of Maggie's competence, her skill as a craftsperson, and her spiritual knowledge and powers and with the impression that the dominant local explanation for the book was to blame the anthropologist who had published inadequately translated stories to produce a book that "should not have been written." Chagrined by my $300 speeding ticket and by my recognition that there were people at Manitou Rapids who rejected Ruth Landes's presentation of women's lives, I wondered if I should pursue the work I had started.

But I also left more certain than ever that the local emotion "the book" roused signaled that women's experience was of deep and critical importance to understanding Ojibwa society—precisely the kind of "unorthodox" experience Ruth Landes would look for and would want to document to get behind dominant culturally endorsed patterns of behavior.[1]

CHAPTER FOUR

Maggie Wilson and Ojibwa Women's Stories

RUTH LANDES arrived in Fort Frances, Ontario, Canada, on July 6, 1932. For the next three months until her return to New York, she maintained regular correspondence with Ruth Benedict.[1] The letters reveal her first impressions in the field, her frustrations and elation, her keen sense of observation, and her insights into the collected data.

Upon her arrival she met A. E. Spencer, the Indian agent. Following her inquiries of him and other locals concerning several reserves in the vicinity, she opted, as recommended by A. Irving Hallowell, for Manitou Rapids (RL to RB, July 10, 1932, RFBP). She found lodgings with the Department of Indian Affairs farm instructor and his wife, William and Helen Hayes, the only non-Native family living on the reserve. Her first impressions, unlike mine in 1995 taking in the beauty of the landscape, emphasize the poverty, the shabby living conditions, the rampant tuberculosis. She found the work strenuous, writing in her first letter to Benedict: "The Indians live considerable distances apart. The first house I arrive at requires a hike of 2 miles. Only the divine pursuit of knowledge drove me to make this walk 5 different times under yesterday's blazing sun."

In her first letter she also informs Ruth Benedict that she has hired Mrs. Maggie Wilson as her interpreter for $1.00 a day. A Christian, Wilson was "the one informant recommended by the agents and by Miss Densmore; it turned out too that Mr. Hallowell had used her" (RL to RB, July 10, 1932, RFBP). It was Wilson who would, in the Boasian tradition, serve as Landes's "key informant" for her ethnological research at Manitou.

Within the first few days in the field, she learned that "Midé ceremonies are to be held next week." The midé ceremonies were rites of the Midéwiwin, the religious society and revitalization movement concerned with curing and with the continuity of aboriginal beliefs and cosmology. Landes also learned that the reserve was "divided in two factions: the 'Christian' and the pagan. . . . Christian and pagan practises with regard to the same set of situations coexist in the same individual" (RL to RB, July 10, 1932, RFBP), a dichotomy that, as was made clear to me during my visit with Jeannie, Maggie Wilson's granddaughter, persists if not de facto then as an operative category.

During the summer and fall of 1932, Landes passed most of her days in the company of Maggie Wilson and her married sons and daughters, Leonard, Albert, Christina, and Janet. She worked with Wilson, whom she always referred to as "Mrs. Wilson," and other elders to record midé knowledge: "The work goes along rather nicely—the hours are closely packed. There is considerable to be resuscitated here from the older folks" (RL to RB, July 24, 1932, RFBP).

She also devoted a great deal of time to recording kinship terminology and was impressed by the discrepancies she found between formal marriage rules and actual social practice. She wrote to Benedict: "One interesting thing struck me. I collected an extensive vocabulary of kinship terms; and they showed COMPLETELY all the equivalences that Hallowell has been seeking. But the practise—present, and ancient according to my informants—carefully avoids the implications that might be assumed from the linguistic evidence . . . and the genealogies show there is a great deal of marrying into strange places. Hallowell was here for four days last summer; I wonder what he'll make of his findings."

Twelve days later she wrote "very excitedly": "About these cross-cousin marriages: I finally pinned three old people down to definite independently unanimous statements that these marriages have been discountenanced since the beginning of time; that the first degree cross-cousin marriages in the environs are recent, within the history of their own lifetimes; and that they are associated with a general relaxation of the old ways. What do you think of that with which to confront Hallowell: cross-cousin marriage as a symptom of breakdown? . . . The situation tickles me. However I would not consider this explanation complete. Of course the genealogies would be the crux" (RL to RB, August 5, 1932, RFBP). What is striking is that in this first effort in anthropological fieldwork Landes collected a wealth of information in less than a month and had the temerity to contradict Hallowell. The letters also reveal two strengths repeatedly marking her research: her excellence in the field and her eye for disparities and inconsistencies within the professed norms.

Ojibwa Sociology, published in 1937, was Ruth Landes's first presentation of the data she collected at Manitou Rapids. A conventional scientific ethnological report, it was written and published to fulfill the requirements for the Ph.D. The analysis was organized under the headings Political Organization, Kinship Organization, Gens Organization, Marriage, and Property. Against the historical context of shattering sociopolitical and economic changes, Landes identified continuities in the values of a people who had once lived a nomadic lifestyle relying on hunting and foraging scattered and seasonally available resources. She described the importance of autonomy for individuals and families; respect, "kindness," and egalitarianism in social relations; indulgence of the young and respect for elders; teasing, humor, and ridicule, but never shame, as methods to discipline and control behavior; the importance of romance and sex in conjugal relations; resourcefulness, responsibility, and flexibility in the work of subsistence; the ownership of certain skills and forms of knowledge such as midwifery, curing, dances, and songs that were acquired by individuals through visions or purchase (those who desired access to these services or knowledge were expected to give gifts or payment); and a vibrant imaginative life and spirituality such that everyone (male and female) was encouraged to dream, dreams being the most highly valued personal property.[2]

In this portrait of Ojibwa social values and principles Ruth Landes's doctoral thesis was largely consistent with the work of her contemporaries, but in her descriptions of kinship and property relations she developed two points of difference with them. Building on the genealogical data she had recorded for the 230 residents of Manitou Rapids, she diverged from A. Irving Hallowell's discussion of cross-cousin marriage among the Ojibwa. Landes argued that although cross-cousins are formally classified as "sweethearts" and the relationship between cross-cousins was stylized in incessant ribald joking, among the Rainy River Ojibwa it was not local practice for cross-cousins to marry (Landes 1937b:19–20; cf. Hallowell 1928). Instead Landes argued that the choice of marriage partner was based on personal decision and affection (53). The economic contribution of a partner was valued—especially for widows— but economic considerations were not overriding: a partner had to please. A couple's residence after marriage was also based on congeniality and practicality rather than on prescriptive postmarital residence rules (76). Furthermore, the Manitou Rapids genealogies indicated a high rate of separations and remarriages in this small population rather than long-term partnerships (81). The behavior of both men and women was, Landes said, motivated by a combination of economic necessity and desires for romance and sexual fulfillment rather than by prescribed rules and kinship classifications. Her description contrasted with her contemporaries' formalist anthropological studies of kinship relations in that she evaluated prescriptive kinship rules against actual social behavior.

Landes's portrait of Ojibwa concepts of usufructuary property rights also diverged from the work of her contemporaries, specifically Frank Speck's 1915 description of the "family hunting territory" as fixed hunting and trapping grounds that were owned and inherited by a group of adult male relatives. In Landes's account, hunting and trapping grounds were inherited or acquired by individuals, not groups, and inheritance was according to ties of affection, not prescription (91). Territories might be lost through disuse and, if abandoned, might be acquired by others who could claim them through use.

Configuration and Contestation

From the beginning a critical tension is present in Landes's writing. She endeavors to establish general principles in Ojibwa social relations, to write in the distanced, authoritative voice that she knows is scientific practice, and to look for the Benedictine "pattern" that served as the integrative mechanism of Ojibwa culture. But instead of pattern, she is struck by the number of ways and instances in which individuals moderate, reinterpret, or ignore the general rule in order to fulfill their own preferences, needs, or desires. She is attracted by "the democratic and individualistic spirit of this culture [that] is always overriding dogma" (1937b:125). Quietly she has begun to diverge from her teacher's concern for pattern and to document the behavior that interested her: the evidence for individual agency. We begin to see that they are different pilgrims: Benedict, the victim who stressed the pattern that the individual rails against, and Landes, the iconoclast who relishes the strategies and behaviors that individuals create to meet their goals.

In her ethnography Landes followed the discursive practice of introducing each topic (cross-cousin relations, marriage prescriptions, residence patterns) by presenting the general rule. She would then offer several specific examples of actual practice of individuals; their behavior inevitably contradicted the rule. As a final illustration, she would provide a direct quotation from a story she had been told (e.g., see Landes 1937b:20–25). According to Landes, this pattern followed Maggie Wilson's teaching: "She would explain the traditional rules impeccably, only to top this with accounts of big violations by individuals. . . . Her discussions always followed this sequence: specific social rules were taught and heavily sanctioned by gens, family, and supernatural powers, but these could be and were universally set aside" (1966:5). Maggie Wilson's method of teaching Landes through storytelling nicely complemented Boasian training to record oral texts from key informants.

This reflexive questioning in the text took Landes's analysis in two directions: the first was to describe individualism as the consistent pattern in Ojibwa society; the other was to begin to theorize culture as a dynamic process that involves not only the formulation of ideal values, norms, and patterns of behavior but also strategic practices by which individuals negotiate and contest cultural norms. Ruth Landes intuitively began to develop a dynamic model of culture.

Landes pursued these two different theoretical directions in two pieces of writing that followed upon the publication of *Ojibwa Sociology*. In "The Ojibwa of Canada" (1937a), the chapter she contributed to *Cooperation and Competition among Primitive Peoples*, edited by Margaret Mead, she elaborated individualism as the psychological configuration unifying (or "integrating") Ojibwa culture. In *The Ojibwa Woman* (1938b) she formally began her career of documenting the subaltern voices of women and "other restless spirits" (Kendall 1985) whose lived experiences, like her own, led them to challenge dominant cultural patterns.

In the fall of 1934 Margaret Mead invited Ruth Landes to join the seminar on "Cooperation and Competition among Primitive Peoples." The Social Science Research Council had recruited Mead to survey available ethnological material on cooperation and conflict in "primitive societies as a background for planning research in this field in our own society" (Mead 1937:ix). The seminar met weekly over the winter of 1934–35 in the Department of Anthropology at Columbia University under Mead's direction. The participants were four graduate students, Irving Goldman, Jeannette Mirsky, Buell Quain, and Bernard Mishkin, and two postdoctoral scholars, May Mandelbaum Edel and Ruth Landes.

In her introduction to *Cooperation and Competition*, the volume that resulted from the seminar, Mead explained that the participants had been asked to "reorganize their original notes in the light of this special problem [i.e., the conditions that generate competitive and cooperative behavior]" (1937:4). Mead wrote a portrait of Manus society that served as a model, and members of the seminar then met to discuss her model and to develop hypotheses concerning their own ethnographic cases. The seminar identified the ecological environment and the technology of subsistence as the key factors and saw the social structure and socialization processes as, respectively, the third and fourth levels of analysis. The group participants developed a detailed set of questions in each of these four areas, and each contributor then organized his or her data in response to these questions. It was in response to the seminar's questions about the nature of the food supply and the type of social organization that most efficiently captured that food supply that Landes linked individualism (which the Mead seminar called "atomism") to Ojibwa reliance on sparse, seasonally available and unpredictable resources, an argument that some scholars later critiqued (Hickerson 1967).

In "The Ojibwa of Canada" (1937a), the essay she contributed to *Cooperation and Competition*, Landes argued that the opposing terms *cooperation* and *competition* were ethnocentrically rooted in American social values and were not appropriate to describe social relations in Ojibwa society. She suggested that the term *individualism* more closely approached the character of Ojibwa social relations, by which she meant that a primary motivation in Ojibwa society is that individuals seek to be self-reliant. Rather than *atomism*, Landes's term *individualism* may be understood as a theoretical precursor for the concept of *autonomy* as it is used in more recent work on subarctic societies (Albers 1989; Buffalohead 1983; E. Leacock 1954; Sharp 1994).

Economic production, wrote Landes, is "objectively but not subjectively cooperative" (1937a:125); "a cooperative situation . . . phrased individualistically" (96). When people appear to work cooperatively as in the rice harvest, for example, individuals are in fact working side by side for sociability, but they maintain economic independence and control over the rice they harvest. Individuals cooperate as members of small nuclear or extended-family households but retain control over the products of their individual labor. Autonomy was maintained even within the household between husbands and wives who cooperated in subsistence production but independently controlled their own time, labor, and the products of their labor. Landes's Ojibwa are not only autonomous in the sphere of economic production but also in the sphere of social reproduction. Men and women have equal rights to choose their partners, to expect respect and affection, and, because property is not exchanged at marriage, to leave a marriage where these are not present.

The deductive approach of the Cooperation and Competition seminar contrasts with the inductive approach Landes was to take, in collaboration with Maggie Wilson, in her next writing project, *The Ojibwa Woman* (1938b), a pioneering attempt to develop a theoretical framework for the analysis of gender relations or "sex differences," as they were then called.

Maggie Wilson, Ethnologist

Maggie Wilson became for Ruth Landes her third great teacher, after Boas and Benedict. To fully appreciate Wilson's profound influence on Ruth Landes's anthropology it is necessary to understand who she was and how and why she and Landes came together in a collaboration that would result in one of the first critical studies of gender in the discipline.

Twice Landes's age, Maggie Wilson was born about 1879 at the

Little Forks Indian Reserve on the Rainy River west of Fort Frances. She was the first child of Benjamin and Elizabeth Spence. The previous year her parents had begun receiving payments from the Canadian government under Treaty 3 as members of the Little Forks band. Elizabeth was the daughter of a Scottish Hudson Bay Company trader and a woman whom Maggie describes as a "Cree halfbreed woman." Maggie Wilson introduced herself to Ruth Landes through the following story of her mother's life.

Elizabeth was about five years old (ca. 1865) when her father decided to return to Scotland and to take his Native wife and their three small daughters to live with him there. Elizabeth's mother, however, refused to go, and he left for Scotland alone; Elizabeth never saw her father again.[3] Soon afterward her mother married a Cree man, and the new family camped near Fort Alexander on Lake Winnipeg. The stepfather, however, was abusive, and the little girls were soon taken into the care of their mother's sisters, who were also married to Scottish men. At the age of seven, Elizabeth went to live with a cousin who was married to a Hudson Bay Company man to help care for their young daughter. Elizabeth endured years of abuse with this couple: she was regularly beaten, deprived of food, and locked alone in the company warehouse. When the man was transferred to Fort Frances, Elizabeth accompanied the family. She finally ran away when she was 14 and found work at the Anglican minister's house. Here she met Ben Spence, who worked as a driver taking the minister by dog team throughout the Rainy River district.

Elizabeth and Ben married the following summer and moved to Little Forks reserve to live with his parents. Ben's father, Peter Spence, was a bilingual (English-speaking) Cree from Fort Alexander who taught at the Church Missionary Society school in Little Forks. Ben took a succession of seasonal jobs working for land surveyors or on the steamers that plied the Rainy River between Fort Frances and Kenora. Maggie recalls interminable conflict between Elizabeth and her mother-in-law over rights to the wages, trade goods, and purchased items, such as cloth ("print") and food that Ben brought home. When Peter Spence was moved to the Anglican mission at Long Sault reserve in 1881, Ben rented a house in Fort Frances and brought Elizabeth and Maggie there to live for the winter. Maggie was then about three years old. In the spring they joined Peter Spence at Long Sault. Ben went to work on the riverboats for the summer, and Elizabeth cleared land for a garden and planted corn and potatoes. Maggie reports that she and her mother nearly starved that summer until Ben returned, bringing with him blankets, a shawl, cotton yard goods, tea, flour, and other groceries and "things that were nice to eat." For several years, they farmed at Long Sault, and Ben worked on the riverboats in the summers. In March 1885, when Maggie was six years old, Ben and Elizabeth's second child, also a daughter, was born. That year the Anglican Church moved Peter Spence and his family back to Little Forks, and Maggie's parents decided to join them and to accept treaty provisions to farm there. Ben cleared land, and Maggie describes four happy years during which her grandparents "were different people," doting on their new granddaughter and now being kind to Maggie and Elizabeth. Elizabeth began her profession as a midwife, receiving payment in food and animals — her first pay was a young calf from a non-Native woman whose baby she had safely delivered at Little Forks. The small farm apparently prospered as the Spences raised cows, pigs, and chickens and grew potatoes and corn.

Then tragedy struck, a tragedy from which Maggie's parents and grandparents never fully recovered. One of Ben's brothers became seriously ill. On the last steamboat before freeze-up in the fall of 1888 the entire Spence family, including Ben, Elizabeth, and their children, moved into Kenora to be near the hospital. In November Maggie's uncle died. Then in March 1889, when Maggie was 10 years old, her 4-year-old sister contracted measles and died. Her grandparents' world was shattered. They both began to drink heavily. When the ice was out in the spring the grieving family returned by steamboat from Kenora to Little Forks and took up farming again. They gardened and raised pigs, cows, and poultry for the next few years. Maggie recalls that her parents often quarreled and blamed one another for their young daughter's death. One summer Maggie's father, distraught, simply left them and moved into Kenora. In September Maggie, then 14 years of age, went by boat to Kenora to find her father and refused to leave him until he returned to Little Forks with her. When they returned they brought with them her father's 17-year old orphaned cousin,

Thomas Spence. Ben died a few years later, and Elizabeth married Thomas Spence and moved to Long Sault, where she lived until Thomas Spence died 16 years later. She then married John Bunyan at Manitou Rapids in 1914 or 1915. As Elizabeth Bunyan, she died in the fall of 1932 (the day after Ruth Landes left Manitou to return to New York).

Shortly after her father's death Maggie, then 16, also married, but her husband died within the year. She then married Tom Wilson of the Hungry Hall band and moved to Hungry Hall, further west on the Rainy River. Their first child, a daughter, Christina, was born September 14, 1902, when Maggie was in her early 20s. A son, Leonard, was born February 20, 1908. Her second husband's death is noted on the Hungry Hall annuity pay list of June 1911, and Maggie's son Albert was born on February 26, 1912.[4]

People at Manitou Rapids told Landes that, within a remarkably short time after her husband's death, Maggie had collected the wealth she needed to leave her in-laws. They claimed that as a woman she could not have done this on her own, that a lover must have assisted her, and that "This was wrong and punishable, for she should have been celibate and sorrowing — sorrowing in guilt, as the survivor" (Landes n.d., "Wilson"). Maggie apparently asserted her autonomy too prominently, and through gossip other community members sought to discipline and control her. Landes, however, expressed admiration for Maggie's individualism, resourcefulness, and courage and pointed out that, as a widow with three young children, she might otherwise have been "forced into service for her husband's kin" ("Wilson"). Maggie, it was clear, was determined to control her own destiny. Under such difficult conditions, it is a considerable feat that she managed to keep her children with her and that they all remained emotionally close to one another throughout their lives.

Maggie continued living at Hungry Hall until 1914 when she moved to Manitou Rapids and married Chief Namepok's son, John Wilson. Their daughter, Janet, was born in 1915, and Maggie's last child, a girl, was born about 1919 when Maggie was 40, but she died within her first year. Six years later, Maggie Wilson adopted a non-Native baby boy who had been left at her door. He was known simply as "Shaganash," meaning "white boy," and he went everywhere with Maggie Wilson and Ruth Landes. I interviewed Gus "Shaganash" Wilson in 1996, and he recalled that "Mrs. Wilson," as she was known at Manitou Rapids, was loving and meticulous in her care for him: "I was nothing but skin and bone. She fed me Eagle Brand condensed milk to fatten me up and that was expensive in those days and people were poor. She was a clever woman. Her family stood by her. She mothered an abandoned white boy."[5]

The stories of Maggie and her mother introduced Landes to the themes of illness, separation, relocation, death, widowhood, remarriage, resourcefulness, and survival that patterned Ojibwa women's lives. Wilson also described the larger political and economic changes that had occurred during her lifetime and the context of acculturation that Landes would need to know if she was to appreciate the meaning and significance of the stories of women's lives that Wilson would tell her.

Social and Economic Changes at Manitou Rapids

Maggie was born a few years after the Rainy River bands had signed Treaty 3 with the Canadian government in 1873 and had settled on reserves under the administration of the Department of Indian Affairs in Ottawa. With the signing of the treaty, the territory opened for Euro-Canadian settlement, and the Ojibwa were limited to specific hunting, fishing, and gardening sites. By the time Maggie died around 1940, these reserve lands, with the exception of the Manitou Rapids reserve, had also been appropriated by the government, and the seven formerly autonomous Rainy River bands had been consolidated as one band under the administrative authority of the Indian agent in Fort Frances.

Maggie well remembered the seasonality of life during her childhood. From the summer "village" at Little Forks, she traveled with her father and mother up and down both shores of the Rainy River harvesting berries and fishing sturgeon, which they smoked for winter food. Summer was also the time for communality: games, ceremonial life, courtship, and romance. In fall Maggie camped with her parents and grandparents near the wild rice beds on Rainy Lake, where they spent several weeks harvesting and preparing the rice for winter storage. In the late fall they used to gather at her grandfather's fishing grounds at Whitefish Creek on the American side of the Rainy River, three miles below Fort Frances, and for the winter they moved to her father's hunting and trapping grounds north of Little Forks. As spring approached and the sap began to run, Maggie, her father, her mother, and her father's cousin used to work a sugar bush stand of about 300 maple trees on the American side of the mouth of the Little Forks River, a stand that had belonged to her father's mother. They collected the sap and made maple sugar, which could be stored and later eaten with wild rice, vegetables, and fish. After the making of maple sugar, they returned to Little Forks to plant their gardens of wheat, barley, oats, potatoes, and corn, and the seasonal round began again (Landes 1937b:87–102).

In the late 19th century, when Maggie was a girl, the Ojibwa living along the Rainy River faced increasing difficulties in sustaining a viable livelihood. In 1881 the federal government had passed legislation that prevented Ojibwa from selling their produce to the non-Indian fur traders, logging companies, and settlers who had previously bought their corn and potatoes. This legislation permanently undermined Ojibwa attempts to farm. In 1887 a dam built at the mouth of the Rainy River at Lake of the Woods flooded many Ojibwa gardens and rice fields so that even raising food for household subsistence became difficult. By the 1890s many people were starving. The closing of the markets for their produce, lack of training in farming techniques, poor-quality seed and implements, appropriation of the most arable reserve lands for Euro-Canadian settlers, starvation, and sickness all contributed to Ojibwa demoralization and the failure of the farm instruction program the government instituted at Manitou Rapids after the relocation (Waisberg and Holzkamm 1993).

Maggie described to Landes the efforts people made to farm at Manitou. Her husband John cleared a few acres, built a two-story frame house, and planted wheat, barley, oats, potatoes, and corn. When Christina, Maggie's eldest daughter, married in 1916 at the age of 14, she and her husband cleared bush for farmland adjacent to John and Maggie's farm. Maggie and John gave her son Albert land on which to farm and build a house when he married. John was ill and unable to cultivate all his land by the time their daughter

Janet married at the age of 13 in 1927, and he invited his new son-in-law, James, into partnership with him. James contributed a horse and plough and helped his father-in-law to farm the land, and they divided the produce between them. James also cleared additional new land for himself.

In 1932 when Ruth Landes arrived at Manitou, the people relied on an annual subsistence round of diverse activities, exploiting resources that included deer and other game, fish, wild rice, berries, maple sugar, and garden produce. Fur trapping and seasonal work in local resource industries (logging, timber mills, commercial fisheries, and mining) offered limited and unpredictable wage earnings for some men. Chronic destitution was the lot of most. Maggie Wilson supported herself and her asthmatic husband by selling crafts, working as a midwife and herbal healer, performing naming ceremonies, and serving as an interpreter.

The Canadian government had consolidated the seven Rainy River bands at Manitou Rapids in the fall of 1914, and the population suddenly more than quadrupled to 277. The people had never lived in villages of more than 40 to 60 people, and then only seasonally during the summer months. Little Forks, for example, was a reserve of 49 people when Maggie was born. There had been no village-wide political organization: the summer village was simply a collection of autonomous extended families who congregated annually at productive summer fishing stations on the river. Small groups of related families who came together at summer villages disbanded for winter hunting. Individual autonomy and closeness of family ties were the key Ojibwa principles in interpersonal relations, and "kindness" was the primary attitude relatives expressed toward one another. Social groups or "bands" were thus autonomous extended family units organized around subsistence activities, and decision making at both household and "village" levels was by consensus. With the consolidation and sedentarization of seven formerly autonomous seasonally nomadic "bands" of extended families at Manitou and the centralization of political authority under the Manitou Rapids band, questions of political authority and leadership arose. Not recognizing aboriginal notions of individual autonomy, the Canadian government had appointed a male chief and councilors as political heads of the new band.

The forced co-residence of members of different bands at Manitou required the negotiation of new social relationships as unrelated families developed new patterns of social interaction as neighbors and as members of one community.

Maggie Wilson also described increased stresses in marriages on the reserve as well as new restrictions on marriage and divorce that the Indian agent sought to enforce. Historically the choice of marriage partners was an individual decision based on personal choice and affection, although family members, especially mothers, could become involved; Maggie recalled how her own mother had forbidden her from marrying her first sweetheart, who was also her fourth cousin. Notions of romantic love and sexual fulfillment, Maggie emphasized, were traditionally important components of a successful marriage, and separations and remarriages had been common occurrences. There was little ceremony and no exchange of property at marriage, and it was an individual's choice to remain in or to leave a marriage.

On the reserve, however, women were less free to leave unhappy marriages or abusive partners because there were no longer other villages or social groups to go to, and the surrounding territory was now in the hands of non-Native settlers. Furthermore, the Indian agent now took an active hand in keeping intact those marriages that would not have survived previously. If a couple separated, the agent would penalize the individuals by withdrawing material resources they desperately needed and by refusing to provide them with the seed, tools, and farming instruction that were treaty rights. Maggie described the life of a neighbor whose abusive husband was continually frustrated and disappointed in his attempts to farm. He had taken up gambling and often stayed away from home for days. This young neighbor would often cry herself to sleep at Maggie's house, or Maggie would find her at home in bed "helpless from her husband's kicks." Maggie explained to Landes: "That's why she's so thin and unhappy. But the Agent said they had to live together, otherwise he wouldn't help [her husband] with his wheat. I tried to tell the Agent that they should separate, but he said no" (Landes 1937b:81–83). Abuse of women was a direct effect of government policies, but the Indian agent chose to disregard the women's concerns and instead imposed Christian and legal notions of morality onto marriage tensions. Maggie Wilson observed this, and Ruth Landes, unlike other anthropologists of the time, chose to record the problem of domestic violence in the context of rapid social change and forced acculturation.

Thus Maggie Wilson reported how, in addition to the constraints of poverty, the people at Manitou Rapids struggled against marital tensions, new jealousies created by jockeying for political leadership and the bureaucratic interventions of the Indian agent. She described how she herself had experienced these as the result of a ritual leadership role she at first reluctantly assumed and later, also reluctantly, relinquished.

Maggie Wilson's Vision

Ruth Landes was especially moved by Maggie Wilson's account of her trepidation in the face of a powerful vision-dream and her continuing search for salvation. Ironically, throughout her career and beginning with the Harlem Jews, Landes, the daughter of secular, even anti-religious, socialists, would seek spiritual knowledge and experience in anthropological fieldwork. In the years to come, Wilson's spiritual resilience offered Ruth Landes a valuable touchstone in her own pilgrim's search for resolution.

Maggie was a 35-year-old widow and mother of three in 1914 when she moved to Manitou Rapids and married John Wilson. On her first night at Manitou, she had a vision that was to recur in a sequence of vision-dreams, each lasting several nights. In the vision, supernatural thunderbirds accompanied by a veiled woman with feathered wings told her to perform a dance to save her son-in-law, Christina's husband, and the other Ojibwa soldiers who were fighting overseas in the First World War. For a long while Maggie feared and resisted the visions. "The head Thunderbird [came], saying they were going to take me somewhere—and I did not want to go. I heard them singing. I wakened, got out of bed, thought about the dream, returned to bed, and dreamt again. They repeated that they wanted me to go with them, to a big mountain." Maggie was afraid, but they assured her that they meant to console and "amuse" her. When she continued to resist, the thunderbirds threatened: "something will befall your family and all the people" (Landes 1968b: 208).

In vivid visions thunderbirds transported Maggie to the world of owls and thunderbirds and eagles, a supernatural mountain, where they taught her dance sequences, drum patterns, and 80 songs. "I dreamt so much that at last it seemed no longer like a dream but like a person talking to me. It was so plain!" (Landes 1968b:209). Sixty thunderbirds appeared in the visions. They told her to make a drum and to recruit 60 villagers to represent them in the dance. As Maggie explained:

People were glad to help and join the dance for I dreamt that the soldiers would come back if their relatives danced. . . . This would be a new war dance. The head Thunderbird told me to name the dance the Union Star Dance. The sixty birds all came in a flock, flying with a tremendous noise, like a rattling train. They would tell me how to lead the dance and how to fix things. I would dream and waken and return to dream from the place where I had left off. They said, "Count us — as many as we are, so many will you have in the dance." I would sit awake for the dream to leave me alone — I couldn't understand it for a long time. But it would come back. I do not know what would have happened if I had not obeyed the dream. Maybe I wouldn't have lived. (Landes 1968b:210)

After having the vision for several years, Maggie gave the dance for the first time in September of 1918 and oversaw its performance for the next several years. "During the seven or eight years that I gave the dance, other people had dreams about it. They would not understand their dreams and talked to me about them. Several people dreamt songs that I put into the dance." Maggie continued to dream and to learn new songs during the years she sponsored the dance: "I would wake up singing," she told Ruth Landes (1968b:211). Landes was tremendously impressed: "It is remarkable that an untrained woman could have organized large numbers to join a religious performance that she planned in every detail, and which was resumed annually. Psychologically, it is extraordinary that the whole thing emerged below the level of consciousness. . . . The fact that she dwelt on the wonderful dreams in our talks showed that she had not sought them in the men's way, for boys and men are forbidden to discuss their Manido experiences, under pain of supernatural punishments" (Landes n.d., "Remembering":8).

Although neither Ruth Landes nor Maggie Wilson suggest this,

Maggie's leadership in the Union Star dance may have offered a focal point around which the dislocated people from different bands could unify and experience communality in the new social entity of the Manitou Rapids Indian Reserve. Maggie recalled: "All who danced and who came to the dance brought tobacco, food, some print [cloth], which we offered to the Thunderbirds, asking protection. . . . The dance was given fall and spring because Thunderbird leaves in the fall and returns in the spring. You seldom hear the Bird in winter. But sometimes we gave the dance oftener because the Birds told me to commercialize it. The Indian agent helped. We gave it at a ball ground near Fort Frances and charged twenty-five cents admission. We all shared and did well. Sometimes we gave the dance five times a year: at Christmas, New Year's, spring, summer, fall. The dance had to run two to four nights" (Landes 1968b:212).

Despite this popularity, Maggie said, the people "turned against" her, and she had to stop. "But after seven or eight years, the people became mean and jealous, and the whole thing too expensive. If anyone sickened or died, it was blamed on me. Then my leg became too sore to dance. And about four years ago [circa 1928] we turned Christian. So we gave up the dance. We laid all the furnishings in the bush to rot. But I still dream of Thunders and I do not think they are angry at me for having quit" (Landes 1968b:212).

Maggie also met tragedy and disappointment during these years. A year after she started the dance she gave birth to her last child, the daughter who died in infancy, and Maggie attributed the death to people's jealousy and sorcery. Her son-in-law did die in the war overseas, and Maggie blamed herself because she had initially been reluctant to perform the dance. Her husband became ill, and so did Maggie. In the summer of 1932 when she met Landes, Maggie lived a rather solitary life, surrounded by her family but isolated from the social life of the community. She often told Landes that she felt "hollow" and "empty" since the community had discredited her and her dance. Landes said, "She felt severely punished and suffered incurable ailments. . . . She could not relinquish the awful sense of her tragedy, of her loss of fame, of her creative identity. To use a current phrase, her feminism had reached heights, and then been dashed to nothing." Landes commented, "Considering

Maggie's extreme poverty, her ailments, the narrow confines of her life, and her fall from the exhilarating heights of the mystic Dance, I am impressed by the courage that carried her and that I know sustained her family" (Landes n.d., "Remembering":8, 12).

In the 1930s when Ruth Landes knew her, Maggie's songs were "still sung at native dances within an area of about one hundred square miles, often by people who never saw her, always by people who are not interested in her personally although they know that 'the songs come from her dance'" (Landes 1938b:130).[6] Jealous of her autonomy and spiritual powers and enforcing values of community egalitarianism, people sought to control Maggie Wilson through gossip and ostracization. In Landes's view she had also been especially harshly disciplined as a woman for exercising power through vision experiences, a domain that was culturally sanctioned for men, not women. Maggie had hoped conversion to Christianity would be "a refuge from terror and pain and consolation for the loss of her Star Dance" (Landes n.d., "Remembering":14), but Landes "surmise[d] the burden of the Vision, the exhaustion, the shock when it was denied by the people, the emptiness which she tried to fill through Conversion . . . [and that] after [Maggie] lost her Vision or it was taken away from her by her fellows who withdrew their faith, she had no self" (Landes n.d., "Wilson":4).

Ruth Landes wrote these words 50 years later in a short biographical sketch of Maggie Wilson. By this time she had herself experienced ostracization and exclusion from opportunities to practice her profession. She, like Maggie, experienced these as losses of self, and she remembered Maggie as a model of endurance and courage. Her empathy for Maggie grew over the years, and she wished that Maggie "could know that her life is not forgotten, that she has an audience." Landes considered "the moving stories she assembled for me — each one a tale of a woman's lone struggle for dignified survival — were a last spurt of creativity, that without which no artist or scientist can endure" (Landes n.d., "Remembering":14, 12).

* * *

The Ojibwa Woman is one of the first ethnographies to pay attention to women's words, and Ruth Landes was the first anthropologist to document Ojibwa women's lives. This surprised Landes: "Why does one never hear about the Indian matriarchs who certainly acted among these hunting, trapping, rice- and berry-gathering people?" (Landes n.d., "Remembering":4). She credits Maggie Wilson: "The ethnography was a product of her genius and my conscientiousness" (Landes n.d., "Wilson":5). As Landes wrote to Ruth Benedict from Manitou Rapids: "I consider her a gem and believe that we will have her with us till she gives up the ghost. I think that by now she is as good an ethnologist as any of us. I gave her some instruction this summer, which she snapped up. She gets the real point of what we want" (October 12, 1933, RFBP). Later, in the preface to the second edition of *The Ojibwa Woman*, Landes wrote: "I did not tell her what kinds of stories to report, but she knew from our intensive studies that I wanted the whole life — its warm breath, its traditional forms. She had the storyteller's instinct and a dramatic flair. These biographical accounts are unique as a gifted woman's view of her fellow women, usually under stress. Since the characters come alive despite the crude English, how powerfully they must have emerged in the original Ojibwa!" (1971:viii).

Wilson's intellect and careful attention to detail were key to the success of their work together, Landes said. "Above all, there was her immense reliability, conducted with immense intelligence. . . . In her photograph you can see her bright shrewd eyes and her repressed humorous smile. I would not trust any projective test to convey a meaningful impression of this subtle woman. Given half the chances we all enjoy she would have stood out in any enlightened circle. I used to compare her to Mrs. Eleanor Roosevelt, the President's wife, but I think Maggie was more versatile, and a true matriarch. . . . Her family showed her true respect" (n.d., "Remembering":4–5). "To complete her picture" Landes wrote:

A hard life had uglified her physically, but in youth she may have been beautiful. I infer this from the remembered facial traits of her oldest daughter, Christina Bombay, which composed one of the loveliest faces I've ever seen. She had the curly dark hair of her mother, beautifully triangular green eyes (her mother's were black), an endearingly heart-shaped face, a tiny smile; and she had the presence of one accustomed to admiration, despite the heavy body of much child-bearing. Her husband . . . loved her passionately, and she reciprocated. They had beautiful children from the eldest, a girl of 14 years, down to a boy nursing at his mother. . . . You should have seen the tenderness among these people. (4–5)

Landes knew that there was probably much in Maggie Wilson's accounts that she missed:

[Maggie] loved to ponder and talk reflectively in the Ojibwa's rather whining, nasal, light tones; she embroidered with porcupine quills for which she used native grassy dyes; she embroidered also with trader's beads; she tanned hides of deer, elk and moose, and cut them up for moccasins and "firebags" (carrying tinder for tobacco); and she bit designs into new birchbark. . . . Seeing her shining, shrewd black eyes peer through rimless spectacles (worn only when embroidering), one would not have supposed she was a mystic who had produced mighty "dreams." Those eyes, the broad cheekbones, the tight-clamped mouth exposing constant harassment, belonged to her needle-sharp mind, ever at grips with reality. She had a sardonic humor that my young self could record but not truly follow. (Landes 1971:vii)

Landes did not claim that their ethnographic collaboration rested on a special intimacy or friendship, and she was aware that the economic exchange between them signified an inequality in their relationship: "Maggie sensed, I think, something patronizing in my research presence for she threw it at me that I was there to exploit the people by writing a book about them. Perhaps she was bitter at the lost chance to write a better book. She knew her life was not dead, though its circumstances were unfair" (1976a:9). "I never supposed that she liked me," Landes wrote, "but she treated me well in every way. The times were desperately poor, so I made a point of paying her one dollar at the close of each day, besides small extras. She respected this punctilio, which happened to coincide with Ojibwa requirements surrounding the relationship of teacher and learner. Her work habits were meticulous and I surmise she respected my own conscientiousness" (1971:vii).

She condemned herself to sit opposite me, listening and answering my questions, because I paid her a dollar a day and small gifts — she needed the cash desperately for her unemployed husband and children and grandchildren. I have no idea what she thought of me; she never looked at me but kept her eyes on her handwork when she was sitting down: cutting and sew-

ing moosehide and deerhide for moccasins that she sold, and embroidering them with beads in the now standard French-inspired floral patterns; she bit patterns in new tender birchbark for me; her poor teeth were worn to the gums from a lifetime of chewing hides. She would rise to fry bannock bread in old lard, a horrible concoction that I loved, and which put pounds on me. In exchange I gave her the thick tasteless cheese-sandwiches made up for my lunch by the reserve's agriculturalist (from Leicestershire, England with whose family I roomed, ate, and sponge-bathed from a tin washtub). Her English speech had no tone, perhaps deliberately so but when suddenly she screamed to her family, there was the lilting Ojibwa character. (Landes n.d., "Remembering":3–4)

Nonetheless, Landes was convinced that their collaboration was exceptional.

It apparently was not typical. Deborah Gordon (1993) has described how women anthropologists held an attitude of liberal reformism and "matronization" and projected idealized passive maternal and feminine roles onto aboriginal women.[7] Gordon referred, as an example, to Gladys Reichard's *Dezba: Woman of the Desert*, published in 1939, the year after *The Ojibwa Woman*. "Dezba" is a fictional composite Navaho woman, the self-sacrificing defender of household needs and community values, an archetypal "communal mother." By contrast, *The Ojibwa Woman* tells stories of diverse women's lives, does not idealize gender roles and relations, and instead records women's courage and tenacity in the face of separation and divorce, child and wife abuse, incest, rape, and infanticide. Why did the Landes-Wilson collaboration take such a different course?

According to Landes, despite their differences in age, cultural background, and material resources, she and Maggie Wilson shared the experience of social marginality: "We were truly outsiders, on a most provisional footing, joined by my ability to relieve her poverty a bit, and by her desire to avenge the villagers' condemnation of her visionary feats by selling knowledge to me" (1976a:4). Deborah Gordon's women anthropologists were all raised as members of established old New England families. Their liberal reformism was the response of a particular social class to conditions in early-20th-century American society. Ruth Landes, the immigrant daughter, was an outsider to that society; her termination of her brief marriage had also strained relations with her family and placed her outside her own ethnic milieu, which prescribed marriage and motherhood. At Manitou Rapids, Maggie Wilson was ostracized for her visionary powers. She recognized in Landes a keen fellow observer and social critic. And Landes, after her failed marriage, was especially sensitized to hear Maggie's stories about other women's experiences of marriage, separation, and divorce.

Anthropology and Women's Stories

Dear Ruth,

This is a story of an Indian woman named [Two Skies]. She was a doctor woman, in Indian, Na na da wi i we. She went through a rough life. She got married to an Indian named [Forever Standing]. He was married already so she had a [co-wife]. He was a great hunter and he went out with her to hunt ducks. They upset the canoe and he swam ashore but she hung onto the boat and she was blown away by the wind for about four hours. She came to a grassy point but still she couldn't reach the shore. . . . At last she swam ashore and dragged the boat along 'til finally she landed. She was soaking wet and cold. She had no matches to light a fire and no paddle to use. There was a little wind so she took her clothes off and hung them up to dry. Then she raced around the bush to keep herself warm. She used to say that was the hardest part of it as she was cold and had nothing to eat. She was about nine or ten miles away from home. There were no people close . . . and the wind was blowing against her. So she went along the beach in the canoe with a stick for a paddle. She kept along the shore until it got so dark that she couldn't see at all. She put ashore and . . . lay down and . . . finally she slept. It was daylight when she woke and then the wind was still against her and it was blowing harder then the day before. She kept right on again going the same way and she had about six miles to go yet before she would reach the nearest house. So at last the next evening she finally came to the house. The people gave her a good drink of whiskey and put her to bed and for four days she was unconscious and at last she came to and got better. Her husband came as soon as he heard she got there and then he took her home. So they kept on living that way hunting and fishing. She had three children and every time the child would come to the same age they would die. Her husband would be fighting her, kicking her, and was awfully mean to her. Then his two wives would get after him and

they would lick him. Then she parted with him and she started with her
Na na da wi i we. She was getting nice things for it. She got along so fine
with all kinds of nice things and she was a great woman to tan hides . . .
she went away to the Lake of the Woods and that was where she was living
fine when she got in with a young man and married him. . . . They had a
little boy and she had to support him herself. [Her husband] was good for
nothing but he was good to her so she had him rigged up in bead work at
last so he would trade . . . the boy was about three years old and . . . in the
winter time they came to Hungry Hall. The man she was first married to
lived there. He wanted to take her back from her young husband and the
old man scared them so much that the young man ran away and she had
to go back to the old man but she never did like him. Her little boy got
sick and died. He was lonesome for his father. After the boy died she used
to fight this old man and he used to say all kinds of wishes so the young
man would die. . . . At last they heard that the young man froze to death
and soon after that the old man got blind and was sick. Then he died and
she was left a widow again and was free from her husbands. Her mother-
in-law and father-in-law and the two brothers and sister of this old man
wanted her to stay with them. That fall they went back to their hunting
grounds and they nearly starved. They could not even kill a rabbit. It was
this other young man's parents that were doing all their bad dreams to
make them unlucky so they would starve to death. They were mad 'cause it
was this old man's work, the reason why he died. So they moved away and
left her there alone 'cause she cut her foot. She didn't have anything to eat.
She hardly cut wood for herself. They told her they would come back for her
and she waited five days but nobody showed up. So she started off and it
took her four days to get there. . . . She knew they were going to make a slave
of her. She did everything, cutting wood and tanning hides for them. So
she did not stay there at all but went to another place and then from there
she went home to where she belonged to and the young man's parents were
glad to see her back and were good to her. She made a home with her own
parents and sisters and the next summer she went around with her own
sister. That was two years after her husband died and she met her brothers-
in-law and sisters-in-law. They fought her. They tore all her clothes and
cut her hair and cut up her canoe and tent and beat her. They were mad
just because she had on good clothes and was making a good living for
herself. That was the style of the Indians long ago. When the husband or
wife dies the in-laws take everything the widow has if he or she doesn't

give anything in place of the one she married. So after all her bedding and things were taken away from her she sat there and didn't know what to do so she left word there and said that she was going to get married the first chance she had and wasn't going to give them the pile of stuff they wanted her to give them. Some kind people then lent them a canoe to go back with and they went home. She was coming there to make a visit at her old man's grave the time they tore her clothes and canoe but she never came again after that. Then a year after she got married to an older man at Whitefish Bay. He was a widow like herself. . . . He was all kinds of manito kaso: gisuki [conjurer who conducts Shaking Tent ceremony] and Grand Medicine king and a kind of Indian fortune teller. He knew what was going to happen ahead of time and nearly all the time his dreams came true. And he had lots of bad medicine. People used to say that he wished to keep other people's luck and they claimed that he used to make people crazy. Every body was scared to make him mad and he used to be the only one to kill game or fish and the other people wouldn't kill any thing and that was the reason why people thought him bad. So they kept on like that for many years and he cured lots of people and he was a great old gambler. So she lived there with him all this time as his wife 'til all her in-laws with the first husband . . . were all dead and he put her through the Grand Medicine dance. He got sick with small pox and died so she was left a widow again and she started with Na na da wi i we doctoring and she was a hunter. She killed furs and fish and made rice and made a good living. She was a real Indian woman. She dressed like an Indian. She dreamed of all kinds of games such as the Indian dice game and snake game and the caribou bone game. She gives these out to her namesakes and she gives out songs she dreams of and all kinds of other games and songs. She did not have any children but just the four that died. None are living. She's still living yet today. She is very old but she's still on her manito kaso and naming lots of children and giving out dance songs and these games of all kinds. She used to make a nice big cooking and pretend she was having a feast with the dead people and she would make a speech over it. Then she would pretend she was sending it to the dead people and she would pick the people out that's living and they would eat it and she would say that the God of these dead people would send the dishes back filled with life for them. She had lots of other kinds of feasts and she would make the people believe she had visitors from heaven. When she would doctor any one she would tell them to go through the Grand Medicine and she would dress them up herself

putting red paint and everything on their faces. Sometimes they would live but sometimes they wouldn't get better. She was just trying to keep up the same way as her old man . . . and lots of other rough life that is not fit to tell. She's living alone, hardly any relatives, at Whitefish Bay. She's old and helpless as a baby. Now this is all I know of her. The end"
    Mrs. Wilson[8]

This is one of the stories that Maggie Wilson sent in more than 40 story-letters she mailed to Ruth Landes in New York after Landes left Manitou Rapids. Landes later recalled: "The flood of materials . . . was determined by the meeting of traditional values and skills with particular immediacies, i.e. the vision discipline + imposed literacy + real hunger + love of storytelling and philosophical rumination + the sacredness of contract + my interest and rewards. Surely, besides, the individualities of informants were determining; for example, Mrs. Wilson's genius and steadiness gave me the idea of absentee writing" (1966:8). Wilson, who could speak but not write English, dictated stories to her daughter Janet, who wrote them down and sent them as letters to Ruth Landes. The letters were a kind of anthropological piecework: Columbia University paid Wilson "$1.00 per fifteen pages one side" (RL to RB, June 11, 1933, RFBP). The typical opening is: "Dear Ruth, This is the story of . . . She was an Ojibwa woman who . . ." Wilson punctuates her stories with statements such as "She lived a rough life; she was a real Indian woman."[9] Receiving a batch of Wilson's story-letters, Landes wrote to Benedict on March 20, 1935: "I find these excellent. One is her old and thorough line about the woman deserted, mistreated, rewarded, shamed, combatted over, etc. The theme is damned familiar to us by now" (RFBP).

Typical is the story of "Hawk-Woman," whose husband, after years of beatings and repeated desertions, finally abandoned her one day when the couple was out moose-hunting. Wilson relates:

They travelled by canoe up the Lake for two days. The third night they stopped on the shore. The next day they killed two big moose, and she cleaned them, and dried the meat. So they (separately) went up into the woods to get some birch to make a birchbark wigwam, and also birchbark for a canoe. She came down with her load of birchbark, and saw their gun there, so she took it along and went back for another load. When she re-

turned, their canoe was gone, also her husband. So she was left there alone with no canoe. But everything else was there ... her kettles, tea pail, knives, all her clothing and blankets, and she also had the gun. She walked along the shore thinking that her husband was out paddling, but it got so dark that she returned to the wigwam and went to bed. The next day she waited, and still he didn't come. Then she knew that her husband had left her there for good. She made up her mind to stay until death came to her. She made birchbarks, tanned the moose-hides, and pounded meat, and then she got some cedar and made the frame of a canoe. She stayed there and did all her work, made mats, and all kinds of things. She had her sewing with her. One evening she went around the point of the bay and sat there. She saw a moose in the water. She waited until it came closer, and then she shot and killed it. (Landes 1938b:87–88)

Hawk Woman survived by doing the work of a man, in addition to using her womanly skills. Eventually, she met and happily married a younger man. In Maggie Wilson's stories, the common denominators of women's lives emerge in a pattern that became "damned familiar" to Ruth Landes. The sheer volume of the stories and the repetitiveness of the themes required that she pay attention to the testimony. Viewed through Maggie Wilson's stories, Ojibwa women emerge as survivors despite victimization.

The Ojibwa Woman and Gender Theory

The Ojibwa Woman introduced to anthropology the possibilities that gender offered as a theoretical domain for the illumination of Ojibwa culture. First published in 1938 and reissued in 1971 and 1997, *The Ojibwa Woman* is an important early contribution to the anthropology of gender for three specific and central components of its analytical framework. First, the method of data collection and presentation relies on the recording of life stories of individuals. Second, the analysis gives priority to work ("occupations") and marriage as the keys to understanding women's place in society. These domains — under the terms *production* and *reproduction* — became central analytical categories in late-20th-century feminist scholarship (see Moore 1988). Third, Landes recognized that gender (which she, like other scholars in the 1930s, called "sex") comprised both a set of sociological practices and an ideological code of cultural norms and that these two domains could, and did, coexist in contradiction.

Ruth Landes used the life history method to illustrate the contradictions between practice and ideology. As we have seen, her analysis of marriage and kinship is a far remove from the formalist analyses of her contemporaries. The life stories she records illustrate not how individuals reproduce cultural norms but how they negotiate and contest cultural rules to address the particular circumstances of their individual lives. In the foreword to The Ojibwa Woman, Landes writes: "The Ojibwa material shows that the social norms institutionalized in even a simple nomadic culture do not provide for all of the population, nor for the entire range of tribal activities" (vii). Landes's ethnographic focus reflected her personal interest in the dynamic tension between individualism and constraint in her own life, and her ethnographic focus is on the elaboration of moments of engagement between individual lives and the constraints of society, environment, and history.

The remarkable achievement of the collaboration is that the two women spoke across the cultural chasm between them. Maggie Wilson told the anthropologist stories of women's lives to provide testimony of Ojibwa women's experience. As a grandmother situated in a culture that prescribed storytelling for women, she also told the stories to educate the younger woman, who had had trouble in marriage and who was seeking to develop her own skills as an autonomous woman.

Wilson's stories tell how women overcome hardship through resourcefulness and knowledge learned from other women. They describe women who, because they did not limit themselves to prescribed roles, were able then to endure starvation, abandonment, abuse, and loss. The stories highlight women's responses to predicaments such as a husband's laziness, adultery, or desertion. Stories tell of women paddling long distances, hunting and butchering a moose, and surviving alone in the wilderness. They portray women making choices in their lives. The stories report that some widows choose to remarry and preserve the conventional gendered division of labor, whereas others choose not to remarry and choose to employ "masculine" skills in order to maintain their independence (83–84). The stories tell how some women leave polygynous marriages and others choose to stay because they value the companionship of a co-wife (71). Wilson's stories are cautionary tales told by older women enjoining younger women to develop practical skills and personal autonomy to survive challenges that may arise in their marriages and in the wider conditions of their lives.

There is a paradox in Maggie Wilson's storytelling. Although the stories urge that personal autonomy is the key to women's survival, their very telling created a sense of community among women in a culture that Ruth Landes said idealized masculine roles. Ojibwa women, like Maggie Wilson, told stories of their own and other women's lives in order to create a cultural space for women's experience. Anthropologist Julie Cruikshank has described similar storytelling practices among Yukon Athapaskan and Tlingit women and suggests that "Individual autonomy is only a means to an end for these protagonists; their goal is reconnection with the community" (1990:355). The stories may be understood as "narrative resources" (Passerini 1989) deployed by women rather than as historical or biographical accounts of specific women's lives. The historical truth of events in the stories is not the primary concern of the narrator. Rather, the stories and the events they recount are metaphors of experience, lessons in living, and their retellings help to create and maintain social spaces for women.[10]

The Ojibwa Woman is written in five parts: "Youth," "Marriage," "Occupations," "Abnormalities," and "Life Histories." More than half of the discussion in the book is devoted to descriptions of women's work ("occupations") and marriage practices. The ethnographic data illustrate the diversity of ways in which women (and, to a lesser extent, men) experience the institution of marriage and redefine norms of women's and men's occupational roles.

In the chapter entitled "Occupations" Landes uses excerpts from Maggie Wilson's stories to illustrate how Ojibwa women both fulfill and negotiate the culturally constructed gendered division of labor according to which men hunt and procure raw materials and women process raw materials and manufacture clothing, shelter and utilitarian objects. The stories of Sky Woman (138–139), Half Sky (154), and Kota (161–162), for example, are of women who not only excelled at "feminine" tasks but who were also well known as hunters and trappers, athletes, or shamans and healers—skills the Ojibwa defined as "masculine." Stories like those of Thunder Cloud (163) and Gaybay (169) reveal that most women at some point in their lives will be required to take up "masculine" occupations. The stories urge all women to develop occupational versatility and flexibility regarding their gender identities. Gaybay, for example, as a girl had learned to hunt with her mother after her father died. Later, married and widowed several times herself, Gaybay "during the married intervals functioned like a conventional woman inasmuch as she never hunted, trapped or fished, but confined herself to the sedentary activities connected with the wigwam and to assisting her husband on the hunt when so requested. But during the periods of widowhood, which were far longer than those of marriage, she found no difficulty in adjusting to the occupational life of a man" (169).

According to Landes: "Even the most conservative women usually find it necessary to take up some prescriptively masculine work at one time or another. The cultural view of the normal woman remains unchallenged and finds expression in the training that is usual for young girls. Those women whose behaviour is exceptional are not judged with reference to the conventional standard but with reference to their individual fortunes only. The conduct of the ideal woman, therefore, and the behaviour of any individual woman may be quite at variance" (1938b:135).

In the chapter entitled "Marriage," Maggie Wilson's stories illustrate how, although a lifelong cooperative economic partnership was the cultural ideal, in practice both men and women often had several marriage partners over the course of their lives in a pattern of serial monogamy. Landes writes:

The general attitude in the community regarding love and sex . . . [is that] [t]hese are considered very enjoyable, socially and sensually. The culture-hero myths contain a great number of incidents that express this taste, and often incidents are told by men in friendly small talk; the incidents are told broadly and humorously and sound as though inspired by the intercourse of cross-cousins. Other legendary and semi-historical tales, and even gossipy tales are concerned with sexual and romantic relations. Through the winter months older women often tell their life histories and devote a great amount of time and interest to elaborating their past affairs with lovers and husbands. (1938b:42)

Landes later wrote that such stories were the life's breath of Ojibwa society: "Scholars of the 1930s assumed that Indian cultures were 'dying'. I never felt that I was even in a 'sick society', so lusty it was. . . . Amenities for Ojibwa lay, as I know from the women's stories, in the traditional prizing of romance . . . i.e. sensuous, gallant love between the sexes, where individuals vault social barriers. Amenities lay also in exploits of war, feud, hunt, sports, spinning ballads and risqué tales, fervid discussion of ideas of Midéwiwin and vision pursuits, and appreciation of individual characters" (1966:9).

Ruth Landes was especially interested in stories that told how marriages were established and terminated; these were also stories that Maggie Wilson was culturally inclined to tell. Their collaborative portrait is one of gender egalitarianism: men and women had similar rights, expectations, and responsibilities within marriage. Although some gift giving might take place in the case of first marriages, marriage was not an exchange of property and was formalized by night visiting and by a man "sleeping through the dawn" in a woman's home. According to Landes: "Marriages are from the start private, independent affairs, and are usually contracted with equal good will by both parties" (1938b:56).

Ruth Landes, the New Woman, found that Ojibwa marriages practiced the romantic ideals of companionate marriage that had been missing in her own marriage: "Marriage is theoretically the union of two people who like each other deeply, and in practice this is borne out. Divorce is supposed to be a natural consequence of indifference, or of offence, and this is also normally the case" (119–120). "Women often desert a husband when they have conceived a passion for another man" (97), and "divorce [achieved by simple desertion] is nearly as common as marriage" (85). Landes stressed: "The people do not brand [a woman's] conduct as irresponsible, for marital responsibility is not recognized as the motivation of an adult's life. It is so thoroughly recognized that a person follows only his private inclinations" (100). And in a statement that appears to reflect Landes's own view of marriage, she writes: "Clearly, it [marriage] is a very limited social experience, especially for a monogamous couple. But every cultural effort has been made to charge it with excitement and beauty" (123).

Finally, the analysis of gender in *The Ojibwa Woman* is both cultural and sociological: Landes distinguishes the ideological constructions of gender from the actual behavior and social relations of men and women. She describes how gender ideals do not represent actual gender relations, men's and women's activities, or men's and women's contributions. Rather, contradiction and contestation characterize local gender practice. Gender relations, in Landes's view, require individual strategies for accommodating differences and contesting hegemonies, whether societies are pre- or postcontact, whether in equilibrium or in flux. This is because, both in Landes's own experience and in the ethnographic research, the relations between men and women—especially within marriage—are the relations that also often define rights of access to resources, privilege, and status in the wider society. It is within relations of intimacy that men and women negotiate these broader relations and initiate strategies to better position themselves socially and economically. It is also in the context of strategizing and negotiating that gender becomes symbolically loaded.

For Landes, contestation and contradiction are intrinsic components of gender practice in human societies. Maggie Wilson's stories highlight the skills and values that one society taught women in order to negotiate gender and to survive as individuals. Wilson's women are actors in history and makers of culture. Through her storytelling Maggie Wilson both serves as witness to women's experience and teaches Ojibwa women to uphold the ideals of autonomy, resourcefulness, courage, and endurance. In *The Ojibwa Woman* Ruth Landes makes women visible in anthropological analysis and communicates Maggie Wilson's teachings to women across cultures.

Reception in the Discipline

A. Irving Hallowell praised Landes's achievement in *The Ojibwa Woman*. He recognized that not only had she collected data on the then-standard topics of kinship and religion but she had followed her intuition and employed her acute observation skills to bring women into the analysis of Ojibwa culture. In his review of the book for *American Sociological Review* in 1938, he wrote:

Since male ethnographers have given us most of our accounts of the life of native peoples, it is well to have a culture systematically studied and presented from a feminine point of view. Landes has been successful in carrying this out, as I can testify from my own investigation of a western branch of the Ojibwa. . . . Since, in Ojibwa society the role of women, as culturally phrased, is very much more circumscribed than that of men, one might gain a totally false impression of the actual life of women without such data as Landes gives. She is able to show, and rightly I believe, that women not only have an immense amount of freedom in this very individualistic society, but that they are often successful in flaunting customs and vetoing traditional standards. (892–893)

This is strong acknowledgment for the work of the junior scholar.

Despite Hallowell's recognition of the value of paying attention to women's experience, the "real Indian woman" narratively constructed by Wilson and recorded by Landes remained absent from subsequent Ojibwa ethnography.[11] The Landes-Wilson portrait of pleasure and pain in love and marriage was not provided for in the anthropology of the time that was concerned with norms often elicited about prereservation cultures. It was also absent from later hunter-gatherer studies where formulaic descriptions of a naturalized sexual division of labor silenced gender differences in experience, knowledge, and interpretation. The Landes-Wilson portrait was not the one being developed by anthropologists seeking to reconstruct the social lives of primordial "primitive man." For example, in a classic Ojibwa ethnography, *Social and Economic Change among the Northern Ojibwa*, William Dunning describes marriage practices within the conventional mid-20th-century anthropological understanding of marriage in hunter-gatherer studies as a life-long economic partnership in which women are "passive" and "submissive" to husbands who are "active and gregarious" (1959: 131). According to Dunning, marriage choices followed prescribed cultural rules, not individual choice, and he does not mention love, conflict, separation, or divorce — topics that interested Maggie Wilson and Ruth Landes and that form the basis of *The Ojibwa Woman*.

When the second edition of *The Ojibwa Woman* was published

in 1971, second-wave feminists described the book as "flawed and male-centred" (Green 1980) and criticized Landes for "downgrading . . . women . . . [in] unexamined and ethnocentric phraseology" (E. Leacock 1978). They focused on Landes's statement that there was a cultural bias in favor of men and that the cultural ideal was the male shaman. Passages such as the following, reprinted in the 1971 edition, fueled their critiques:

The same culture that has laid down a glamorous course for men has provided no distinct line of conduct for women. Women therefore attempt nearly everything available in the culture — and by so doing, alter the formulated nature of much that they engage in, heedless of the occupational demarcation so painstakingly taught to the men. Individual variations among women show up conspicuously as difference in objectives, technical accomplishments, and perseverance; whereas among men such minor variations are only in degree of accomplishment. If men are thought of as the specialized instruments of Ojibwa culture, women are the unspecialized; if men are considered inheritors of the culture's wealth, women are the dispossessed and underprivileged; if men are the material selected arbitrarily to be the finest medium for the expression of Ojibwa ideals, women are second-rate, or perhaps reserve, material. (1938b:177)

In my analysis I have emphasized Landes's subaltern voice and gender critique, which are, as I see it, her distinctive contribution. But in her written work Landes never fully extricated her analysis from Benedictine generalizations, and these leave her open to feminist critics. This is one of the weaknesses of her work and produces contradictions such as the one above between her argument for women's autonomy and her glossing of male dominance. I argue that these contradictions arise because Landes herself wavered between contestation and compliance in her strategies to find a place for herself in the discipline. She was the iconoclastic observer in the field, but she was the insecure subordinate in the academy. She complied with Benedict by making generalizations about cultural patterns that inevitably ran roughshod over Landes's own opposing evidence, which she so carefully lays out for us in detailed and rich ethnographic descriptions based on her own field observations and interviews.

It should also be recognized that Landes implicitly *was* making a theoretical argument that differed from the arguments of late-20th-century feminists. In *The Ojibwa Woman*, her concern was to analyze what she called "the moot problem of men and women" (1938b:v)—a problem she saw as crossing cultural boundaries, space, and time—that is, a universal problem. In the 1970s feminist anthropologists such as Eleanor Leacock were interested in women's status, the origins of gender inequality, and the possibilities for future gender egalitarianism. They sought to document that historically gender egalitarianism had existed in hunter-gatherer societies (Moore 1988).

There are fundamental differences in these theoretical approaches: for Landes, the "problem" of men and women is universal and "moot"; gender differences are a central organizing principle in all societies, and gendered experiences create different foundations of knowledge for women and men within the same society. For Leacock, the problem of men and women is a problem of gender hierarchy that was introduced through historical processes of European colonization and is not indigenous to hunter-gatherer societies such as the Ojibwa (Etienne and Leacock 1980; E. Leacock 1978). A historical materialist, Leacock interpreted gender relations as rooted in the relations of economic production. She argued that the male dominance that Landes described in *The Ojibwa Woman*, the higher status symbolically awarded masculine roles in Ojibwa society, was a product of the transformation from an egalitarian foraging society to a stratified society based on commodity relations first of the fur trade and later of a capitalist wage economy. Leacock criticized Landes for lacking a historical materialist analysis of how the social and economic changes of wage labor, forced relocation, and the increasing intrusiveness of Indian agents had affected gender relations.

Nonfeminists also criticized the second edition. Unlike Hallowell, who 40 years earlier had seen Landes's attention to women as a strength of her work, Herbert Alexander, in reviewing *The Ojibwa Woman* for *American Anthropologist* in 1975, considered that "women interpreting women's viewpoints derived from women informants" results in work that is "less than scientific" (1975:111). He found that Landes's reliance upon Maggie Wilson's stories created "the risk of an idiosyncratic female viewpoint of Ojibwa life."

Landes responded to Alexander in a letter to the editor of *American Anthropologist*, a revised version of which was published in the journal:

Dr. Alexander should understand that there was no full-length anthropological study of women 'in a primitive society' during my time; and that when this one appeared it met with no enthusiasm outside of our Columbia University circle. More, I had not set out to study women; it was they who came to talk to me. . . . The women simply wished to talk about their lives to this young, inquiring outsider. The 'few informants', as Dr. Alexander puts it, were actually a large number. . . . The 'idiosyncratic female viewpoint' suggested by the reviewer was no more so than the male viewpoint that dominates the other two Ojibwa books of mine (Ojibwa Sociology and Ojibwa Religion and the Midéwiwin). I mean that both reveal the culture . . . dealing chiefly with men. . . . Standing alone for some time, the study neither followed 'fads', as the reviewer puts it, nor inspired any. I thought my Ojibwa people were just acting humanly, like those I knew in New York. . . . Ojibwa women were . . . great realists, doing what had to be done even when this was called male.

She continued:

Every woman field worker has forced on her the knowledge that women undergo experiences not conceptualized by men; and this is true of the host culture's women too. Dr. Alexander appears to deplore this as 'women interpreting women's viewpoints derived from women informants.' . . . Culture is an absolute barrier, even within a common society, between the sex categories. . . . It has always struck me that, among the numerous 'primitive' and contemporary cultures I've studied, women (besides men) have talked to me in ways and about matters not recorded by male observers. I'm sure men do not 'hear' the women's affairs that we women record, unless the women's affairs are presented in a culturally stylized way. (May 27, 1975, RLP, box 2)

Refusal to "hear" women's affairs continues. A third edition of *The Ojibwa Woman* was published in 1997, and in a clear dismissal of the different forms women's knowledge takes and of the different experiences upon which it is based, a reviewer in the *European Review of Native American Studies* described the book as "gossip as ethnography" (Anonymous 1999).

Ruth Landes, Author

Landes was bright and ambitious, and she knew that the reading public was interested in women's lives in other cultures. Once she had extracted from her field notes the formal data she needed for her Ph.D. dissertation, she began to imagine a book that would record women's experiences growing up and living in Ojibwa culture.[12] She knew that Maggie Wilson's stories offered a rich portrait, and she envisioned a book that would sell. Mead's *Coming of Age in Samoa* (1928) and *Sex and Temperament in Three Primitive Societies* (1935), not to mention Benedict's *Patterns of Culture* (1934), were best-sellers.

Landes had written the first draft of *The Ojibwa Woman* during the winter of 1934-35 when she was a postdoctoral fellow participating in Mead's Cooperation and Competition seminar. To achieve credibility in the profession and establish herself in an academic career she would need to adopt an authoritative analytical voice in her scientific writing. She was conflicted about the audience for *The Ojibwa Woman* and about the kind of text she wanted to produce. She was torn between her Boasian attention to microscopic details and particular individuals and Benedict's concern for pattern and generalization. As a scientist she was required to step back from the array of data and draw general conclusions or principles. This she attempted to do through her arguments about individualism and male dominance. But she was clearly reluctant to have her book be *about* these generalizations. She and Benedict debated the analysis of "abnormalities." In a letter dated April 24, 1935 Landes expressed the hope that Benedict would "come around to the [Abnormalities] chapter of the WOMAN" (RL to RB, April 24, 1935, RFBP).

Ruth Landes sought to write a book that might capture the creativity—not only the "abnormality"—in Ojibwa women's struggles and resilience. Maggie Wilson's stories of women's survival, she knew, were also autobiographical. Through storytelling Maggie transformed her life from memory to narrative to emerge as an actor in history, a participant in culture, and author of her own life. For Landes, the stories also echoed the restlessness of her own pilgrim's search. *The Ojibwa Woman* was not only an anthropological account of women's lives in another culture. It was about the lives of women like herself—about life itself.

How could she write a text that would have legitimacy in the discipline? How could she at the same time produce a text that would keep intact the experiential world of contradiction and constraint and celebrate the particular ways that individual women overcame hardship and asserted agency within the world? These women's stories offered contesting voices to anthropological constructions of homogeneous, coherent, cultural wholes.

Landes struggled. On the one hand, in Benedictine fashion, she argued that individualism was the central ethos or dominant pattern in Ojibwa culture. On the other hand, she could not fail to note the cultural visibility given to men's skills and accomplishments and the symbolic value given to the role of the male shaman, that is, that male dominance was also a dominant pattern. If in seeking autonomy individual women were fulfilling cultural ideals, collectively they could be seen as a subordinate group within a culture that was not a unified whole but that contained within it diverse and contesting interests. In the end Landes produced a text where the analytical voice of the scientist weaves in and out of a text full of contradictory women's experiences, where generalizations and unruly experience jockey for the reader's attention. She chose to end *The Ojibwa Woman* not with general conclusions but instead with three women's life stories, the final words of the last story being: "So her bad luck never ended. But in spite of it all, she was happy. She and her husband grew very old. . . . That is all."

Because she was unemployed, Landes remained in a dependent relationship with her teacher, Benedict, and when in the spring of 1935 Benedict arranged a $1,500 grant for Landes to return to the field, Landes accepted it as a means to be able to support herself without relying on her parents and as an avenue to continuing professionalization that she hoped one day would lead her to a permanent position in anthropology. She left *The Ojibwa Woman* manuscript with Benedict when she went to the field, and Benedict and her companion, Nathalie Raymond, read and edited it, sending sections to Landes to revise while in the field.[13] Being immersed in new data and a new field situation hardly provided Landes with ideal conditions to revise the book. It was Benedict who in March 1936 submitted the manuscript to Harcourt Brace and who a month later reported to Landes that it had been rejected "as too specialized and for a university press" (RB to RL, April 11, 1936, RFBP). When Landes returned to New York in the summer of 1936, she sent the manuscript to Macmillan, and in August she wrote to Benedict at her summer home, Shattuck Farm, that Macmillan had received "an extremely favorable report . . . recommending publication because not specialized! and because first book to give a full-length picture of women and children in one primitive culture—for which there are frequent requests." But by April 1937 Macmillan had rejected *The Ojibwa Woman* because it had "no general appeal," and Oxford had also turned down the book, saying it was "overburdened with manuscripts to publish." Benedict eventually arranged for Columbia University Press to publish *The Ojibwa Woman* in 1938 in its Contributions to Anthropology series, which she herself edited.

In *Primate Visions* Donna Haraway proposes that "scientific practices are storytelling practices" and that like other storytelling practices they are "historically specific practices of interpretation and testimony" (1989:331). Ethnographic texts are anthropology's storytelling. Landes's professional aspirations in the discipline required that she engage the storytelling practices of scientific storytelling. Her personal dilemmas, however, were so eloquently mirrored in Maggie Wilson's life stories that autobiographical practices also motivated *The Ojibwa Woman*. Feminist literary critics write of the "micropolitical practices" at work in women's autobiographical storytelling (de Lauretis 1984) and explore how practices of self-representation "illuminate the contradictory, multiple construction of subjectivity at the intersections, but also in the interstices of ideologies of gender, race and sexuality" (Martin 1988:2). In *The Ojibwa Woman* Ruth Landes, through her insistence on recording the contradictions and constraints in women's lives, tapped the microcultural politics in the interstitial zones of Ojibwa culture. In *The Ojibwa Woman* she confirms that it is not Benedict's patterns but the cracks in the patterns that really concern her in anthropology. The cracks symbolized the social spaces where she felt she led her own life, and they motivated her observations in the field.

CHAPTER FIVE

Lusty Shamans in the Midwest

BEFORE HER LANDMARK study of Afro-Brazilian religion, *The City of Women* (1947), Ruth Landes made two more extended field trips to Native American communities during the Great Depression years, both funded by grants to Columbia University managed by Ruth Benedict. "The immediate drive behind my Columbia-sponsored research was boundless regard for the characters and geniuses of [Franz Boas and Ruth Benedict]" she later recalled (1970a:v). Landes welcomed the opportunity to continue to develop her field observation skills and to collect data to publish, but she also needed the work. Since her separation from her husband she had found herself, now 24 years of age, again financially dependent upon her parents and living with them in their apartment. At least when she was in the field she could live on her own and regain some sense of independence by supporting herself. The grants were to cover her living costs and research expenses while away, but there would be nothing left to live on when back in New York. If, at least in the short term, the arrangement helped Ruth Landes, it also suited Ruth Benedict. Benedict could benefit from Ruth Landes's already sophisticated powers of observation and recording and from the hard work and youthful energy of a student seeking to impress her.

In the summer and fall of 1933 Landes was based at Red Lake, Minnesota where she worked particularly with Chippewa (Ojibwa) shaman or midé Will Rogers and continued the study of Ojibwa religion she had begun with Maggie Wilson. In the fall and winter of 1935–36 Ruth would conduct field research with two groups: the easternmost Siouan-language speakers near Red Wing, Minnesota, whose way of life closely resembled their Algonquian-speaking neighbors, the Ojibwa; and the southernmost Algonquian speakers, the Potawatomi in Kansas.

In these field studies Landes would collect standard kinship data, record myths, and observe and document religious rituals. She would also follow her intuition and with increasing depth record her observations of acculturation and the cultural creativity of marginalized peoples. She was shocked by the poverty on the reservations in the 1930s, but she was impressed beyond measure by the peoples' resilience and cultural innovation and by the personalities she encountered. In her writing she chose to highlight the peoples' strong will to maintain cultural beliefs and practices. She documented the creative intellectual and social practices by which people reinterpreted their beliefs and continually modified their practices to invest them with meaning and vitality. Her approach was to focus on certain key individuals whose personalities illuminated the contradictions, struggles, and determination of the group.

Based on this work she wrote three book manuscripts in the late 1930s. These remained unpublished for three decades: *Ojibwa Religion and the Midéwiwin* and *The Mystic Lake Sioux* were published in 1968. *The Prairie Potawatomi* was published in 1970.

The first of these books, *Ojibwa Religion and the Midéwiwin*, is the product of her work with Maggie Wilson and Will Rogers. In the interval that lapsed between the time Landes wrote *Ojibwa Religion* and the time it was published, the Ojibwa became known to anthropologists as "the classic case of the Guardian Spirit ethic, a people whose world was filled with spirit forces and whose existence depended on gaining power over these forces, both benign and malevolent" (Dunning 1968). But when Ruth Landes conducted research, the only published study of Ojibwa religious practices was Hoffman's 1891 Bureau of American Ethnology report, "The Midéwiwin or 'Grand Medicine Society,'" which was based on secondary sources and not on firsthand observation and fieldwork. *Ojibwa Religion* would be "the first detailed account of Ojibwa Midéwiwin ritual since W. J. Hoffman's report in 1891" (Barnouw 1969).

Letters from the Field

Ruth Landes arrived at Red Lake in northeastern Minnesota on June 13, 1933, "after very miscellaneous travel." The next day she hired a car and driver to travel several hundred miles to visit the neighboring reservations of Ponemah, Cass Lake, and Leech Lake: "Everyone most kind and Government buildings are almost country clubs by contrast with Canadian ones" she reported to Benedict (June 14, 1933, RFBP).

Her initial enthusiasm had dampened when she wrote two weeks later on June 29, 1933: "I have felt so discouraged that I have almost packed up and returned to Canada. First, Red Lake and Cass Lake and now large parts of Ponemah are in a condition of cultural leprosy . . . it is amazing how large parts of the whole are just dropping away." Finding informants was a second problem. A forestation program, one of the Roosevelt administration's New Deal employment programs to alleviate rural poverty, was hiring ablebodied Chippewa men at $30 per month plus room and board. Landes's informants' fees could not compete: "The ones who remain are the old ones who speak no English and the women. I have tried the women repeatedly, and for my purposes they are hopeless. . . . I suppose a Mrs. Wilson [is] just [a] freak . . . of accident."

A few weeks later, on July 15, 1933, Landes wrote that she had been "exceedingly occupied with little difficulties that sum up to mountains, and for which the ease of last summer's work little prepared me." She was becoming more hopeful about the research now that she had solved one of her main problems — transportation — by purchasing a 1929 Ford for $200. She had also increased her payment to informants from $1 to $2 daily and had found some informants who were willing to work with her:

I am getting tales from two bright men. One man is quite remarkable. He is a young man of 26 years, with a mind of brilliant promise. He is married to a white girl . . . he is convalescing from TB . . . because he is weak I cannot work with him steadily but I am having him write traditional stories for me . . . I am typing them just as he wrote them. I told him that if he writes 50–100 of them we can get them published. So he is writing. I give him $1.00 for 10 pages — because he is too much my equal (his attitude) to be paid for our discussions, therefore he must be paid at a higher rate for the stories. The other bright man is the one for whom I had to raise my daily bidding. But he can secure several big medicine men to work with me, so the raise will secure good returns.

On July 19, 1933, Benedict wrote to say that she would increase Landes's monthly allowance to $150 to cover the higher than expected costs of the fieldwork. She reminded Landes "affectionately" that in addition to her reports on data collection "I want to know how comfortably you are making out in the things of this world too."[1] On July 25, 1933, Ruth Landes replied: "At present, in trying to do aboriginal ethnology, I must resort to a kind of archeology. I must take an interpreter to sit down with me and dig away at the dim passages of an informant's memory. This is a grueling task for the informants and I myself feel quite worn out from holding the people down and in good temper. (But there are some good results.) All this makes [Manitou] culture seem vividly alive."

She reported that she "turn[ed] to the stories as generally-speaking the most vigorous survivals" because, although "a considerable body of aboriginal thinking persists at Ponemah, especially in the field of religion . . . one can just see the attenuation in process." She described witnessing "a medicine dance which fell very far short indeed of Hoffman's description, and where indifference was striking. And the head men were tottering drunk. There are large gaps in the knowledge of even the most earnest and intelligent of the young Indians: a *dzisaki* ["juggler," shaman] who is not considered heretical for dzisakiing without tent and at the age of 20 years; a man who has been through five degrees of the Mide yet can give only fragments of the philosophy that should have been thoroughly taught him." "I think I need an occasional letter from you to cheer me up," she concluded, because "the generally intensive assimilation program that our government tries to further is simply devastating to one's spirits."

Benedict replied on August 2, 1933: "My heart goes out to you in your "archeological" weeks. [Manitou] was such good luck that I hoped perhaps it might continue — though I knew by all the precedents it couldn't. I never shall forget Reo Fortune's despair when he first struck the Omaha. Any ethnology that depended on what was obtainable among people like that was bunk by definition. But in the end he had to admit that his efforts had been well worth the investment. It's a bore that we didn't live a century ago" (RLP, box 4).

Margaret Mead and her second husband, Reo Fortune, had conducted fieldwork together among the Omaha (whom they called the "Antlers"). Mead's report on the work published the preceding year had stressed the negative impacts of acculturation. Benedict and Mead shared this then-prevalent view in the discipline that focused more on salvaging the culture that had been "lost" than on developing theory and methodology to analyze the cultural processes that were at work on reservations in the 1930s. At this moment in her career Landes was on the cusp between these two approaches.

Reminding Landes that overcoming adversity is part of fieldwork, Benedict tried to cheer her up by relaying a report from another of her students, Jules Henry, who had been living and working with the Kaingáng in southeastern Brazil since December 1932: "Have you had a letter from Jules? The rains had come, and a flu epidemic had struck. Eduardo's five children, wife and servants were down with it, and the baby had died. The country is half under water. Two of his best informants had died, and another was going soon. Nevertheless he said, 'I've every reason to be pleased with the ethnology I've been able to get' and that from Jules made me feel that all was not lost. For that will make him sleep comfortably at night no matter what goes on around him" (August 2, 1933, RLP, box 4).[2]

Benedict also responded to Landes's report on July 25 that University of Chicago anthropologist Sol Tax had "passed through" and that he had "been through 3 or 4 or more reservations, from where he secured kinship schedules." "How is Sol Tax now that he is a disciple of Radcliffe-Brown's?" inquired Benedict. "I'm sure he told you that he's a master hand at kinship systems now, but did you get any facts from him that were of interest?"

Ruth Landes wrote on August 15, 1933, that receiving Benedict's letter "has been the greater pleasure because it has reached me while on a dysentery rack! . . . The pain and the weakness!" She also expressed her relief that Benedict had "broken the ice," and now "the horror I nursed can out":

I thought Sol Tax sounded like a Radcliffe-Brown disciple . . . or a CCNY [City College of New York] graduate. He just knows it all, and has the most beautiful mimeographed set of kinship forms i.e. blanks. He has a numerous collection of Chippewa kinship schedules, collected in the past weeks, and yet has not abstracted a single principle therefrom. He went through the courtly gesture of asking me what I knew about my own Ojibway schedules, and then tried to prove me wrong . . . but he had to admit defeat. I guess he hadn't been with Radcliffe-Brown long enough. Then I tried to show him the functional variations that the same kinship schedule had undergone — but that was too much for Chicago. (RFBP)

Their correspondence from now on, in addition to discussing Landes's field research, would include exchanging gossip and observations on the work of their colleagues. Although the "ice was broken," Landes would continue to address Benedict as "Dr. Benedict."

Landes also happily reported that she had begun intensive work with a shaman, Will Rogers:

Yesterday I attempted to drag myself out of the awful sickness that a paregoric diet brings, and I attempted some ethnology. The old fellow is both deaf and has a sense of humor — so I suppose I cannot attribute the collapse that came after a few hours to the dysentery solely. . . . [He] is 83–93 years old, possessing a good street English and an active though senile mind. He had . . . got it into his head that he would tell me "everything." His "everything" is the Midéwiwin — he is a priest of highest ranking. I am getting full texts from him. . . . Already I see one point that delights my controversial soul, and which I had previously suspected . . . [that] there were two original supreme beings, one earth, the other sky, i.e. a dual supreme god-head not monotheism as Chippewa religion is always described. (August 15, 1933, RFBP)

Once her "controversial soul" had been touched, Landes's interest increased, and she "fell into a morass of steady work from which it has been impossible to be extricated," she wrote Benedict on October 12, 1933. "So I was in a nunnery until a week ago." Landes and Will Rogers had worked together every day for two months. She told Benedict that she felt she would need another month in the field (and another $150) to "rework for errors and refinement." But she was in a dilemma: she wasn't sure she wanted to delay preparing for exams, and she was anxious to start writing her dissertation.[3] In addition, she was worried about her future job opportunities: "Do there seem to be any possibilities for me at the AMNH [American Museum of Natural history]?" Landes asked Benedict.

Pindigegizig/Hole-in-the-Sky/Will Rogers

Will Rogers, or "Hole-in-the-Sky," was in his 80s and nearing the end of a productive career as a midé (shaman) when Ruth Landes met him at his home in Cass Lake. She brought him to Red Lake, where they worked together from early August to late October 1933. She paid for his room and board with a local family who feared his supernatural powers but needed the money Landes offered.

Rogers described himself to Landes as both *midé* and *manitou* (spirit-power) (1968b:11). To represent Will/"Hole"'s multiple subjectivity and his fluid identity as a human spirit medium, Landes used both names in her writing "according to the situation": "When we dealt with secular matters, I call him Will, as others did. When he acted the shaman by tutoring me, I should have used a kinship term like "Grandfather," and occasionally did. In [writing] I use his Ojibwa 'mystic' name Pindigegizig, meaning Hole-in-the-Sky. I retain the two names as indicators of the secular or mystic nature of the situations in which they figured" (16).

Will Rogers's reputation as a midé built on those of his father and uncles who had also been shamans. He spoke unaccented English, the result of his years of work in the Minnesota logging industry, yet he "thought in Ojibwa forms and habitually 'talked sacredly' with Supernaturals, especially his 'twin brother,' Thunderbird" (18). He was lonely when Landes met him. She said he had been put out of the house by his last wife and adult stepson. After Landes left in the late fall, "they had him committed to a mental hospital as a nuisance; he wrote me sad letters from there," she recalled (18). Will welcomed the respect Landes showed for his midé knowledge, and the work offered him relief from loneliness. Landes described their relationship to Benedict:

There has developed one of those beautiful ties that are made in heaven, or in the mauve decade. He has become very attached to me. He has adopted me as his namesake (this is a serious tie, whereby namer and namee are identified as one body) and regularly treats me with sweat baths and herbs. All this has a powerful bearing naturally on the Mide information he gives me. At first he was merely conscientious in filling up the day with texts, etc. that skirted the profounder esoterica; but now the esoterica just pour out. The whole business now is to be had for the bare asking. . . . The com-

parative Midéwiwin information is exciting . . . my life with the old man is many-faceted! Since I do everything but sleep with him, the ethnological by-product of our association is well-rounded. (October 12, 1933, RFBP)

Landes was careful to pay for the cultural knowledge, recognizing that "legalistically, he 'owned' this material and the 'right' to teach it" (1968b:123–124): "Daily we pored over his birchbark scrolls depicting midéwiwin lore. I provided the other necessaries, which were the tobacco that sanctioned talking to and about Supernaturals, Will's daily fee that also sanctioned any instruction, and his food and lodging. And he stinted nothing" (19–20). Describing one of their work sessions, she wrote: "Hole reproduced the song for me, in his aged but true voice, gazing intently, devoutly, at some remote horizon; first he offered tobacco, silently. During such mystic reproductions, I felt he summoned the effort from emotional depths. I could not tell whether his attitude contained some apology for possible blasphemy, singing or praying in this unusual secular situation" (123–124). Outsiders, she wrote, "could not imagine the great energies and tensions behind a midé rite, binding its shamans, patients and witnesses with fierce interests. . . . While I spent a few short months being tutored by Will in the midé texts and rites that follow, the Indians spent their lives in the heavy shadows cast by midé and other shamanistic personages" (71–72).

Sexual banter, however, was a source of "fun" in Ojibwa culture that appealed to Ruth Landes and became an important idiom of communication for Landes and Will Rogers. Will asked her to "marry" him: "Teaching me midéwiwin under conditions required by dogma, Will proposed that we marry to consolidate our shamanistic partnership. He said, 'With your brains and my knowledge, we should rule the world.' He pursued this seriously, using the courtship cross-cousin ["sweetheart"] terms and conduct until I terminated matters by driving him back to Cass Lake, forty miles away. Yet a week later, under the blistering sun, he trudged back and we resumed uncousinly instruction" (19). Their parting was solemn when it came time for Landes to return to New York:

At the end he gave me a "powerful" name (of an eagle manito), the promise of guarding me after his reincarnation as a Thunderbird, also his sacred scrolls . . . little sacks of protective magic or "medicine," his handsome, large redstone peacepipe, and two fine new quilts just earned for serving midé rites at Red Lake. When we parted under a snowfall at Cass Lake and I let him out of the car, he stood erect by my window, reached for my hand, asked me to return, then removed his glasses to dry his tears. So the Ojibwa begged ritual "pity" of a guardian spirit, seeking "power" after humbling himself physically and mentally, and weeping. He wrote me until his death a few years later. At my present writing, he should be stationed above Niagara Falls in his Thunderbird aspect, as he anticipated. (20)

The Academy of Shamans: Ojibwa Religion and the Midéwiwin

Landes's *Ojibwa Religion and the Midéwiwin* is divided into three parts. The first discusses Ojibwa religion in terms of cosmology, the vision quest, shamanism, and sorcery. The second concentrates on the Midéwiwin, describing its organization, origin myths, rituals, and variations. The third part contains appendixes: an account of Maggie Wilson's war vision, a discussion of "common dreams," brief descriptions of midé birch bark scrolls, and a description of a Midéwiwin public rite that Landes attended.

Landes described Ojibwa religion as personal and individualized, an ancient belief system that emerged from the solitary hunting lifestyle. Individuals who opened themselves to the manitous through fasting or the solitary vision quest in isolated spiritual places gained "power" ("medicine") through dreams or visions. "Ojibwa tradition created its intensest religious expression through pursuit of a private guardian spirit who revealed (or yielded) himself in 'dreams' or visions," she wrote (1968b:8). Hole-in-the-Sky described the vision experience as "dying," that is, giving one's life over to the manitous and opening oneself to receiving visions and thus knowledge (88). Individuals developed personal relationships with manitous, who served as lifelong patron guardian spirit-powers. Landes recalled how "watching Will pray to his own Thunderbird guardian" or "listening . . . to Mrs. Wilson narrate for me the 'power' dream of her World War I Star Dance, I sensed that to each visionary, his own experience was uniquely worthy and could be subordinated to others only against the deepest protest" (32).

The concept of "power" was at the core of the religious system and pervaded all aspects of the culture, guiding the actions and thoughts of the people. "Power" resided within the individual and did not form the basis for an organized religion with a congregation of worshippers. Importantly, this allowed individuals to act independently of others. People feared "power" and could never be sure who possessed it and to what degree; they thus tended to fear one another and avoided intimate contacts with individuals who were not close kin. Individuals readily admitted that their fears of others were due to the fear of the possibility of sorcery. Landes described how terrified Wilson was when she came to Red Lake to work with Landes for three weeks during that summer; Maggie feared Will Rogers's "power." Occasional elder women evolved into feared shamans, but a male shaman was "the Ojibwa ideal strong man, defining and holding [at] bay the terrible forces of existence, manito and human. His skills were inseparable from his alarming personality, seen in the manifestations described as jealous, greedy, bullying, and extremely ambitious" (1968b:59).

Landes interpreted Ojibwa visions, sorcery, and rituals as cultural responses to fears "about hunger, sickness, crippling, infidelity, betrayal, ridicule, failure in trapping, games, and war, about weather and poisonings and insanity" (1968b:22). The Ojibwa, she said, lived "expecting Evil to triumph but ever optimistic about Good. This gave their ethos an ironical, sophisticated aspect free of despair" (2). She suggested that the conditions of extreme poverty in Ojibwa communities in the 1930s and the related high rates of infant mortality and illness had increased people's fears that others were using their "power" for evil and increased their reliance on midé shamans and on the rites of the Midéwiwin (57).

According to Basil Johnston, the goal of the Midéwiwin, the religious and curing society known to ethnologists of Landes's time as "The Grand Medicine Society," is to bring health and long life to the Ojibwa and to preserve traditional knowledge (1982:96). Historically there were eight degrees of membership or levels of training to become a midé (a member, a curer, a shaman). A candidate would spend years learning the songs, rituals, ethics, and medicinal knowledge. The midés used picture writing on birch bark scrolls as mnemonic devices to assist in recalling the hundreds of songs and rites of the Midéwiwin. Infinite variations in the myths and songs existed because these were communicated orally, and each midé had a personal repertoire. Consistent with her earlier ethnography of Ojibwa individualism and gender autonomy, Landes found that individuals personalized their relations with a spirit world, and as in her other Ojibwa writing, she insisted on recording variability rather than "dogma." Much of Maggie Wilson's and Will Rogers's testimony described how ritual practices and knowledge varied locally and among individual practitioners. They were concerned to distinguish their own personal knowledge from that of other midé specialists. In Landes's words, "the towering prestige of the midé shamans rested mainly on their private vision achievements; seen thus, the Midé Society was the academy of shamans" (Landes 1968b:42).

Although "the Indians always said that they were transferring faithfully the teachings of past times" (Landes 1968b:112), Landes recorded different versions of the origin myths and described how their telling was a source of both entertainment and intellectual debate for the midé shamans: "There is no firm limit to the number of elaborations about the midé tale. Hole and others . . . revealed that imaginative men liked to speculate on ethical, philosophic, therapeutic, and even novelistic implications hidden in the tale" (109). She described how "midé officers stayed up late debating these matters, talking with unusual freedom and disregarding jealousies under the influences of quiet nights, ample tobacco, and fellow scholars (109).

After weeks of studying the origin myth with Hole, transcribing text from his speeches and the pictographs of his scroll, working out the allusions, Landes found that "when finally systematized, it seemed slight, much dramatized in the telling and by other ritual enactments and much repeated" (1968b:96). "The tales' slightness was partly a literary form, even a religious one, for value was laid on great understatement" (136). She observed that while repetitions often appeared contradictory, "this may well be the illusion of outside (research) standards" (96). "Consistency and order," she said, "cannot be expected from an oral tradition . . . in a community that [does not] tabu open questioning and criticism" (96).

The voices of her two key informants are clearly heard in the text, and Landes's empathy with them is evident. One reviewer called the book a "descriptive study of Ojibwa supernatural practices by Will Rogers and Maggie Wilson, edited or collected by Ruth Landes" (Dunning 1968). Landes credited the powerful descriptions in *Ojibwa Religion* to Maggie Wilson and Will Rogers, whom she described as "by our standards, energetic, intellectually keen, and sophisticated . . . wary, brilliant, immensely alert and curious about events. . . . [T]hey worked superbly despite illness, destitution, and a deep restlessness within . . . they expressed high points of their culture; to me they seemed immensely civilized" (1968b:16–17).

Ojibwa Religion and the Midéwiwin, although published in 1968, is largely unchanged from the original manuscript written in the 1930s. Landes integrated little of the scholarly research that had taken place during the intervening years, and the book was something of an anachronism by the time it appeared in print. Its portrait of Ojibwa beliefs is, however, consistent with that of later scholars (Brown in collaboration with Matthews 1993; Hallowell 1955; 1992; Johnston 1982; Matthews and Roulette 1996; Rogers 1962; Vennum 1982). Because the book was not published at the time it was written, Landes's research did not contribute to the study of Native American religion in the way that it might have. Despite its delayed appearance in print, noted Ojibwa scholars Victor Barnouw, Edward Rogers, and William Dunning all favorably reviewed the book, indicating that her research might have helped solidify Landes's professional stature had she been able to publish it in the 1930s.

Edward S. Rogers, writing in *American Anthropologist* (1969), observed that Landes had identified the key characteristics of Ojibwa religion that have since preoccupied scholars: the fluid ways in which individuals combine Christian and aboriginal beliefs to develop personalized belief systems, the belief that "power" resides within all individuals, and the importance of dreams. Recalling his own field experience among the Round Lake Ojibwa of northern Ontario, Rogers said that Ojibwa are reluctant to reveal information about the Midéwiwin to outsiders, and he considered Landes's work with Maggie Wilson and Will Rogers exceptional. He described the Ojibwa as "not particularly articulate [and] . . . no amount of prodding can alter the situation" (1962:4). Landes believed that her youth and "perhaps also my low-ranked femaleness reduced Ojibwa caution" (1968b:16–17).

In his review in *Pacific Northwest Quarterly* (1969), Chippewa scholar Victor Barnouw called *Ojibwa Religion* "a tour de force about the Ojibwa world view" and discussed the effect the delay in its publication has upon the reader:

Ojibwa Religion and the Midéwiwin . . . is a kind of Rip Van Winkle, making the current scene after a back-drawer slumber of more than thirty years. As in the case of Rip, there is an air of strangeness in this latter-day emergence, for the book differs in some ways from more recent anthropological publications. This is not to say that it is 'out of date' or failing in some fashionable new virtue, for Ojibwa Religion and the Midéwiwin is an excellent piece of work, much like the author's earlier publications on the Ojibwa, and written in the same lively, sometimes dramatic style. . . . One can see in Ojibwa Religion the strong influence of Ruth Benedict. There is a searching effort here to see the Ojibwa world whole and to assess the effect of that cultural configuration upon the individual. Intuition and insight, as well as reason and deduction, have gone into the making of this work. I suspect that most of today's anthropology graduate students would not have so much faith in their own intuitions and would not dare to generalize as boldly as Ruth Landes did in the 1930s. We now have a more cautious generation of scholars, concerned with more manageable issues. This may be well enough, but perhaps something has been lost in the process.

A Third Season of Fieldwork

In the spring of 1935, Ruth Benedict arranged a further $1,500 research grant from Columbia University for Ruth Landes — now "Dr. Landes" — to undertake a third season of field research, this time among the Prairie Potawatomi of Kansas, who were thought to represent the southernmost extent of Algonquian-speaking peoples and whose religious practices were said to include a form of the Midéwiwin. Landes recalled that Benedict proposed the study "as a proper sequel to my work among the Ojibwa of Ontario and Minnesota. . . . [She] expected Potawatomi data [to exemplify] Central Algonkian and possibly Plains influences upon an originally Ojibwa-like base . . . and she expected data to advance speculations about theories of 'culture area' and 'culture change'" (1970a:30). En route, Landes planned to visit Maggie Wilson in Ontario and Will Rogers in Cass Lake and to spend several weeks consulting with ethnomusicologist Frances Densmore in Red Wing, Minnesota.

On August 2, 1935, she left New York by train for St. Paul, where she purchased a second-hand Model A Ford coupe "whose high carriage would navigate the gumbo roads" (Landes 1970a:9). Over the next nine months she was to travel several thousand miles in the Ford, endure breakdowns and delays for repairs, and even sleep alone in the car one night by the road in Kansas when a sudden winter snowstorm had made the road impassable. There being no accommodation on the reservations, she stayed in small hotels in the nearby towns — "no less drab than the dwellings on the reservation, though perhaps in better repair" (9). Daily she drove to the reservations, her arrival always heralded and never inconspicuous. Her driving glasses were a particular source of mystique and comment: "For driving I wore glasses, which became a detail in attributing sorcery to me, evidencing eyes made sore from contact with my magical concoctions" (9).

She reported on her trip in a letter to Benedict on August 16 — addressing her now as "Ruth dear" — and described a

crazily hectic 2–3 weeks. . . . I started on a 300 mile trek north to the Manitou reserve . . . 70 miles out of St. Paul needed new tires. . . . So I continued on to Duluth where I stayed over night and the next day went on to Ft. Frances and [Manitou]. . . . Mrs. Wilson was not in but I located her by Sat. afternoon, passed the most loving time of day and made arrangements to commence work the coming Monday (she does not work Sundays, being Christian or whatever). So I stayed at the "hotel" at Emo, the most sinfully horrible place in the world outside of Dickens — [a] proprietor . . . who does not bathe, a captain in the Canadian and Imperial reserves . . . who lets out a pigsty at $1.50 a night and permits you to use a toilet seat ringed round with ancient faeces and excreta. Mon. and Tues. I worked with Maggie . . . by Tues night my work with Maggie was done so I commenced to turn south for I want to do some Santee work in Red Wing, Minn. and by October want to go on to Kansas . . . but Wed. engine would not start on car . . . need for repairs before leaving . . . am now holed up for the weekend on the north shore of Lake Superior to rest and catch up on typing. . . . I hope

*you feel for me. . . . I have wished to see you the more that I have not seen
you and I do hope that you will be within reach when I return next year.*
(RFBP)

She had hoped to stop in Red Lake to visit Will Rogers on her way
south to Red Wing, but upon learning that he was in the hospital
in Fergus Falls, Minnesota, she decided to head straight south and
to try instead to visit him on a weekend trip from Red Wing.

Improvisation with Frances Densmore in Red Wing

In Red Wing Landes introduced herself to Frances Densmore. Born
in Red Wing in 1867, Densmore grew up in the family home over-
looking the Mississippi River and was fascinated by the drumming she could hear in the nearby Dakota Sioux encampment.
She studied music at Oberlin Conservatory and later at Harvard,
where she read Alice Cunningham Fletcher's study of Omaha music
when it was first published in 1893 and was impressed by Fletcher's
method of interpreting music in relation to cultural context. Under Fletcher's guidance for the next ten years she read widely in the
published sources on Native American cultures. In 1905 she made
her first field trip, transcribing by ear songs of the Chippewa on
Lake Superior at Grand Portage. In 1907 she made the first recordings of Chippewa songs, and upon submitting these to the Bureau of American Ethnology she began a 50-year association with
that institution, which thereafter provided her with $3,000 annu-
ally for her research. Between 1907 and 1925 she recorded songs
of the Ojibwa (Chippewa) of the reservations at White Earth, Red
Lake, Cass Lake, Leech Lake, and Mille Lacs in Minnesota, at the Lac
Courte Oreilles reservation in Wisconsin, and at Manitou Rapids in
Ontario, where Maggie Wilson had been one of her key informants.

Since 1911 she had also been recording songs and conducting research with the Dakota Sioux. In addition to sound recordings,
she collected and preserved musical instruments, crafts, and other
items of material culture and made detailed ethnographic observations of daily life, customs, and religion. She had published her
Ojibwa ethnology in 1929 in her book *Chippewa Customs*. Earlier
books included *Chippewa Music* (1910), *Chippewa Music II* (1913), and
Teton Sioux Music (1918). Densmore was also deeply interested in

the close relationship between music and medicine among Native Americans, and she collected botanical specimens of medicinal herbs and recorded the healing songs of the Midéwiwin and the private and public ceremonial curing methods of men and women in many groups. Over her lifetime she recorded more than 3,000 songs of 76 Native American groups; her publications include more than 20 books and more than 100 articles. One of the most important figures in 20th-century American Indian music research, Densmore worked in relative isolation from other scholars, accompanied by her sister Margaret, who was cook and driver on the field trips. She died in "quiet obscurity" in Red Wing in 1957 at the age of 90 (Frisbie 1989:51–58; Lurie 1966:69–72).

Reporting that the "car continued on its career of going bad" and that "the rush and strain have been so continuous as to prohibit writing," Landes wrote to Benedict on September 2 to describe meeting Densmore, "who as you must know is a hoary native of Red Wing." She continued: "I do not know what to say about her: if you know her, it is not necessary. She has collected some nice music and herb texts, but she really ends nearly just there. Societal and psychological mechanisms are completely foreign to her; and her attitudes diverge not a whit from the proper ones of a Red Wing Episcopal member. I can't say that I like her, though she has tried wonderfully to be nice. She has not been a real help in any way, which was not unexpected; but besides she has taken offense because I have refused to traipse around Wisconsin with her to interview Fair Indians. But she did recommend one good informant... I must not forget that!" (RFBP). One can only imagine what the 68-year-old Episcopalian Midwestern spinster thought of the 27-year-old urbane New York divorcee! They worked together for the month of September and seemed to reach an understanding and appreciation for each other. On September 29 Landes wrote, "I must remark on Miss Densmore's courtesy to me—which she wishes me to remark on. She really has helped lots and feels that she can't do too much. She always wishes greetings sent to you and to Prof. Boas." And on October 3: "I have spent much time with Miss Densmore: evgs that last from 7:30 to one, and then I get away by main force! I have grown to like her. She tries so hard to be obliging. Her limitations I think are those inevitable to her sex in her generation in her town (Red Wing is the home of her family since 1834). I have reread her Chippewa music bulletins, and the material she has there (though piecemeal and collected only to make a context for the songs) is gorgeous. Obviously she was a hard worker, and honest, and daring too in view of the circle from which she originates" (RFBP). Landes found especially "absorbing" Densmore's collection of photos "showing women of various tribes in various stages of their handicrafts" and suggested to Benedict that they "might be useful to Prof Boas' gesture project" (October 3, 1935, RFBP).

Densmore told Landes of "a number of very live Chippewa localities" in Minnesota east of Red Lake. "She has objects from these places that make my mouth water, for neither the Manitou nor the Red Lake people can do anything of the sort: bead work; bark dishes; quill work; weaving with bark, etc. Her Chippewa make these objects commercially, but that does not vitiate the fact of their excellent existence." Landes hypothesized that "if these aboriginal objects are surviving there is a chance that aboriginal institutions may be surviving there too." With pleasure, she began to plan future research with Frances Densmore, writing to Benedict: "For a month or two on my next trip I would like to traipse among these Ojibwa. I would not be treading on Miss D's toes, as she herself says, for she does no ethnology as we know it . . . she records songs, collects objects and herbology. And she does know Minnesota in a wonderfully useful way for she has lived and travelled in it all of her certainly 60 years" (October 3, 1935, RFBP). Landes, however, would be unable to fulfill these plans because her next Columbia-sponsored field research would take her far from Red Wing and to Brazil.

Frances Densmore had introduced Landes to a 37-year-old Santee Dakota interpreter, Grace Rouillard, at Prairie Island, the nearby Sioux community—"a bare spot islanded in the surrounding woods" (RL to RB, September 29, 1935, RLP, box 2), "not a reservation but land privately owned by individual Indians" (RL to RB, September 2, 1935, RFBP). Rouillard, whom Landes describes as "good-looking and meticulous in every way" (1968a:114), had recruited her 54-year-old uncle, Moses Wells, to work with Landes for several weeks. Although Siouan-speakers and not Algonquian, the Santee Sioux lived in the eastern woodlands and had adopted the subsistence practices of their Ojibwa neighbors. They were the traditional enemies of the Ojibwa and had figured prominently in the Ojibwa war myths Landes had previously recorded. While living in Red Wing, Landes decided to conduct fieldwork with the Santee Sioux, driving the 17 miles north to Prairie Island each day to work with Moses Wells and returning to Red Wing to work in the evenings with Frances Densmore. As Wells spoke only Dakota, Landes also hired Rouillard to translate from Dakota to English.

Moses Wells was one of the few members of the community who had an interest in ritual, but his knowledge relied on his memory of what he had heard as a child from his parents and grandparents. Landes found him "the opposite of skeptical and he resents questioning." Furthermore, she could not observe religious ritual at Prairie Island because it was a community of "only 50 souls" and had "no political organization and no ceremonial life." The people traveled west to other Sioux communities to participate in dances and rituals. Genealogical data was also "lacking woefully." What genealogical and ceremonial data she did obtain was "as through a glass darkly," and in frustration she was "nearly jumping out of my skin most of the time," she told Benedict (September 29, 1935, RLP, box 2).

What did fascinate Moses Wells and other community members and what Landes was able to record were stories of Santee history, of their exile to Santee, Nebraska, from Minnesota following the Dakota uprising in 1862, and of their various migrations and the eventual return of a few families to Prairie Island. The stories that Wells wished to tell and that he spent hours relating to Ruth Landes and his enthralled niece, Grace Rouillard, were different versions of Santee history. He also recounted tales of raids and war parties against the Ojibwa to the north, and he described in detail subsistence activities, especially deer hunting, harvesting rice, and maple sugaring, that resembled Ojibwa practices. "Time levels may appear to merge occasionally in the tales," Landes noted, "so that it is not always clear whether events recounted occurred in the lifetime of the narrator or in earlier generations; this is partly a stylistic trait of epics whose mystic 'power' survives and partly because the tellers actually found the old days still vivid" (1968a:17–18). Landes recalled: "Though I secured information only laboriously from a few aged and young tribespeople, who were morose generally, I was lastingly impressed by the reality in their minds of the culture they were expounding. They brought the Sioux humanity alive."

The Mystic Lake Sioux: Sociology of the Mdewakantonwan Sioux (1968a) is organized in four chapters: "History," "Political Organization," "Kinship and Marriage," and "Occupations." Landes did not discuss religion except as an adjunct activity in these other domains. In this respect the book resembles her first study, *Ojibwa Sociology* (1937b). Her work is partly retrospective, reconstructing Santee social organization before their exile in 1862, and partly a description of the community as she found it in 1935. Her discussion of social relations in the community is the innovative contribution of the book. Instead of interpreting the material poverty and absence of religious ritual as a sign of cultural deterioration, as she had in her first letters from the field and as did many of her contemporaries (including Ruth Benedict, as is evident in her letters), Landes interpreted the social behavior she observed as a creative response. This approach she would further elaborate in her Potawatomi ethnography. She reminded her readers that the "general demoralization that impressed observers of the Prairie Island Santee in 1935 was not sudden" (1968a:18); the people had withstood more than a century of assimilative intrusions and dislocations. Landes's personal experiences of acculturation had taught her that the process involves not only loss but also transformation and continuity. She chose to document culture making rather than cultural loss.

Although she predicted that it would "provide rather beautiful distributive and comparative material," Landes found the actual field experience at Prairie Island taxing: "The nervous cost!" she wrote Benedict on September 2. "I live in hourly dread of the announcement that someone's feelings have finally been mortally hurt and that that someone needs leave my service." She was also worried that field expenses were "not too slight," and she detailed these to Benedict: She paid "the usual dollar a day" to both interpreter and informant "tho' Miss Densmore says they should be given 50 cents an hour!" Landes also provided tobacco and other extras that averaged another 15 cents apiece daily. Because there was no place to stay except in Red Wing she paid $12 a month for a hotel room, "short of a dollar a day" for food, and gas expenses to drive 34 miles each day to work with her informants at Prairie Island (RFBP).

On September 29 she wrote "out of the deeps of the blues" and "to relieve myself of the topmost foam." The Prairie Island people had left to "dance at a fair some 200 miles west of here." Landes "welcomed this" as an opportunity to go to St. Paul to catch up on her reading and writing and to work at the State Historical Society and Museum, "with which institutions Miss Densmore has most kindly made connections for me." She was also looking forward to seeing her father, who was coming to St. Paul to visit her for the weekend. "I spent some sleepless nights just over being happy over the coming Sabbatical." On Saturday she had driven into St. Paul, introduced herself at the Museum, and made elaborate working arrangements: "They gave me access to storerooms, manuscripts of the early 1800's, library, photographic equipment . . . just everything." She met her father, "got a hairwash," and the next day woke up with 103 degrees of fever and extreme muscular pain. Her father moved her to a more comfortable hotel in Minneapolis, "the only available room at $2.50 the day!" and "[h]ere I have been chafing all week. All my plans and grand arrangements shot." Joseph Schlossberg postponed his return to New York because he was worried about her. Meanwhile, Landes was worried about expenses "for I maintained my room in Red Wing; though my father has paid the major portion of my hotel bill." On the first day she had ventured out, "weak and achy," she had even got a traffic ticket for ignoring a highway sign—"another $3.00." "So my blueness is deeper than that of indigo," she told Benedict. She also reported that her father had advanced her $500 to buy traveler's checks to take to Kansas and asked Benedict to reimburse him from the remains of the $1,500 grant (RLP, box 2).

But all was not deeper than indigo. "Until this grippe or whatever had come on me, I had thought life was pretty grand." She explained: "For this Minnesota country is wonderfully gorgeous and various, ranging from luxuriant pine forests and biting cold, to pretty valleys landscaped naturally by elm and maple and willow, and cottonwood too, with suitable balmy temperatures. And I did a lot of travelling. So, a few weeks ago I drove from Red Wing to Red Lake (which is a round trip of some 830 miles). And may I say that I was terribly happy to see some of the Indians with whom I had become friendly two years ago; and I was delighted with their warmth, and felt with Miss Densmore that they are the 'nicest' people" (September 29, 1935). But, a few days later, on October 3, she was writing to Benedict "in a most gasp-y state" because her informant was "on a bender," and her interpreter and her husband, who were to have driven with her to introduce her to relatives at Morton, had gone ahead without her: "I am reluctant to follow them," she wrote, "because they will think they can treat me any way — they have behaved badly all along, taking whole afternoons off, coming late or not at all and I have indulged them; but I feel that I should halt — and I can hardly go to work at Morton without them." She continued: "I have given you this long spiel because I have just discussed the situation with Miss Densmore and she feels strongly that I should go; but I continue to disagree with her; still, I am sufficiently disturbed by her objection to feel that the case should be presented to you." Landes suggested that she could "pick up the Morton Santee during my next field trip; and a week there at this time under the present circumstances would probably not clarify the problems that developed from the work of the past 5 weeks." She reminded Benedict that "the Sioux are not my main problem and so are not entitled to this disproportionate expenditure of time, money and energy" (October 3, 1935, RFBP).

She did not go to Morton. On October 6 Landes reported that she worked "on the botany all day with F. Densmore." In mid October she spent a week in St. Paul working at the historical society and museum, and by the end of October she was settled in Kansas for the winter's work with the Potawatomi.

Santee Innovations and Ojibwa Comparisons

Victor Barnouw notes, "Since Ruth Landes worked among different adjacent American Indian tribes, she was able to make comparisons and contrasts . . . which serve, as in Ruth Benedict's work, to highlight the special characteristics and tendencies of each particular culture" (1969). Although subsistence pursuits of the Santee Sioux strongly resembled those of the Red Lake and Manitou Rapids Ojibwa, there were differences in social relations and values that struck Ruth Landes forcefully. The Sioux emphasized communality, not individualism, and personal autonomy, so important to the

Ojibwa, was not stressed by the Santee. "Among the Santee, everyone had the right to know about all. Among the Ojibwa, the privacy of a life, of all personal experiences and property, was paramount," she observed (1968a:36). Landes attributed the differences to the communal buffalo hunt, which had, a century earlier, been the focal point of annual activity in Dakota communities. Organization of labor for the summer hunt had required that the village function as a corporate unit and that individuals subordinate their behavior and aspirations to those required by the group at large.

Landes noted that communality, village solidarity, and sharing were still dominant values at Prairie Island in the 1930s and provided evidence of cultural continuity. She described, for example, how welfare rations were shared with others no matter how destitute the original recipient and how the entire village assumed responsibility for widows, the poor, and the disabled. Each Dakota community was conceptually a kin group, and Santee marriages were arranged by parents and followed strict rules of village exogamy. In contrast to the Ojibwa, who stressed personal, romantic, and individualistic sentiments in marriage, the Santee respected "honorable marriage," one in which both spouses were faithful and "often continent, as evident by their few offspring" (1968a:130).

Landes found that in 1935 "kinship obligations functioned vigorously at Prairie Island village, dominating personal lives," and that "behavior within the village was always determined by kin prescriptions." "Even I, the complete outsider," she wrote, "got trapped in them to a degree for which I was unprepared by my prior experiences with Ojibwa." "Among Ojibwa," she said, "a person was as much a free individual as a kinsman [but] among the Santee there was no choice but commitment to or against a kin complex (1968a:95).

Landes described how her position as Grace Rouillard's patron, confidante, and daily companion embroiled her in local kin relations and culminated in an encounter that she called an attempted rape. "I finally was nearly raped by a drunken Indian," she dramatically reported to Benedict: "This is a man who is obsessed with sex, who hates his sister-in-law (my interpreter), who is jealous of the work, and who feels the need to assert his equality with other whites, for he is half white. He came round and carried on at length in Dakota which of course I did not understand; I knew only that he was getting into a fight with his sister-in-law, and that she was crying; so I felt it my place to stay with her; and then suddenly he reached for me; and so I went off" (September 29, 1935, RLP, box 2). Siblings-in-law were conceptually equated with cross-cousins (and potential spouses under local practices of levirate and sororate remarriage). Prescribed relations and accepted behavior between siblings-in-law as between cross-cousins allowed "extensive and boorish flirting privileges [and] merciless teasing that charged encounters with hostility" (1968b:98). Members of the opposite sex within this category were those with whom one can "joke and play sexually, whom [one] can humiliate in public, and against whom [one] may never hold offence" (102). Grace and her brother-in-law, Emmanuel (a pseudonym), enacted extremes of acceptable sibling-in-law behavior that were rendered to Landes in English translation as "hate" and "rape." Landes observed how this prescribed behavior also allowed the release of tension and conflict within the small community. Grace explained to Ruth that Emmanuel was "jealous his wife isn't doing this work, he wants to take it away from me" (120). Moses Wells, who had also been present at the encounter, said that "if Emmanuel had gone so far as to try rape, well, [I] would have knocked him down!" (122). Grace would later refuse to serve as a witness against Emmanuel when his own wife brought a court case against him. Community members thus remained secure in the knowledge that, in genuine crisis, kin would support one another.

Ruth Landes was always acutely observant of quotidian interpersonal relations and encounters. She was also theoretically as much interested in innovation and change as in norms and prescriptions. These combined to enable her to make perhaps her most important and prescient contribution in *The Mystic Lake Sioux*. At Prairie Island in 1935, she noted a social division within the community into "two adjacent neighborhoods" organized around what she called two "kinships centers" (1968a:105). The kinship centers were two focal families who were also more well-off than the others, owning larger houses and more land. These centers incorporated and protected poorer relations (as essentially squatters) in exchange for different kinds of services. Landes wrote: "Each attracted a fringe of persons more interested in it than in the adjoining family-center. The people of each neighborhood constantly visited and borrowed and quarreled, but preserved distant, courteous ties with the adjoining neighborhood" (105). Grace Rouillard was poor, landless, and dependent on the good will of kin for the house she lived in and the plot of land she gardened. It was her skill as an interpreter that was her social and economic capital and that had gained her membership in one of the protective kinship centers. Her skill was also a source of jealousy from kin who were dependent upon her to act as an interpreter for them at court cases, hospitals, and government agencies in Red Wing—often at great personal cost and inconvenience to her.

Ruth Landes's description of Santee neighborhood relations and exchanges of goods and services in the 1930s anticipates anthropological studies of kinship relations in contemporary societies in the 1960s, of which Carol Stack's *All Our Kin* (1974), a study of residence patterns and domestic networks in an African American community, is an elegant example. Landes developed her analysis intuitively through her relationship with her interpreter, Grace Rouillard, and through her participant observation of daily life in Prairie Island.

That Landes did not limit her ethnography to reconstructing the past and that she provided detailed description of contemporary social practices was commended by some of her reviewers. Charles Callender in his 1969 review in *American Anthropologist* described *The Mystic Lake Sioux* as "an important contribution to studies of American Indian social organization" "that plac[ed] the Santee in a better cultural perspective." Callender was impressed with the complexity of Landes's description of kinship relations as involving both obligation and resentment. He saw the incident with Grace and her brother-in-law as an example of how prescriptive joking behavior (in this case between cross-sexed siblings-in-law) also served to express hostility. Others, however, were uneasy with her gendered descriptions of conflictual relations in a small community, where the anonymity of participants is hard to preserve. One such critical reader charged that she recorded "community gossip" and that her "very frank characterizations of people" raised a question of professional ethics because "the Prairie Island Indians are not primitives from the interior of New Guinea," and they would read the book (Meyer 1969). This reviewer for *Minnesota History* discredited Landes's description of "what she regarded as an indecent assault on her person" and was more concerned with the portrait she had painted of the man involved in the encounter.

One anonymous reader who was reviewing the manuscript for a prospective publisher in the 1960s was also concerned with "the intimacy of some of the detail for a small community" because "Prairie Island is not Mexico City" — here referring to similar intimacies detailed in the Mexican life histories then recently published by Oscar Lewis in *Children of Sanchez* (1961), where, unlike Prairie Island, "individuals are lost in the anonymity of a large community." This reviewer went on to acknowledge: "This is not to say that it creates a false impression of aspects of Indian life. I wish that it were so. Some of the facts observed could be presented in better context to balance the picture and satisfy potential readers who have enshrined the 'noble savage,' but I would never question that the author is accurately reporting what she saw" (June 8, 1966, RLP). *The Mystic Lake Sioux* was published in the 1960s in the heyday of "Man the Hunter" notions about social relations in Native American societies. This reader was expressing how the discipline was concerned at least as much for the integrity of its concept of the "noble savage" as it was for the privacy of community members. The ethical dilemmas of protecting privacy and the politics behind what is regarded as appropriate contextualization, of course, continue to challenge ethnographers.

In reporting the "rape" encounter and describing the ambivalences in contemporary kinship relations, Ruth Landes was not merely gossiping. She was unabashedly stating her allegiance to Grace Rouillard and her empathy for a woman who like herself faced the outsider-insider dilemmas of biculturalism. Her ability to appreciate the complexity of her interpreter's social position as a mediator provided a case study that Landes analyzed with acumen and that opened a new window onto reservation life in the 1930s. Once again, Ruth Landes's own experiences of acculturation led her to new theoretical insights.

A Kansas Winter

In October 1935 Ruth Landes moved to Kansas to begin work with the Prairie Potawatomi. Her letters from Kansas report her many ups and downs during the seven-month field period including homesickness, unending car troubles and expenses, the weather, and factionalism on the reservation. To reduce the cost and inconvenience of car repairs, she decided to live in a hotel in Holton, not on the reservation. As she had with Will Rogers at Red Lake, she brought her key Potawatomi informant, septuagenarian Tom Topash, to town to live for the winter in a small rooming house near her hotel, where they could work together everyday, and "[t]o keep him accessible, since ice and encrusted snow often sealed off the reservation." "It nearly broke my heart," she wrote to Benedict on October 30, "not to speak of my conscience to be forced to live as I do [but] I know well that the present arrangements are best for the Kansas winter in view of my sinus troubles and respiratory propensities and that I am saving on energy and medical bills; still I am troubled by the artificiality, and have come to regard the Manitou situation and even the Red Lake one as paradise-like."

Landes asked for news of friends and colleagues: "I know you have little time for chatty letters . . . but perhaps sometime you can tell me more about my colleagues. How is Jules [Henry]? What is Ruth Bunzel doing? And Jeanette [Mirsky]? and [William] Whitman [III]? and [Martha] Champion? You know your letters mean a lot to me . . . and go a long way in jacking me up in my troughs. I always look forward to them" (RFBP).

Diversions from homesickness were soon provided by entanglements in the intricacies of the friendships and enmities of her key informants. She was quickly worn down by the constant need to navigate through the factions that ruled daily life on the reservation, writing to Benedict on January 6, 1936: "These damned Indians have frazzled my morale completely." Two weeks later she reported: "I still continue being a loved object around here, and it is very wearing; for everyone under the sun comes to my room mornings and evenings and privacy is for me a dream glimmering goldenly in an ashen past." But she said that she was "getting good Pot material" and that "Pots should be followed up in Canada, Oklahoma, the Lake states, and Mexico," hastening to tell Benedict *not* to "take this as a plea on my part. Send someone who needs chastising, and at the same time has an appearance of consummate gentle poise" (January 30, 1936, RFBP). On March 4 Landes reported that "One of the disaffected witchcraft groups I spoke of plans to write Columbia complaints about me. Don't mind if they do. It's this group that agitates constantly on the reservation, tries to libel or oust everyone" (RFBP). She was tempted, she said, to title her manuscript "Potawatomi Hooligans."

After almost five months in the field she wrote on March 20:

I have reached the stage of my Pot work where the people are first workable. If I stayed another 6 months I could get simply corking material, live, textual, detailed and very scrw-y. I'll simply have to come again and I hope I can commence where I will now be leaving off. The fight here (against the Indians and the weather) has been . . . well, it defies precise wording. . . . And I don't begin to have Pot institutions down with any precision . . . when I compare this material with my Ojibwa material, my heart sinks . . . god, it does. Yet I've put infinitely more into the Pot work; and am accepted and even liked now as I never was by the Ojibwa. And they'll tell me anything now . . . now when I have not the money. (RFBP)

The Prairie Potawatomi: Tradition and Ritual in the Twentieth Century (1970a) is largely devoted to a description of the "medicine bundle society" and "personal medicines" and visions of Potawatomi shamanism. There are shorter discussions of two more recent revitalization movements, the Religion Dance and the Peyote religious movement. Of the book's seven chapters, five are devoted to these religious movements because, in Landes's view, they "comprised the bulk of the life" of the Potawatomi in the 1930s (RL to RB, March 26, 1938, RFBP). She described how membership in these different religious societies was not mutually exclusive: the then-recently introduced Religion or Drum Dance incorporated certain syncretic Christian features and was dogmatically antagonistic to the older bundle and vision movements, yet many of its leading participants were bundle chiefs who had a reputation as great shamans. Two chapters also describe the name-group (which Landes called "gens") and kinship systems. Appendix A provides a list of the names and gens affiliations of 270 individuals. Appendix B compares details of her description of the Religion Dance with S. A. Barrett's 1911 description in *The Dream Dance of the Chippewa and Menominee Indians of Northern Wisconsin*. Appendix C is a phonetic transcription of informant Tom Topash's Prayer.

In her 1970 introduction Landes reminded readers: "In the terms of the thirties, my four field trips to the three tribes were to 'dead' or 'dying' cultures. The grim metaphor arose from our critical awareness . . . of all the tribes' utter defeat at our country's hands, sometimes emphasized as military and political, sometimes as economic, always as cultural" (1970a:4). In the 1930s "anthropologists hastened to record the remains of aboriginal concepts and practices, to preserve them for themselves and as material for speculations about human and cultural evolution" (5). Landes described the poverty on the reservation and the impact of the Roosevelt administration's public works and federal relief programs, the prejudice against Indians, which "was general in the United States of the 1930s" (5), and the Potawatomi refusal to accept the federal Indian Reorganization Act of 1934, which offered constitutional self-government on the condition that bands limit membership on the basis of residence and blood ancestry, a condition the Potawatomi refused. She emphasized that "despite the 'dead' state of aboriginal cultures," she had found "extraordinary vigor, social and individual," among the Prairie Potawatomi: "Daily I confronted their other world, organized about its own rules and values, obliging behavior that I found difficult to learn and emulate, often rousing fears, yet fostering real friendships. The individuals and groups I knew, who considered themselves shoved aside, exploited, and poor, and who fought back with suspicions of everyone, were no museum dolls salvaged from history's dumps. They were men and women evolved clearly from their ancestors' ways" (1970a:6). She continued, "Far from dying culturally, they have always seized life with a will" (38).

It was the "lustiness" of religious life that struck her most forcibly. In religion she found the stage for cultural creativity and the social space for individual agency. Religious rites offered a stage on which to dramatize community tensions and concerns: "The Religion, or Drum Dance ritual, was understood clearly to be also a drama within which conflicting interests wrestled. No single interest was more important than another, nor were they separable from each other" (1970a:258). "Most [rituals] . . . carried two or more interpretations. . . . The interpretations were not mutually contradictory but revealed a range of linked possibilities, each one intelligible upon explanation. There was no concept of 'truth' being 'one' as the white community expected; it might or might not be a plurality where the parts were linked within a greater context. . . . The ranging opinions were known to all I talked with, and not disputed" (267–268).

As Landes observed: "Mystic powers were now a mass of learning, bought and inherited, interpreted and reinterpreted" (1970a:195). "The specific evidences of syncretism fascinated me," Landes wrote. "It is one thing to say axiomatically that the culture borrows from others; it is another experience to witness *individuals* enacting the process that blends the borrowed with the traditional. To me, Potawatomi informants seemed open to innovations, whether approaching eighty like Topash [a key male informant] or approaching twenty-one like Louise Mazhi [a key female informant] . . . what arrested me . . . was . . . their creativity in meshing other-culture items with tribal traditions that they refused to abandon, ranging from mystic concepts to the kinship system" (268–269).

Thus, the prevailing culture pattern — what reviewer Robert Bee (1970) called "the shamanic tonic chord" of Landes's Potawatomi study — is dynamic and adaptive, not static and unchanging. Landes maintained: "Their special ethos cannot be viewed apart from the reality that, by 1935, the Potawatomi had been on hostile and mistrustful terms with Americans for over a hundred years . . . the tribesmen said over and over again that they were victims of government neglect and dishonesty. . . . Bundle leaders were tireless in fighting the Indian Agent" (1970a:38–39). She interpreted the revitalization movement and the florescence of bundles as creative responses to the pervasiveness of racism and the intrusion of the federal Indian administration in Potawatomi lives — a form of psychological warfare.

As she always did, Ruth Landes developed friendships and strong sympathies with her key informants, whose lives she tells between the lines of her ethnography. Tom Topash as a young man in the 1890s had been one of those who had led local resistance to the implementation of the Dawes Act and the allotment of reserve lands (Clifton 1977:394). By the time Ruth Landes met him, he was a widower in his 70s who "never fretted about, and barely mentioned, the passing of the old ways . . . he had long found his place in the dominant society and in the tribal one. He applauded the successful adaptations of his family" (Landes 1970a:117). Topash represented the "hard-working families on the reservation in 1935–36 . . . opposed to the popular leadership . . . associated with the bundle societies; they considered themselves 'good' because they upheld conservative traditions of their ancestors and of the general American world (such as hard work, maintaining credit, responsibleness towards family and friends, good manners) and refrained from bundle activities in favor of adherence to the officially Christianized anti-bundle Religion or Drum Dance cult" (34–35). Topash, Landes writes, "took me everywhere, interpreted, dictated texts to me, and analyzed minutely and tirelessly. He was highly intelligent, with a craftsmen's love of excellence. . . . He was a meticulous shaman, father, farmer, and work partner" (8–10). Like Will Rogers, Topash also proposed marriage over the course of their work together. Through Topash Landes also met her close women friends on the reservation, Louise Masha Nocktonick and her elderly mother.

By contrast, angry young shaman Joe Masquat was a man in his 30s whose grandmother had trained him in midé practices and bequeathed him her medicine bundle. He "never ceased to rage at the destiny that placed him after his proper time" (Landes 1970a:116–117). He despised the Christian and Peyote religious movements, considered himself the "last Indian," and insisted that Landes record, through him, his grandmother's midé knowledge (53). He addressed Landes as "grandmother," she said, "because of my study of Ojibwa Midéwiwin in Minnesota, with a principal shaman; he respected immensely the Ojibwa institution as did other tribes of the region" (106). Ruth Landes recalled:

This vigorous young man of the desperate 1930s bestrides my memories, talking always with harassed awareness of the fading Potawatomi religious tradition and the onrush of an alien modernity. His miserableness over the lost Indian epoch and destiny was amazing and, in my experience, unique.

It rooted in unassuageable longing for his dead shamaness-grandmother, his mentor and protector in his private and mystic careers. The shaman personalities I met and heard of were indeed towering and resourceful, among the Potawatomi and the Ojibwa. They were the only company Joe wished to keep, the only ones to rouse his imagination and sense of aliveness. As they died and were not replaced, he lost his orientations, his sense of identity, and definition of purpose. (105)

He wrote troubled letters to Landes for many years afterward.

In her analysis of Potawatomi syncretism and revitalization movements, Ruth Landes continued to develop her model of culture as dynamic and creative. She understood and conveyed her empathy for the people who, she said, "*enjoyed their sorcery, both the practice as professionals and the anticipation as victims. This zest may have been the key to their balance*" (1970a:58). It gave them sensations of empowerment, vitality, pride, and dignity above the everyday humiliations of racial hatred, economic impoverishment, and political subordination. Well aware of the prevailing views, both in American society at large and within the discipline of anthropology, that processes of acculturation eroded Native American cultures, Landes sought to record people's resilience and the agency of their cultural production. She observed: "In 1936, despite notions of 'dying' cultures, one could feel no sickroom tenderness for the Band's lusty shamans, who were of both sexes and several generations" (25). She was fascinated by syncretism and by competing local discourses on cultural change. Noting that the solitary vision quest, central to other Algonquian speakers, seemed to have given way to the more communal rites of the bundles, Drum Dance, and Peyote religious movements, she mused on how and why this should be so: "The Potawatomi shift of emphasis raises conjectures about the sources of change. What provocations lie within a culture and what in the contacts between two or more peoples?" (194).

When *The Prairie Potawatomi* was published in 1970, it was appreciated for its lively portrait of a people who were "no museum dolls" and for the cultural knowledge that Landes had recorded and thus "salvaged" about reservation life in the 1930s (Barwick 1971). Most of the data are "irretrievable," Robert Bee (1970) noted. But the book was also criticized. Although Landes had updated her original manuscript following two brief visits with the Potawatomi in the 1950s and 1960s and in consultation with James A. Clifton and other younger scholars, its 1930s Boasian and Benedictine foundation remained. Her book exemplified all that Leslie White (1949, 1959) and Marvin Harris (1968) had since railed against in Boasian anthropology. Landes was devoted to presenting the Native point of view through a focus on the lives of particular individuals, and her approach was largely descriptive. Her interpretation of religious syncretism essentially as a form of psychological warfare against the forces of acculturation was considered inadequate. "Landes's style conveys warmth and empathy with her subjects, largely at the expense of intensive theoretical analysis," Bee wrote in his 1970 review in the *American Anthropologist*. "Those interested in elaborate theoretical models or extended statements on methodology may be disappointed, but she makes no pretentious claims to such qualities." Anthropologists in the 1970s sought explanations in political and economic factors, which Landes had not treated with any depth. They were also more pessimistic than Landes had been about acculturation. They saw her optimistic focus on creativity as a "bias in data collection" (Pollnac 1971). Structural forces prevailed over individual agency in 1970s anthropology. Had the book been published when it was written, it would have been read by a more sympathetic audience, reviewers acknowledged.

It is hard to resist repeating the words of a review of *The Prairie Potawatomi* published in the *Independent Press Telegram* in Long Beach, California on February 12, 1970. The reviewer, Nat Honig, had previously read Landes's *City of Women* and had found "it was impossible to put the book down." He had been struck by her photo on the jacket cover of that book: "You could have knocked me over with a feather, for in my naivete I didn't expect that a young female anthropologist would be beautiful." On the crest of this experience he had ordered *Ojibwa Religion and the Midéwiwin* and *The Mystic Lake Sioux* and had recently reviewed them for the *Telegram*. He considered the books "indispensable in the library of anyone for whom the American Indian and his culture hold fascination." In *The Prairie Potawatomi*, he wrote, "Ruth Landes, as always, takes the reader into the heart of the very special world of the tribal group she studied." He concluded his highly favorable review: "This is a fine work, scholarly and sprightly. So a salute to Ruth Landes, and while we're at it, a salute to such other 'lady anthropologists' as the late, great Ruth Benedict, one of Ruth Landes' mentors. Let's be glad that this has not been an entirely 'Ruthless' world. And lest we forget, the back flap of this volume too has a picture of a stunningly beautiful anthropologist." The combination of beauty and brains was a shock. Ruth Landes did not conform to the stereotype of academic women.

Gender Diversity

Ruth Landes is one of a handful of her generation of anthropologists to record both what she observed and what people told her about variant genders. Scholars of gender diversity are among those who most frequently cite her Potawatomi and Sioux studies (Blackwood 1984; Callender and Kochems 1983; Greenberg 1986; Lang 1997, 1998; Medicine 1983; Roscoe 1991, 1998; Whitehead 1981; Williams 1992).[4] Her own propensities and her apprenticeships with Ruth Benedict, Maggie Wilson, and Will Rogers inclined and prepared her to document the particular configuration of spirituality, individuality, and androgyny of the *berdache* — the male transvestite who preferred domestic tasks to warfare and buffalo hunting.[5] The critical approach to gender relations that Landes and Wilson had shared also led her to observe that notions of male superiority nonetheless remained firmly in place and were expressed "in the belief that even men who repudiate their masculinity and adopt the role of a female, do feminine work better than the best of women" (1938b:136).

As was also her propensity, Landes had looked for the cultural response to Santee and Potawatomi women who transgressed conventional gender roles, and she had found that "there was no female berdache-like concept allowing women to switch their sex-linked social assignments." Among the Santee Dakota "women never reached the height of social maleness, which was to lead a hunt, though occasionally they instigated avenging war parties [and] medicine dances" (1968a:50). If "despite this dogma" a few individual women in each village did "drive buffalo on horseback, and did stalk, scalp, and mutilate the enemy . . . their deeds were accepted simply by the men, who not only failed to criticize them but even accorded them the honors of career men" (49). Similarly Potawatomi women received "brave" titles designed for men when they "gloriously replaced inept husbands at war and ceremonials" (1970a:37).

Unlike the transgressing female, the male berdache was given a particular social status in Sioux and Potawatomi societies, and the role was linked to heightened spirituality. Individuals were said to identify with the role following a childhood vision, and as they matured, they variously adopted feminine traits including dress, gestures and speech patterns, and occupations. When berdache performed "feminine" tasks such as curing meat and hides or tailoring clothes, the work took on "great mystic aspects" (1970a: 36–37). Landes described the Potawatomi berdache (m'nuhto or m'nuhtokwae) as "male transvestites possessing great skill in female pursuits" (195), strong personal "power" (41), and "visions all their own" (183, 190–191).

Landes recorded the life history of a Potawatomi berdache who had worked as cook and housekeeper for the family of one of her informants in the 1870s and 1880s (1970a:197–201). His name was Louis, but her informant said he had been pleased when the family took to calling him Louise. He was a superb cook and a meticulous dishwasher and house cleaner, and he won blue ribbons at county fairs for his baking. He sewed women's clothing for himself—an apron, dress, jacket, hat—and he loved to wear jewelry and a fur neckpiece, decorated his long hair with women's combs, and always wore a corset, which he proudly hung to air on the clothesline. Landes's informant recalled:

At my father's dances, he danced like a woman with a male partner. He rode horses sidesaddle, like a woman . . . he spoke like a woman, in a female kind of voice. He had no face-hair, though he had a man's face and hands right enough and was strong at any heavy work. He used the woman's language [speech forms of grammar and idiom] in Potawatomi. He took short steps, like a woman. . . . But he, or "she"—Louise liked the "she"—was so tall, taller than most men, that he didn't look much like a woman. . . . When walking he kept looking at himself, pulling his-"her" dress so that

1. Ruth Landes, 1912. With kind permission of Emily Sosnow.

2. Anna Grossman and Joseph Schlossberg, Ruth's parents. With kind permission of Emily Sosnow.

3. Joseph Schlossberg, Ruth, and brother "Mattie."
With kind permission of Emily Sosnow.

4. Anna Grossman, Ruth, and brother "Mattie" at Big Indian,
New York. With kind permission of Emily Sosnow.

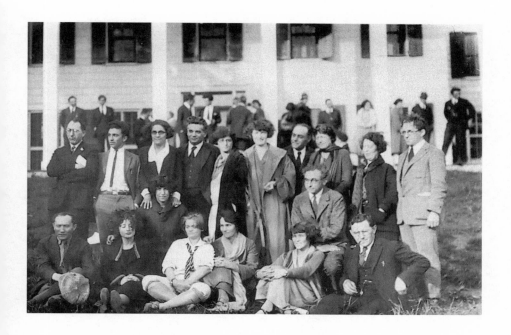

5. Brookwood School graduation, May 30, 1924. Ruth is seated, second from the left. With kind permission of Emily Sosnow.

6. Ruth, summer 1929, married. With kind permission of Emily Sosnow.

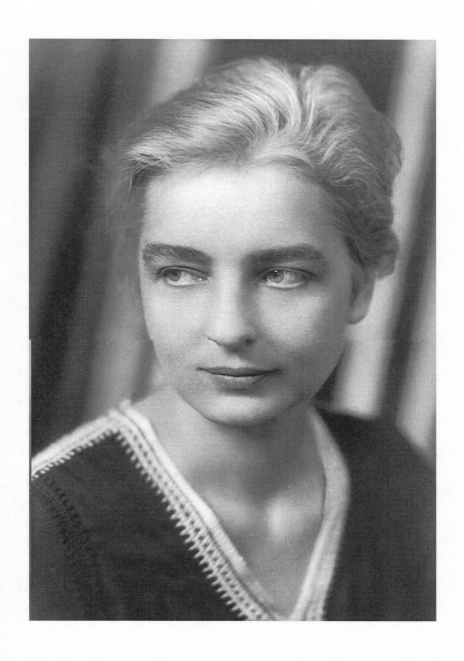

7. Ruth Benedict, 1930. With kind permission of Ellen Wall.

8. Ruth at Red Lake, 1933. Photo by Will Rogers.
With kind permission of Ellen Wall.

9. Maggie Wilson, Manitou Rapids, 1932. Photo by Ruth Landes. Research Institute for the Study of Man, New York (originally published in *Ojibwa Religion and the Midéwiwin* by Ruth Landes).

10. Will Rogers, Red Lake, 1933. Photo by Ruth Landes.
Research Institute for the Study of Man, New York (originally
published in *Ojibwa Religion and the Midéwiwin* by Ruth Landes).

11. In the garden of the Museu Nacional de Rio de Janeiro,
March 1939. *From left*: Edison Carneiro, Raimundo Lopes,
Charles Wagley, Heloisa Alberto Torres, Claude Levi-Strauss, Ruth
Landes, and Luis Castro Faria. With kind permission of Ellen Wall.

12. Sabina's festa de Iemanja, Bahia, 1939. Photo by Ruth Landes.
National Anthropological Archives, Smithsonian Institution/13.

13. A Festa da Lavagem do Bonfim, Bahia, 1939. Photo by Ruth
Landes. National Anthropological Archives, Smithsonian Institution/10.

14. Edison Carneiro, Bahia, 1939. Photo by Ruth Landes.
National Anthropological Archives, Smithsonian Institution/14.

15. E. S. Imes, ca. 1937. With kind permission of Ellen Wall.

16. Ruth in London, England, 1951. With kind permission of Ellen Wall.

17. Ruth in Los Angeles, 1963. With kind permission of Ellen Wall.

everything hung just so. He'd never let himself go the [careless] way I do now!... Louise never used filthy talk or cursed.... He never drank, chewed tobacco, or smoked. His manners were beautiful. My younger sister and I always felt with him that we were with a woman. We never thought twice about it.... Louise died in the grippe epidemic and was buried in women's clothes he had made himself— a brown silk dress with fine tucks. He, or "she", was buried in the Catholic cemetery on the reservation. No, indeed, the Indians never made light of him. They thought "she" had some great power. (1970a:198–201)

Landes similarly described the process by which a young man became a *winkta* among the Santee Sioux. Following visions, a boy began to take up women's occupations, and as he matured he adopted additional feminine traits including dress, gestures, and female speech patterns. Santee said the winkta "had a dream to be like a woman, so he had to act like one or die" (1968a:207). Landes saw the winkta as an individual expression of gender identity, for she said the winkta "served no economic or political purpose." The winkta was "classed with shamans because of his wonderful strangeness, his real abilities, and because he experienced a mystic communion" (66). He was "an unassimilable Dakota, a man who from earliest youth disliked hunting and war, and preferred the sedentary crafts of women. Never a sluggard, the winkta manifested social and artistic gifts" (112–113).

Landes stressed that the berdache role was associated with the enactment of women's social roles, not with same-sex sexuality, and that it in fact reinforced kinship categories and prescriptions (Landes 1970a:201). A Santee village was a patrilineal clan, and the winkta was related to all of the men of his village. If a winkta assumed the cousin's or sister-in-law's joking behavior with men in his natal village, he would be exiled to a neighboring village. Landes argued this was not because same-sex sexual relations were censured but because his sexuality threatened local kinship categories, incest taboos, and clan exogamy. She described the "kindliest and most mournful" ritual of social death by which the winkta was "made dead to kin and village" and banished, "for there was no other way of fitting him into the careful categories" (1968a:31–32). But in a foreign village where "all were 'strangers' to him . . . he recommended himself to women by his industry and helpfulness, and to men by his complete hospitality." He was on joking terms with everyone, "as if all were cousins or siblings-in-law. He was the clown of his village of exile, the one recognized tart" (112–113). Landes linked the ridicule, flirtatious teasing, and bawdiness that often characterized winkta social interactions to the behavior typical of the cross-cousin joking relationship, that is, to protocols of kinship, not sexuality (cf. Callender 1969; Greenberg 1986).

Landes made two observations whose explanations continue to challenge gender scholars. The first came from her comparison of the gender role systems of the Santee and Potawatomi with the Ojibwa. She contrasted the rigidity in male socialization among the Ojibwa with the apparently greater flexibility in male gender identification among the Sioux and Potawatomi. She had recorded no instances of Ojibwa men who developed skill in "feminine" occupations or assumed a gender variant status (see Goulet 1997). If Ojibwa women might "casually, under the pressure of circumstances or of personal inclination," take up so-called masculine occupations, she observed, "the attitude towards [Ojibwa] men's work . . . permits of no leniency. Boys are consistently trained to a categorical male consciousness" (1938b:136). She noted that there was a wider range of publicly recognized offices or statuses for women in the more centralized political systems of Sioux and Potawatomi societies. Santee women, for example, served in the tribal government and as "police" to handle women's problems publicly (Medicine 1983). Landes hypothesized that the wider public stage for women made possible the cultural expression of male transvestism. She would make similar observations about the male transvestites who entered the women's world of candomblé in Bahia.

Her second remarkable insight emerged intuitively and stemmed from her own gendered experiences of the contradictions of acculturation. In contrast to her vivid descriptions of increasing religious diversity, Landes described increasing rigidity in gender roles and relations. She described how the berdache was disappearing under forces of acculturation that were accompanied by increasing dichotomization of gender roles and the stigma of (incorrectly assumed) homosexuality in American society. Moses Wells, for example, "considered berdachery too bawdy for polite ears." But other Sioux and Potawatomi people expressed their regret that the berdache might disappear. As one Potawatomi woman told Landes, "He is . . . something unusual. The Good Spirit put [her] here for a purpose" (Landes 1970a:196). Landes described young men who in the past "would have been guided (by elders and their own visions) to mature as berdache" but who chose instead to work in crafts production or in occupations such as school teaching because the community in the 1930s no longer provided sanctions for the berdache (1970a:26; 1968a:113).

Back to New York

When it came time to return to New York, Landes was reluctant to leave Kansas, determined to return, and thrilled with the ethnographic data. Overnighting in Des Moines on April 14, 1936, after leaving the Potawatomi, she wrote: "Thought of my Pots all the time I miss them so! and am so glad I can return in January. My next visit ought to reap a harvest" (RL to RB, April 14, 1936, RFBP). Benedict had confirmed that she could arrange another $1,000 for Landes to return the following winter. Landes planned to finish writing the *Ojibwa Religion* manuscript in December and return to "the Pots" for five months.

During the next winter Landes received funds from Benedict to complete the *Ojibwa Religion* manuscript and earned some income from teaching a course at Brooklyn College. She lived again with her parents. Her plans to return to Kansas were derailed when Columbia University committed Rockefeller funding for anthropological research in South America, and Ruth Benedict invited Landes to join the Columbia team of researchers. Landes was to return to her original interest in African cultures in the Americas and go to Bahia, Brazil, to study "race relations." Although she had often asked Ruth Benedict to remind Boas of his "half-promises" to her regarding funding for African American research, Landes was caught off-guard and initially was reluctant to abandon the Potawatomi research (RL to RB, April 30, 1936, RFBP). She would not return to Kansas until the 1950s. Instead the winter of 1937–38 would find her in Nashville, Tennessee, teaching at Fisk University and making preparations to go to Brazil. While there she would write a book manuscript based on her first season of Potawatomi research. On completion of the manuscript, she wrote to Benedict from Nashville: "The material is gorgeous! Really good and shot with life. . . . Nightmarish people, but they've got their plots all worked out, though deviously, and it's a delicious lunatic journey to follow each Napoleon on his way!" (March 2, 1938, RFBP).

PART THREE

She-Bull in Brazil's China Closet

Prologue

WAR AND AGGRESSION, incest taboos and infanticide, female circumcision and menstrual taboos: conventional topics of anthropological study. But when Ruth Landes turned the anthropological "spy glass" (Hurston 1935) to "matriarchy" and homosexuality in urban black Brazil, she placed herself permanently on the margins of the discipline.

Matriarchy, the dominance of women as a class over men and a system by which rights and duties descend through the mother's line, was the term used by 19th-century social evolutionists such as Johann Bachofen and Lewis Henry Morgan, who argued that the earliest forms of human social life had been organized around the rule and authority of the mother. Matriarchy was superseded by patriarchy in their universal models of the evolution of civil society. Landes used *matriarchy* to describe the public recognition of women's power and authority in the ritual centers (*terreiros*) of the Afro-Brazilian spirit possession religion, candomblé. The terreiros were, as she described them, women-centered mutual aid associations providing social, emotional, and economic support to women who lived in the poorest black neighborhoods of Bahia. Within the terreiros, rights and knowledge were inherited matrilineally, and junior women were apprenticed to female elders in an elaborate and lengthy initiation to the rites of candomblé. Landes's contemporaries simply could not acknowledge these as norms in a modern urban context, especially in the marginalized shantytowns whose residents were disinherited former slaves, migrants from rural plantations. They implicitly accepted the 20th-century idea — that was at that very moment being launched as a theory in the discipline — that the original and natural form of human society was the patrilineal, patrilocal band. Carrying with it notions of "innate male dominance" (Steward 1936), the patrilineal band would be unchallenged in the discipline until the 1970s.

Like matriarchy, homosexuality represented devalued and "unnatural" social relations. Landes was one of the few at the time who recorded her observations on homosexuality and placed these observations within the frame of her analysis of other cultural processes.

Prior to going to Brazil, Landes had consulted University of Chicago sociologist Robert Park, who had recently visited Brazil and was then retired and teaching at Fisk, the African American university in Nashville. Fisk was a heartland of black scholarship in the 1930s.[1] Park's student Donald Pierson had conducted a two-year (1935 to 1937) field study of race relations in Bahia, and he, too, was in residence at Fisk writing his book *Negroes in Brazil* (1942). Park suggested that Landes come to Fisk to consult with them and to use the library's extensive African and African American collections. When African American sociologist Charles Johnson, chair of the Department of Social Science, invited her to teach at Fisk, she was able to combine paid work with preparatory research and to experience life in the segregated South (Landes 1947:3). Landes lived in Nashville from August 1937 until April 1938.

Landes worked very hard that winter at Fisk. In addition to teaching, she read the page proofs of *The Ojibwa Woman* and revised the "Negro Jews" article that she was still trying to publish. She finished the Potawatomi manuscript: "I think the material is so good," she wrote to Benedict, "that I'd like to suggest it's being published ahead of the other manuscripts I wrote (*Ojibwa Religion* and *Santee*)" (March 26, 1938, RFBP). She also conducted library research in preparation for Brazil.

Fisk was located in the "colored" section of segregated Nashville, but Landes lived in a women's residence on the campus that was not segregated. She would later write a fictionalized autobiographical memoir, "Now at Athens," about her experiences that winter, which included a love affair with a black physics professor, Elmer S. Imes, more than twenty years her senior. Educated in Munich, he was a handsome, cosmopolitan friend of James Weldon Johnson and others in the Harlem Renaissance movement. Landes would write and rewrite her memoir, but it was never published. The story portrays tumultuous and conflicted feelings of a young white female New Yorker living for the first time "with Negroes" and carrying on a clandestine affair with a senior black male professor in a southern racially segregated town.[2]

Donald Pierson encouraged Landes to think of working with the women candomblé leaders, the *mães de santo*. He told her that they dominated ritual life in Bahia but that he would not be giving attention to them in his own book. Landes began to ponder the idea of research with the Afro-Brazilian women candomblé specialists, a logical follow-up to her work with Maggie Wilson on women's leadership and autonomy among the Ojibwa. Studying the syncretic Afro-Brazilian religion would also nicely follow her studies of religious syncretism in Native American contexts. Here was a topic that would bring together all of her interests: gender, race relations, acculturation, religion.

Park and Pierson gave Landes letters of introduction to their friends and colleagues in Brazil: Tennessee missionary Dr. Hugh Tucker, who met Landes's boat when she arrived in Rio de Janeiro; white scholar of Afro-Brazilian culture Arthur Ramos (1903–49); Bahian journalist and folklorist Edison Carneiro (1912–72); Afro-Brazilian savant Martiniano do Bonfim, ancient collaborator of the deceased Dr. Raymundo Nina Rodrigues (1862–1906), the founder of a Bahian tradition of scholarship on Afro-Brazilian religion; and *mãe de santo* Anninha (Eugenia Anna dos Santos, 1869–1938), leader of one of the most influential terreiros in Bahia, who unfortunately died a few months before Landes's arrival.

In May 1938 Ruth Landes sailed into the harbor of Rio de Janeiro. Her Columbia colleagues—Walter Lipkind, Buell Quain, and Charles Wagley—all men and all more junior than Landes— would conduct conventional anthropological field research with indigenous peoples in the interior Amazon. Ruth Landes was charting a new territory for Boasian anthropology. She was initiating research in an urban setting and in a field—Afro-Brazilian studies— in which there was already a long tradition of Brazilian scholarship and that, in the 1930s, held a central place in nationalist imaginings of a modern Brazilian state.

She soon introduced herself to Arthur Ramos, then recognized as the national authority on Afro-Brazilian culture. Ramos had, since 1936, been in correspondence with American anthropologist Melville Herskovits, a former student of Boas's. Like Herskovits, Ramos interpreted Afro-Brazilian culture as an African "survival." As a foreigner, Landes presented herself within Brazilian intellectual circles and sought to inform herself of national scholarly traditions. As a woman, however, she found herself subject to gender codes that had not constrained male scholars, such as Donald Pierson. She was restricted in her movement in wider Brazilian society and subordinated in a patron-client relationship with Arthur Ramos. The relationship with Ramos was unproblematic as long as Landes remained compliant, but once she began to collect her own data based on firsthand observation and to develop her own theoretical perspective and interpretation — one that differed from Ramos's — she would be censured.

Not only would Ruth Landes choose to focus her research on such suppressed topics as matriarchy and homosexuality, but she would experiment with unconventional methods of field research and innovative ethnographic writing. Her Brazilian ethnography — first her 1940 article "A Cult Matriarchate and Male Homosexuality" and then her 1947 book, The City of Women — follows the method of cultural analysis she had developed in her Native American research and is consistent with that earlier work. She recorded her field observations in Bahia as she had done with the Potawatomi, Sioux, and Ojibwa, "with her genius for uncovering the covert aspects of a cultural system" (Clifton 1977:427). In interpreting Afro-Brazilian culture as dynamic and contested, however, she would move away from both the Park-Pierson assimilationist analysis of "race relations" and the Ramos-Herskovits school of African survivals. She would also experiment with a personal and reflexive writing style that many of her contemporaries dismissed as unscientific.

When we reread these texts more than half a century later, it is critical to explore at the same time the gendered contexts of canon building — and nation building — within which they were written and judged. As historian of Brazilian anthropology Mariza Corrêa writes: "Without knowing it, Ruth Landes had crossed the threshold into a minefield of theoretical, methodological and political dissensions" (2000:241). Landes would put it more bluntly: "[I was] a woman stumbling into men's affairs . . . I was the American she-bull in Brazil's china closet." (1970b:137, 124).

CHAPTER SIX

Fieldwork in Brazil

"WE HAD HEARD that the large Negro population lived with ease and freedom among the general population, and we wanted to know the details. We wanted also to know how the interracial situation differed from our own." This was the way Landes later chose to explain the original motivation behind her Brazilian research (1947:1). Like other American social scientists, she had been attracted by Gilberto Freyre's description of Brazil as a racial democracy in his landmark book *Casa grande e senzala* (*The Masters and the Slaves*). Published in 1933, the book had made an extraordinary and immediate impact on scholarship and public opinion in both Brazil and the United States, and the idea that Brazil was a racial democracy was then widely accepted. African American activists such as Booker T. Washington and W. E. B. DuBois pointed to race relations in Brazil as a model for the United States. Anthropologists, who would later disclaim it as a myth, at that time hailed racial democracy as a fundamentally modern idea (Fry 2002; Wagley 1979:5–6).

Freyre (1901–87), a white sociologist from Recife, in the state of Pernambuco, whose elite family had strong links to Portugal and whose cousin had been the state governor, had studied with Franz Boas at Columbia University in the early 1920s. The distinction Boas made between *race* and *culture* had enabled Freyre to declare the emergence of a new society in Brazil based on what he saw as the harmonious mixing of African, European, and indigenous peoples. This new society signaled the eventual disappearance, through assimilation and "whitening," of African Brazil, which, Freyre suggested, could be studied by ethnologists as a "disappearing" culture — much like Native Americans were then studied by American anthropologists.

Following the remarkable success of *The Masters and the Slaves*,

Freyre had organized the First Afro-Brazilian Congress in Recife in 1934. In 1937 in the neighboring state of Bahia, Edison Carneiro, a young mulatto journalist and self-taught folklorist with none of Freyre's patrician credentials or international connections, organized the Second Afro-Brazilian Congress in Bahia to challenge Freyre's authority in the field (Carneiro and Ferraz 1940). Carneiro was a member of a group of young artists and writers that included Jorge Amado and Aydano de Couto Ferraz, who had close relationships with Afro-Brazilian religious practitioners, many of whom also gave presentations at the conference. In contrast to the eugenics-influenced discussions at the Recife conference, Carneiro's group highlighted instead the vitality and innovations of Afro-Brazilian cultural life in Bahia. Although Freyre had predicted that without his endorsement the conference would fail, American scholars such as Donald Pierson (who was in Bahia at the time) and Melville Herskovits (who had sent a paper to be read at the congress) lent their support to the endeavor, which Carneiro declared a resounding success (Carneiro and Ferraz 1940).

When Landes arrived in Rio de Janeiro in May 1938, she immediately began working daily with a private Portuguese language tutor. Arthur Ramos provided her with a large bibliography of sources on Afro-Brazilian culture and copies of his own extensive writings, and on May 27 she reported to Benedict, who was once again her main correspondent: "I have placed myself under his general supervision." She added: "I should say that Dr. Ramos is practically self-taught in ethnology and psycho-analysis, as he says, and consequently his methodology is sometimes fuzzy . . . I recommended to him *Patterns of Culture*." Ramos provided her with letters of introduction to his colleagues in Bahia.

Landes also met Heloisa Alberto Torres, the recently appointed director of the Museu Nacional de Rio de Janeiro, which monitored research with Brazil's indigenous populations. The male members of the Columbia team would all work under "Dona Heloisa's" patronage. Landes alone required the endorsement of Arthur Ramos.

Arthur Ramos, Godfather of Afro-Brazilian Studies

In 1938 Arthur Ramos (1903–49) was at an important juncture in his career and poised to move into the international limelight.[1] Trained in medicine, in 1932 he had left his position as director of the Instituto Médical Legal Nina Rodrigues in Bahia to accept a position in Rio de Janeiro with the Department of Education and Culture in the Vargas government. He had been a follower of the scholarly tradition of Raymundo Nina Rodrigues (1862–1906), physician and professor of forensic medicine in Bahia who, in 1896, had published the first major study of Afro-Brazilian culture. Nina Rodrigues had focused on the physiological and neurological characteristics of spirit possession in Afro-Brazilian religion, which he interpreted as a legacy of African heritage that hindered assimilation into national society (1935, 1976).

In Rio, in his 1934 book O negro brasileiro, Ramos began to distance himself from the racial determinism of the Nina Rodrigues school. Through his independent study of psychoanalysis he underwent a disciplinary "conversion" (Cunha 1999) and began to interpret Afro-Brazilian culture as a cultural and ethnic orientation carried from the past in the unconscious. He began scientific investigations to identify the manifestations of this "unconscious past" in contemporary Afro-Brazilian life. In 1936 he began correspondence with Melville Herskovits and gradually moved away from this psychological approach to adopt a cultural anthropological framework that, like Herskovits's program for the study of Afro-American culture, stressed the African origins and survivals in Brazil (Ramos 1942). Brazilian anthropology was then focused on indigenous peoples in the Amazon, and researchers were based in museums, especially the Museu Nacional in Rio de Janeiro. Arthur Ramos initiated a campaign to establish Afro-Brazilian culture as a subject of scientific anthropological investigation, and much as Boas had done in late-19th-century American anthropology, Ramos began a movement to professionalize Brazilian anthropology by defining scientific research as research conducted by university-trained scholars and not museum-based researchers.

Ramos's campaign for disciplinary professionalization had converged with the nation-building project of the Brazilian state when the then-dictator, Getúlio Vargas, had appointed him to organize a week of activities to commemorate the 50th anniversary of the abolition of slavery, held just weeks before Landes's arrival. Vargas had risen to power as head of a military-backed alliance that formed a provisional government in 1930, and he remained in power for the next 15 years. Following a military coup in 1937, he had established the authoritarian Estado Novo (New State) that he ruled as a dictator until 1945.[2] The Vargas years were characterized by centralization of government; strengthening of the armed forces; repressive control of unions and labor unrest; persecution of all leftist parties and organizations, especially the Communist Party of Brazil (PCB); and political patronage. All civil servants were patronage appointments, and state governors were members of local oligarchies who were appointed to serve national interests at the regional level. The Estado Novo promoted Brazil's modernization through industrialization and reflected an alliance between the civilian and military bureaucracy and the industrial bourgeoisie. The state had established the University of São Paulo in 1934 and the Federal University of Rio de Janeiro in 1935 as part of its promotion of higher education to develop a better-trained elite.

Through its control of public media the Estado Novo also sought to promote "nationwide integration by searching for new roots" and claimed that it had "formed a united country . . . and fostered Brazil's entry into modern times" (Fausto 1999:225). Hence Arthur Ramos's appointment to orchestrate the commemoration activities that aimed, through a new look at the past and especially through the production of a new public collective memory of slavery, to resurrect poor and dispossessed former slaves as "noble and cultured Negros" (Cunha 1999). Ramos declared Afro-Brazilian culture was the foundation of Brazilian culture and essential to "knowledge of ourselves as a people, as a nation" (1942:328). Through ennobling Afro-Brazilian culture, the commemoration sought to establish Brazil as a modern and inclusive nation and, not incidentally, to call attention away from worker unrest and the declining standard of living for nonwhites in Brazil in the 1930s.

The anthropological recovery of Afro-Brazilian culture was central to this national project. Among the commemorative activities launched by Arthur Ramos were plans for an Afro-Brazilian encyclopedia and a new anthropology chair at the Federal University. As director of research, Ramos established the topics and named the scholars who would carry out the research for the encyclopedia, and he tried to ensure the preeminence of his own research and theoretical perspective through his choice of contributors as well as of themes. He rigorously evaluated and often rejected manuscripts. Ramos successfully positioned himself as the *dono do assunto* (master of the subject) (Cunha 1999:269) and would himself be appointed to the new national Chair in Anthropology when it was established at the Federal University in Rio de Janeiro in 1939.

Ramos faced challenges within the scientific community in Rio de Janeiro. Biological scientists and criminologists in the 1930s supported eugenics practices to create a homogeneous population through "whitening." A strong eugenics movement sought to purify and strengthen the nation by individualizing weakness (including poverty) and through criminalization of "degenerative" elements including passive homosexuals and blacks and mestizos charged with homicide, alcoholism, and vagrancy.[3] This was a politically charged era of nation building in which the collective dignity of Afro-Brazilian culture was central to Arthur Ramos's commemorative project and in which blacks and passive homosexuals were also individualized and criminalized and were seen as obstacles to a modernizing Brazil. These are important contexts within which to understand the way in which Arthur Ramos was later to critique Ruth Landes's work in Bahia. Unbeknown to Landes, her portrait of women and passive homosexuals as ritual leaders and culture builders in Afro-Brazilian Bahia threatened to emasculate the larger project in which Ramos was engaged: the construction of Afro-Brazilian culture as integral to Brazil's vision of itself as a modern nation.

Landes was, for the moment, unaware of local rivalries. She had more pressing concerns: "Being a woman promises to be very complicating," she wrote to Benedict on June 3, 1938. "Jacks up expenses . . . I must live in hotels, not apartments. . . . Can't live alone in my own house—only 'French' women do that. And of course I try my best to be conservative." Much of Landes's correspondence from Brazil was preoccupied with expenses and procedures for the safe transfer of funds from Ruth Benedict in New York to Landes in Brazil.

Landes found learning Portuguese a challenge: "The pleasure of civilized intercourse with these agreeable people is somewhat marred by the fact that they move in remote linguistic worlds." she wrote Benedict. "These gentlemen think of English as their lingua franca, and great and increasing areas of verbiage and time pass between us uncharted. So now I'm doing it in Portuguese—which I have reached to the point of understanding it by ear, but not of communicating it by tongue. So at present, they talk, and I write."

From the beginning Landes expressed her lack of interest in elite and expatriate social worlds:

I received an enormous cardboard invitation inviting me to . . . attend a ball being given to a visiting Chilean minister. Dress was de rigeur, and my number was #491. I toyed with the idea of not going, when I was told solemnly that that was not done. So I went. The palace is a beautiful affair, pink on the outside, and gold and white on the inside. The hand-somest Brazilians were there . . . and the ladies were outfitted beautifully and variously in things like Empire and pre-Raphaelite gowns, gossamer in texture and most pastel in color . . . they moved up and down the lovely broad, red-carpeted staircases, stepping over one another's trains, waiting for music and champagne. It looked like one of those famous nineteenth century Russian paintings of somebody or other's salon. I took all this in in five minutes' time, and then left. (RL to RB, May 27, 1938, RFBP)

She had "stationed an American acquaintance" to wait outside for her and from there went to the "Casino Atlantico"—"a night club in American style where I saw the samba, rumba, tango." "I've done my duty" she told Benedict, "and seen most of Rio's high and night life (none of it at my own expense—there are too many bored Americans here for that), and now I long for the simple life and Bahia."

After three months Landes was more optimistic about her linguistic ability to begin fieldwork and made plans to sail for Bahia on August 4. She had assembled a working library of scholarly publications as well as Brazilian novels ("that are grand"). She had also met an American zoologist and adventurer, Alexander Daveron, who had spent eight years traveling throughout the interior, and his descriptions of Afro-Brazilian *quilombos* (runaway slave communities) in the interior and scattered along Brazil's northeast coast intrigued her. They had not been studied, and she wrote to Benedict on July 5 that she was wondering about studying one of the *quilombos* or perhaps conducting research in the town of Santo Amaro in the rich tobacco- and sugar-growing zone outside the capital city of Salavador. She was worried that so much had already been written about Afro-Brazilian Bahia that she would not be able to make an original contribution. In recognizing the historical and theoretical importance of studying cultural processes of race and class construction in rural Bahia, Ruth Landes anticipated a project that Charles Wagley and Columbia students would launch in the 1950s (Wagley 1952).

Arthur Ramos, however, soon vetoed this idea. On July 27 Landes reported: "Dr. Ramos ... tells me that my entire stay this trip should be in the Negro sections of and around the city of Bahia." "Other communities," he said, "present no aspects of life that cannot be found in the City (properly called Salvador) . . . Negro life is far more vigorous and intense, and more varied" in Bahia, which "is known as a norm of reference." "Tho' the prospect offers no thrills," Landes said, she decided to work in Salvador as originally planned. She still worried about duplicating work already done, but one consolation was that "it will save money . . . and I have spent a lot . . . on my very good teacher of Portuguese. Next trip of course the language expense, and the long stay in Rio will be saved . . . and I will be knowing how to get around—awfully important in this country." Landes followed the advice of the senior Brazilian scholar. She was beginning to appreciate how the race, class, and gender codes that limited her mobility and increased her living costs as a single, foreign woman in Brazil would also define her research questions.

Salvador, Bahia

Landes sailed for Salvador in late summer. From the moment of her arrival, the old city and the dignity of the Afro-Brazilian candomblé leaders captivated her: "There is a joy of life in Bahia, tangible as the young palm trees framing the churches on the hills and rising dark and vital against the glowing horizon," she later wrote (1947:15).

She quickly realized that her observations "in point of detail and in point of vigor" would differ significantly from scholars who had gone before her. Her first report to Benedict on September 22 is ecstatic. In Rio Landes had found the "large and good" Brazilian literature "very disorienting after one's lone wolf experience with

Indian tribes" because "you have the feeling of needlessly duplicating good work." Once in the field, however, she recognized that
important aspects of Afro-Brazilian life remained undocumented.
These she intended to address in her own research. "I have discovered," she wrote, "that the duplication is chiefly in the formal aspects . . . not in the functional and interpretative aspects. I mean to
say that the gods and ceremonies etc. are named and described . . .
but the meaning of all these social phenomena, and the contributions of the individual are overlooked" (September 22, 1938, RFBP).

Candomblé was the central subject in Afro-Brazilian studies.
Scholars in the Nina Rodrigues school studied candomblé spirit
possession as a medical phenomenon. Arthur Ramos and Melville
Herskovits emphasized African continuities measuring "authenticity." They identified and catalogued evidence of African "survivals" in candomblé practices and beliefs. Donald Pierson took a
functionalist approach describing candomblé as a collective experience of ritual that promoted "solidarity and group consciousness"
among Afro-Brazilians and "tends to slow up the process of acculturation" (1942:304). All of these approaches shared the view that
Afro-Brazilian culture and religion would eventually disappear.

Three and a half million slaves were brought from Angola, the
Congo, and West Africa to labor in the Portuguese colonization of
Brazil from 1538 until abolition in 1888. Passing through the sea-
port of Salvador, Bahia, each new wave of arrivals revitalized and
diversified local knowledges of African traditions, making Bahia
one of the most vibrant centers of African-based cultures in the
Americas. Slaves brought with them a rich ceremonial life cen-
tered on belief in a cosmology of powerful spirit beings (orixás) who
visit the human world through specially designated human priest-
mediums. Perfunctorily baptized in Roman Catholicism upon
their arrival and left to their own devices in the slave quarters on
plantations, slaves freely interpreted Iberian Catholic imagery. The
result was the birth of Afro-Brazilian religions that were neither
African nor Iberian but a blending of the two that took a diversity
of regional forms. In Bahia, the Afro-Brazilian religion is known as
candomblé.

The abolition of slavery initiated a period of social and economic
upheaval for African Brazilians as freed slaves migrated to cities in

search of wage employment. Some observers have suggested that the florescence of candomblé centers in Bahia at the beginning of the 19th century represented the efforts of former slaves, who were now the urban poor, to establish a new cultural identity through an assertion of cultural continuity with their slave history (Butler 1998; Eco 1983:106).[4] By the 1930s there were an estimated 100 candomblé centers, or terreiros, in Bahia, each sanctified by one of a pantheon of orixás, each led by its own high priestess or priest (*mãe de santo* or *pai de santo*) and core of initiates, the female spirit mediums (*filhas de santo*), and each observing its own ceremonial festival days, rituals, and practices. Ruth Landes concentrated her studies on two of the oldest terreiros, Engenho Velho and Gantois, and organized her fieldwork around the ritual calendar of festivals. The expansion of candomblé terreiros in the post-abolition period was viewed as a potential political threat and had unleashed a clandestine police campaign of harassment and repression of the terreiros that was still strong when Ruth Landes arrived in Bahia in 1938 and that would subject her own movements to surveillance.

In Afro-Brazilian religions, to the accompaniment of drumming and in public ritualized dancing, orixás visit the human world by possessing or "riding" selected human — usually female — spirit mediums. Dominant in Bahia in the 1930s were the Yoruban male spirits: Xangô, lightning and thunder; Ogum, war; Omolu, illness; Oxalá, the sky and procreation; and Oxosse, the hunt; and the female spirits: Iemanjá, the sea, salt water; Iança, wind and storm; and Oxum, fresh water. The orixás were not conceived to be persons or gods but rather to be "natural forces . . . cosmic vibrations, water, wind, leaves, rainbow" (Eco 1983:105). Each was associated with particular symbols, colors, clothing, food, ceremonial days or seasons, invocations, and dances. In the Afro-Brazilian religions these African spirits became loosely identified with Christian saints and symbols.

The postslavery proliferation of candomblé combined with poverty, worker unrest, and police repression in Bahia in the 1930s to create the conditions for intense rivalry among the terreiros. Each terreiro tried to outdo the others by displaying the most elaborate ceremonies, costumes, and accessories, offering the most abundant food, claiming the most knowledgeable leaders, and so on. This competition encouraged increasingly rigid definitions of "tradition" and orthodoxy and generated the contested claims to authenticity that Landes would record.

Unlike her contemporaries who predicted that candomblé would disappear, Ruth Landes saw its apparently limitless creative potential. Her interest, as always, in recording challenges to dogma and non-orthodox interpretations of dominant norms led her to new insights. She now knew that she could make an original contribution to Afro-Brazilian studies.

It is Landes's interpretation of candomblé that has stood the test of time. Not only has candomblé persisted, but new variations have emerged that express the increasing regional diversity and socioeconomic and ethnic complexity of Brazil. New generations of scholars continue to study the Afro-Brazilian possession religions (Birman 1988; D. Brown 1994; Fry 1995; Galembo 1993; Leacock and Leacock 1975; Silverstein 1994; Thompson 1993; Wafer 1991), and a visit to a candomblé terreiro is a standard item on tourist itineraries for visitors to Salvador at the beginning of the 21st century.

In her September 1938 report to Benedict, Landes outlined the observations on which she would elaborate in her future writing. She described the candomblé terreiro as "formally, one great family." In the "oldest and most conservative" terreiros the leaders are women, *mães* (mothers), and their female initiates are *filhas* (daughters). The *mães* inherit their positions matrilineally but must undergo rigorous and ascetic training to establish their worthiness. "Occasionally there are some 'sons' and these are all regarded as inverts, and assume obvious female ways (including dress) when in sacred trance. Male heads and 'sons' are looked at askance, in the ways berdaches are among the less extreme American Indian tribes, but are becoming more accepted. For men are simply not supposed to get beside themselves, they are not supposed to be hosts to the gods for then they lose their self control, faint, behave in extreme and unseemly ways — mere instruments in the very toying hands of very whimsical gods" (September 22, 1938). Serving the gods required feminine behavior. Instead, men were recognized to have important positions as drummers and singers at trance ceremonies and as *ogans* who provide financial sponsorship of terreiros. Male scholars such as Raymundo Nina Rodrigues, Arthur Ramos, Edison

Carneiro, and Donald Pierson had all been named *ogans* — a role not open to Ruth Landes.

Landes found that it was "impossible to work or study with a Mother . . . because streams of people are constantly going in and out of the house, asking for advice, reporting on errands she has given them, etc. etc. She and her organization dominate the life . . . of all those connected with candomblé: . . . She arranges marriage, mends or causes separation, acts as god-mother, provides employment, takes care of all the moneys of the group, secretly practices magic, defends them in court, against the world, mediates for them with the supernatural, mourns their death" (September 22, 1938).

Here Ruth Landes begins to develop her thesis that candomblé was not only a religious center but also a women-centered social and economic organization. Only women and children lived in the terreiro itself: the priestess and her biological daughters and female spirit medium initiates and their children. Common-law marriage was the preferred form, and husbands visited their wives in the terreiro and sometimes lived or stayed in huts on the grounds of the center. The women were also usually engaged in various activities in the informal economy — market and street vending, sewing, laundering, midwifery, healing, divining, and administering death rites. Landes would be the first to describe the terreiros as mutual aid societies providing a basis for female solidarity under social and economic conditions of poverty, sickness, discrimination, and other adversities (see also McCarthy Brown 1991; Constantinides 1982; Kendall 1985). Women could obtain loans of money, advice and counsel, cures for illnesses and other misfortunes, and shelter from abuse or homelessness. Financial resources came to the terreiros from husbands, *ogans*, clients who visited the terreiro and paid to consult the *mãe de santo* for her knowledge, expertise, and counsel, and spectators who made cash donations to the priestess at the public ceremonies, which were often attended by several hundred people. Initiates also paid room and board during the months or years of their initiation and offered gifts at each stage in their apprenticeship. Some *mães de santo* achieved wealth and political influence through their position as leader of a terreiro.

In her first report to Benedict, Landes described the intense rivalry between candomblé terreiros and the innovative rituals of the new *caboclo* ("mixed blood") centers that introduced indigenous (Indian or caboclo) symbolic worlds to the Afro-Brazilian: "These caboclo candomblés, I think, represent partly the efforts of those disinherited from the African traditions (for a number of reasons), and partly definite assimilationist trends in the direction of being thought Brazilian rather than African" (September 22, 1938).

She also introduced Edison Carneiro, who was to become her colleague, key informant, and lover: "All my opportunities and all that I know I owe to a young mulatto named Edison Carneiro. . . . He is all of 26, and has already written three books on the Bahian Negro [and is] co-editor of one of the two important newspapers here and editor of the one 'cultural' periodical. . . . He is extremely intelligent and modest, and is intensely devoted (but in a curious "scientific" and esthetic manner) to the Negro life here. He knows all about everything Negro (that is, folk Negro) that is going on, and I am getting the benefit of it. Being a foreigner, a woman, and with a language handicap, I would be in difficulties without him in this country. There will be no way I can think of to thank him" (September 22, 1938). Edison Carneiro was also writing to Arthur Ramos at this time to describe meeting Ruth Landes: "She is wonderful — and much more intelligent than we could have imagined" (Oliveira and Lima 1987:180).

"You see that I am fixed to stay in Bahia," Landes concluded. "The Negro and Negro-Indian communities in the interior (they are many, farflung and said to be interesting) have to, and should wait for another trip. There is too much dancing life here" (RL to RB, September 22, 1938, RFBP).

For the next four months, Landes explored Salvador with Carneiro: "We rode in streetcars up hill and down dale, all over the sprawling city. Always there was music in the air: at five in the morning, troops of people moving to work in singing bands; at ten at night, lone, contralto voices of black vendors; in the hot afternoon hours, radios blaring popular songs. There was continuous movement in the streets" (1947:135). With Carneiro she observed dancing and possession ceremonies in the candomblé centers, accompanied the faithful out to sea to deliver presents to the spirit of Iemanjá, enjoyed samba and the performances of the Afro-Brazilian martial art *capoeira* at the fairs that were an important part of the annual calendar of religious festivals, and marveled at the annual washing of the great church of Nosso Senhor do Bonfim, the patron saint of Bahia. "There was an ecstasy in the air," she wrote in *The City of Women* as she described the procession of women, men, and children clothed in immaculate white and their donkeys, bedecked with flowers, who had come from miles around bearing barrels of water to wash the sacred church on the hot January day. "It was an ocean of humanity, over which the sun burned" (238).

There was no communication from Benedict until a letter dated January 12, 1939, with the news that she would be leaving New York for a year's sabbatical around the time that Landes was scheduled to return from Brazil. In her letter Benedict reported on the work of Landes's colleagues, Lipkind, Quain, and Wagley, and then wrote of her concerns about finding employment for other students, Alexander Lesser and Ruth Bunzel. She responded to Ruth Landes's own worries about what she would do after the field research in Brazil by offering to try to arrange $100 per month for eight months' write-up time in New York. To Landes's description of her Bahian research, Benedict responded simply, "I am no end excited about what you write of your voodoo priestesses." She then asked about contacts and influences between Afro-Brazilians and aboriginal populations, although she acknowledged: "Of course, this is not the emphasis in your own report on Bahia culture."

A disconsolate Landes replied that New York would be "emptied" without Benedict: "I have you as my centre of gravity there." "My Bahia material is unutterably good," she went on. "The enormous amounts that I keep adding serve gratifyingly to support and extend the outlines I have sent you; the data and mad and gorgeous designs corroborate themselves most loyally. And also the data serve up interesting details and 'problems.'" Replying to Benedict's questions about relations between Afro-Brazilian and indigenous populations, Landes wrote that important research could be done on this topic but that this "should be done by a man, preferably by a married couple, since Negro life is she-life. But a white woman cannot go around alone in Brasil." For herself, Landes had now accepted Ramos's view that "Bahia had to be done first, for it is the beginning and the norm of Brasilian Negro life."

Landes then expressed her growing worries about her professional and personal future: "I see no future and [am] too old (I was 30 in October!) to think it's around the corner, and too young to care to go on this way another 40 years," she wrote. She said that she could not live in New York on the $100 per month that Benedict had proposed and asked if the monies could be used instead for her to stay in Rio for several months after leaving Bahia—"And after that I would see about some other way of taking care of this soul and body."

Less than a month later, Landes was forced to leave Bahia sooner than she had planned. "The business is ugly and disgraceful," she wrote Benedict. "Plain clothes' men have been following me for a month, and in the last 10 days it has been a caging so close that I had to stop work" (February 15, 1939, RFBP). Black male undercover agents dressed in business suits trailed Landes, watched her hotel doorway, and placed anonymous phone calls. When she complained about this constant surveillance, police authorities told her that, because of the "delinquency" of the American consul in Bahia, her research visa was no longer valid, and she would have to leave Brazil. Landes confronted the consul and insisted he notify his counterpart in Rio to ensure that her visa was validated for a further six months' research in Rio. She told Benedict that the surveillance was due to police suspicion that she was a communist—"an official tactic for destroying any political opposition" (Landes 1970b:130). She was not (then or ever) a communist—rejecting as she did, all "dogma"—but Edison Carneiro and his circle were members of the PCB, and during this time Carneiro was arrested and spent a week in jail.

"Can you send some sort of a cable to the American Embassy asking them to enable me to stay—say—six months more?" Landes wrote Benedict. "I know they will do it, but after this mess, I would like them to receive an authoritative affirmation of me. I want to spend a few months more (probably 4) in Rio, for I have been learning that there is a lot of material of contrasting value that is to be gotten there, and I want to get it.—Unfortunately, in the past month I have been spending money like water, getting around things." She again asked Benedict to send some of the money that had been intended to pay her for time to write up her research results in New York: "I know it will be used very fruitfully here where I can write in the midst of all the material." With the help of her friend Brazilian anthropologist Maria Julia Pourchet, who happened to be visiting from Rio, Landes boarded a ship bound for Rio, smuggling onboard her notebooks, photos, and artifacts that the police had sought to confiscate (Landes 1970b:136–137).

Springtime in Rio

In late February 1939 Landes settled back in Rio. During that spring she wrote the first draft of her article "A Cult Matriarchate and Male Homosexuality" and outlined the book she wanted to write based on the Bahian fieldwork. Edison Carneiro followed her to Rio at the end of February.

Landes established herself at the Museu Nacional to write and use the library during the spring of 1939. Its director, Heloisa Alberto Torres, was the official who had granted the necessary permits for Ruth Landes and her Columbia colleagues to conduct research in Brazil.

Landes apparently did not meet again with Arthur Ramos. She may have surmised his disapproval of her ethnographic and theoretical focus on women and his indignation that she had removed herself from his patronage and allied with the more junior (and nonwhite) Edison Carneiro. Ramos would also resent her association with the Museu Nacional. His rivalry with its director, "Dona Heloisa" (as she was known to all), has been well documented by Corrêa, who notes: "Dona Heloisa was the godmother of ethnological studies [of indigenous peoples] in the country . . . as Arthur Ramos was the godfather of Afro-Brazilian studies" (2000:241). Ramos was, as we have seen, working to professionalize anthropology in Brazil by enforcing a distinction between the scientific research conducted by university-based scholars and what he considered to be nonprofessional museum-based research. When he assumed the new national Chair of Anthropology that fall, he would become the most important anthropologist in Brazil during the 1940s, founding the Sociedade Brasileira de Antropologia e Etnologia in 1941, effectively replacing Dona Heloisa as the sponsor and gatekeeper of foreign anthropologists in Brazil (Corrêa 1997:25). He viewed Dona Heloisa as a mere bureaucrat and a representative of the "old anthropology of the museum," as opposed to the new scientific cultural anthropology that he believed he represented (29).

There was, in fact, no clearly defined social or intellectual space of belonging for Ruth Landes in Brazil. As a Columbia anthropologist, she was attached to the national museum in Rio, but her research on Afro-Brazilian culture separated her from her Columbia colleagues who were working with indigenous peoples and put her within Ramos's domain. Her theoretical understanding of culture as dynamic, creative, and adaptive and her methodological approach to fieldwork through participant observation in Bahia, however, distinguished her work from Ramos's armchair anthropology and from the discipline of Afro-Brazilian studies that he was building in Brazil. And her social identity as an autonomous, divorced woman and white foreigner separated her from the other women in anthropological circles in Brazil. The only foreign women involved in anthropological research in Brazil were the wives of anthropologists. The lone woman in Brazilian anthropology was Dona Heloisa, who was a 44-year-old unmarried woman who carefully observed prescribed gender and class codes for white, educated women in Brazilian society. Dona Heloisa would travel only in the company of another woman and cultivated a respectable maternal image with young foreign male anthropologists (Corrêa 1997: 38–39). She was reminiscent of the spinster scholars who characterized women in American academe at the beginning of the 20th century, not unlike Frances Densmore. Ruth Landes was an anomaly: a woman anthropologist who sought personal and professional fulfillment aware of her beauty, brains, and sexuality.

Heloisa Alberto Torres (1895–1977) was one of the first women employed in the civil service in Brazil, which she had entered in 1918 as assistant to the director of the Museu Nacional at the age of 23, the year her father, Alberto Torres, a politician and intellectual, died. She had no formal training in anthropology and wrote little over her career (Corrêa 1997: 12). In 1935 she had become vice-director of the Museu Nacional, and in 1938 she had become the director, a position she held until her retirement in 1955. Charles Wagley, one of the young male anthropologists Dona Heloisa nurtured, described her as "our patroness in Brazil": "Using her great prestige and wide network of friends, she guided us through the intricate bureaucracy . . . Dona Heloisa also taught us proper Brazilian manners" (1977:6). According to Wagley, she had written to Franz Boas "asking that young scholars be sent to Brazil" and indicated she "felt a personal obligation toward and interest in those who came."

Buell Quain was more frank about the politics of their relations with Dona Heloisa and wrote to Ruth Landes from Carolina, Maranhão, where he was conducting fieldwork:

I am worried about your relations with Dona Heloisa. You will probably tell me to mind my own business. But I think you must pay for her favors by seeming humble in her presence, saying nothing which sounds like unsympathetic criticism of Brazil, pretending to be interested in the work of Brazilian academicians, and even letting her feel that she is directing your research. . . . If you should get into more trouble, she might be useful. She really has her influence. But you must make her feel that she is a fellow conspirator. . . . I think you should make an effort because of the vague chance of a job for Lipkind or Lesser. She likes to think that Columbia is filled with humble people striving for truth. The trouble with you is you don't look humble. (March 8, 1939, RLP, box 7)

During that spring of 1939, Dona Heloisa was looking for American anthropologists to help develop a program at the museum to train young Brazilians as professional anthropologists, and Ruth Benedict was looking for jobs for her students. In a letter Benedict wrote to Ruth Landes on February 23, 1939, she sympathized about the encounter with the Bahian police, but her main purpose was to enlist Landes's help to find jobs for Columbia graduates. Benedict hoped to secure a position at the Museu Nacional for Walter Lipkind, who, with his wife, had just completed more than a year of fieldwork among Carajá on the Araguaia River in the Amazon basin. Dona Heloisa seemed be resisting this, and Benedict asked Landes to find out why: "What's your impression of the breach between Dr. [sic] Torres and Lipkind? I'm concerned because I think Lipkind would be excellent for the teaching job next year in Rio which evidently Dr. Torres is still hopeful about establishing." Benedict was also worried about Alexander Lesser, who was still unemployed, and wondered in her letter "if Dr. Torres wouldn't go on with the plan if the incumbent was to be Lipkind, then perhaps it could be Lesser or Kennard. What do you think?"

Not once during these or subsequent deliberations would either woman suggest Ruth Landes for the job although Landes had a completed Ph.D., had published two books, and had worked with aboriginal peoples in North America. Instead, they treated Landes as their intermediary. Landes facilitated communication between Ruth Benedict and Dona Heloisa and handled the administrative details of receiving, exchanging, and transmitting funds from Benedict to "the boys" (as Landes referred to them). "I'll be glad to have you in Rio because I can send money through you to Buell," Benedict wrote.

Landes was, at first, unaware of any reason Dona Heloisa might not support Lipkind. She replied to Ruth Benedict on March 12: "I don't think the Lipkind breach is serious. Naturally, Dona H. prefers Buell [Quain] and Chuck [Wagley]: they are better bred, better looking and have more personal charm. . . . [But] I would say that Lipkind is still in the running." Regarding the other Columbia candidates, Landes said, "Since H. likes Buell and Chuck, I imagine that she would like Kennard, at least better than Lesser. For Lesser would dispute a great deal, and would probably wind up being trailed for extreme political ideas." Landes said she had not yet talked about this with Dona H., "tho I may get a chance now that the boys are gone [Quain to Maranhão and Wagley to the Araguaia River]." She commented that Dona Heloisa "does not seem to know of my ethnological bents: because my work here was Negro and not Indian; and she never cares to discuss ethnological problems. I think my situation very funny — as did the boys — but I like her anyway, because she is wholesome and intelligent."

She went on to describe the arrangements she had made to send money to Quain and then reported on herself. She was working on an article on the Bahian "matriarchate" — "always with the hope too that it might be sold for money! . . . The material is marvelous!" But she was "feeling exhausted, drained, dully oppressed by the extraneousness of the life here . . . in the midst of a dead state of aloneness, of emotional and total aloneness . . . after horror. For the last two weeks in Bahia were a horror." She asked Benedict to "please drop me an ethnological idea, some notion of the thoughts you are playing with . . . it would give me the sparkle I need" (March 12, 1939).

Benedict, however, continued to be preoccupied with the lack of jobs for her male students: "There hasn't been even a *chance* of a job this year; I mean no job has been available so it hasn't been a question of Yale or Chicago getting it instead of Columbia," she wrote to Landes on March 30. Benedict still hoped that Lipkind would get the job in Rio. She was also worried that the threat of war would prevent her from going to England and France for her upcoming sabbatical.

Ruth Landes, meanwhile, was becoming more intimate with Dona Heloisa, and at the end of April she reported to Benedict:

[Dona Heloisa] *simply will not have Lipkind. The one she wants is Quain, to whom she is attached personally. Quain said he wouldn't take it . . . she told him bluntly that she would not take Lipkind at all, that she had the privilege of choosing co-workers personally agreeable to her, and that she wanted Quain. If Quain still held out, she would have Wagley (and W. would be willing). What she told me, and did not write to Quain, was that there is a growing anti-Semitism. . . . And she said "I have difficulties enough running my Museum, . . . I refuse to add unnecessarily to my complications." . . . What the hell, it is an ugly situation. . . . Of course, Dona H. has the right to appoint her favorites, especially when the merits are all about the same, but it is the alleged reason that is so unhappy. I told her so, and she only repeated that she is not interested in coping with anti-Semitism. . . . I am very sorry about the Lipkind matter. I did what I could, and came up against this wall of personal feeling that has chosen to call itself anti-Semitism.* (April 28, 1939, RFBP)

In parentheses, Landes referred to her Jewishness for the first and only time in her correspondence with Benedict over the years: "[N]either [Dona Heloisa] nor anyone else imagines that I too am a 'semite', and the effect on me has worn so deep that I have to remind myself as they talk, including me with them and excluding the 'others', that I too belong in the strange abstraction of the damned." Landes claimed that she had "noticed no real anti-Semitism, just the nasty talk about individuals one always hears," but in *City of Women* she would describe her anxiety when she found herself "staring miserably" at portraits of Hitler hanging on the walls of government offices in Brazil (1947:9).

On May 13 Ruth Benedict wrote again, this time with news of a job for Landes: the Carnegie Foundation had established a commission "for the study of Negro personality" under the direction of the Swedish social scientist Gunnar Myrdal. The commission was hiring researchers. Benedict wrote: "The sociologists will tend to be satisfied with statistics on standards of living and on population movements, and you could be a help to them. Then too it would put you in touch with people working in the Negro field." If she was to be considered for a position on the research team, Carnegie organizers would need to interview Landes in New York in June. Benedict understood that this would unsettle Landes, who was well into her writing in Rio and had planned to stay until the end of August. She assured Landes that she would make "close to $1000" available to her "as needed" to allow her to write up the results of her Bahian research after her return to New York.

Landes had mailed Benedict a draft of her first article on the Bahian research and commented, "I'll die waiting for your opinion. . . . I wonder if you'll think the material as fantastic as I do. I think the situation is like nothing recorded in history" (April 6, 1939, RFBP). In her May 13 letter Benedict replied that the "matriarchs' article" is "rich and exciting material" and then asked: "Did you write this particular article with the idea of publishing it for some particular audience? I couldn't quite place the audience." Landes wrote on May 22: "I thought of the 'matriarchs' article for a general audience, and got torn between my desires to make it 'general' and 'scientific.'" She was envisioning selling an article (she had thought of the *New York Times* or *Harper's*) as well as publishing scholarly publications, hence her problem finding an authorial voice.

News of the Carnegie opportunity completely disrupted Landes's research and writing. She was worried about finding a job when she returned to the United States, and the Carnegie project appeared to offer an opportunity to build on her Brazilian research. But there was no guarantee of secure employment, the terms (salary and length of employment) were unknown, and she would have to return to New York even to be considered for the job. Then there were the logistics of arranging sea passage to New York: all ships were booked until the end of June, at which point it might be too late even to be considered for the Carnegie job. She put her name on waiting lists with different passenger lines in the event of a cancellation and replied to Benedict by return mail asking how late in June she could return. She had finally secured the necessary permits to conduct fieldwork in Rio and wanted to remain as long as possible. Nonetheless she thanked Benedict: "You must know how strongly I feel your kindness in advising me of this opportunity. It is difficult to express one's gratitude for a thing like this, and I am trusting to your intuition to aid me" (May 15, 1939).

Landes went on to express again her frustration that Dona Heloisa did not take her seriously as an ethnologist: "Though she seems to like me, and always seeks me out, she seems to overlook entirely the fact that I *am* an ethnologist, that I have been trained in the graduate school, and that my business is to report what I see. She wants to see what Quain wrote about Fiji, but what I have written about Bahia and offered her she ignores."

The other day at tea, she remarked that there were three ethnologists in Brazil from Columbia, and all men. I thought this very funny, and because the same kind of thing had happened so many times before, in different ways, I said, "You know there is a fourth here, a woman, with the longest ethnological experience of the four." She seemed disconcerted and said nothing. . . . Apart from all this, since I have no stakes at all in her classification of me professionally, I think she is a nice and charming person, with a great and naïve and successful will to power; and she has done indispensable things for the boys . . . they simply could not have reached first base without her. Clearly she is not interested in the scientific etc. aspects of her position, but in the personal ones.

A week later, on May 22, Landes wrote to Benedict describing again how difficult it was to arrange transportation back to New York and wondering what to do. Like all freelance workers, she tried to weigh the pros and cons of her options. She was reluctant to interrupt her work in Rio. On the other hand, a Carnegie job might launch her career in the United States, and she had no other job to which to return. She could not possibly know that the Carnegie contract would turn out to be only four months' work and that the assignment would derail, rather than establish, her professional career.

Leaving Brazil and Edison Carneiro

By mid June of 1939 Ruth Landes was on a ship bound for New York. The Brazilian experience had been strenuous. Navigating the social, political, and academic networks had been full of peril. The "spy business" had forced her to leave Bahia prematurely, and she was now leaving Rio two months earlier than she had planned. Arthur Ramos and others would be annoyed that she had not come to say good-bye before she left Brazil (EC to RL, September 18, 1939, RLP). And she was leaving her friend, companion, and lover, Edison Carneiro, whom she described to Benedict as, "in my opinion, the Bahia Negro authority, and the best Brazilian ethnologist" (April 28, 1939).

As their correspondence reveals, Landes and Carneiro had discussed marrying and raising children together and had thought that they might go to England, where Bronislaw Malinowski was encouraging Carneiro to work on a Ph.D. in anthropology at the London School of Economics. In the summer of 1939 Carneiro would apply for a job with the British Broadcasting Corporation as a way to fund his trip to England, but this did not materialize. In New York Landes would try unsuccessfully, through Benedict, to arrange a graduate fellowship for Carneiro to study anthropology at Columbia (RL to RB, July 17, 1939, RFBP). Carneiro applied for a Guggenheim fellowship (Arthur Ramos, Dona Heloisa, Edgar Roquette-Pinto, Ruth Benedict, and Ruth Landes were his references) to come to the United States to study but was informed that there was only one fellowship available for a scholar from Brazil. It was Arthur Ramos who would go to the United States on a Guggenheim fellowship in 1940 and as a visiting scholar to Louisiana.

The summer after Landes left Brazil, Carneiro described feeling like a "widower." The threat of war hampered — and its eventual outbreak finally dashed — any hopes of their reunion. He wrote Landes that Ramos said he would hire Carneiro as his assistant at the university, but he did not do so. In September Carneiro began a contract with the Museu Nacional, and in October he returned to Bahia on a "collecting expedition." However, he fell ill on board the ship to Bahia; he was taken to the hospital to convalesce for several months and was unable to fulfill his contract obligations (EC to RL, November 13, 1939, RLP, box 4).

Landes and Carneiro wrote passionate letters to one another until Christmas 1939. Landes consulted Carneiro on numerous details for her Carnegie report. He sent Brazilian news, helped her with her Portuguese, and encouraged her to write her book. "I'm expecting your book, which I hope will be great, beautiful and serious," he wrote on December 22, 1939.

Carneiro did not write again until October 1940, when he reported that he had spent four months in bed after an operation, his favorite younger brother had died of tuberculosis, and he himself had been out of work since the termination of his contract with the Museu Nacional. He had relocated permanently to Rio, where he was living in poverty—without money, he said, even for postage stamps—and supported himself translating Sinclair Lewis and John Steinbeck along with scholarly works of folklore and social science. He reported that Ramos was in Louisiana and that Donald Pierson was teaching in São Paulo. In this letter Carneiro also told Landes that in February 1940 he had married Magdalena Botelho, a teacher whom he had known in Bahia. He nonetheless affirmed his continuing love: "You were at the crossroad of my life—and you took me by the hand and I took the way you were going and we marched together."[5]

That neither Landes nor Carneiro had money or employment made their reunion impossible. That the American scholar was unemployed and an attractive divorcee and the lover a Brazilian "man of color" also allowed colleagues to construct their affair as a short-term liaison and not as a relationship that, under different conditions, might have led to marriage.[6]

No other single woman would attempt anthropological fieldwork in Brazil until the 1960s (Corrêa 1988). And with few exceptions, such as Buell Quain (who committed suicide in Brazil in August 1939[7]), male anthropologists—Walter Lipkind, Melville Herskovits, Claude Levi-Strauss, David Maybury Lewis, Jules Henry, Ronald Murphy, Donald Pierson, and Roberto DaMatta, for example — would be accompanied by their wives, who provided legitimate companionship, emotional solace, and research assistance. Within this scholarly community Landes's alliance with Carneiro made her scientific research suspect. Arthur Ramos dismissed her work as a study of the "sexual life of Negroes" (Carneiro 1964).

CHAPTER SEVEN

Writing Afro-Brazilian Culture in New York

R UTH LANDES was adrift in New York in the winter following her return. Her nomadism was beginning to affect her work. War had broken out in Europe. Reuniting with Edison Carneiro was unlikely. Elmer Imes had been diagnosed with terminal cancer in Nashville. Ruth Benedict had decided to stay in California for her sabbatical.

Having spent most of the years 1932–36 in Ojibwa, Sioux, and Potawatomi communities, 1937–38 at Fisk, and 1938–39 in Brazil, Landes barely recognized the anthropological world in New York. It did not help that her research contract with the Myrdal Commission was for only three months (later extended to four) and the terms were vague: "Nobody knows what he wants, except 'Negro ethos'" (RL to RB, August 20, 1939, RFBP), she wrote Benedict. There were few job openings in universities. She turned to two unlikely candidates for mentorship: Melville Herskovits and Margaret Mead. On her own initiative, Landes approached Herskovits as one of the few American anthropologists interested in Afro-Brazilian culture, as a colleague of Arthur Ramos and Edison Carneiro, and as the only other cultural anthropologist hired by Gunnar Myrdal for the "Negro in America" Project.[1]

At Benedict's suggestion she contacted Mead (RB to MM, August 24, 1939, RFB). Mead, at 38, was happily preoccupied with her first pregnancy and a poor choice for Benedict's surrogate. On October 22, 1939, she wrote Benedict that "[Ruth Landes] does seem to have a very definite capacity to learn, and I can see how you think she is worth taking trouble over [but] I still find her personally trying" (MMP, box B1). Landes, however, was unaware of Mead's criticism and had written to Benedict just a few days earlier: "I'm very grateful for all your attention, and for Margaret's. . . . I've seen Margaret a lot. . . . She has been generous and stimulating, and lovely [in her pregnancy]. . . . I'd feel very unhappy if Margaret were not here to talk to: she is so consistently interested in ideas and in other people's work. I've been spoiled by you: I can't get along without someone to talk to" (RL to RB, October 17, 1939, RFBP).

Landes had turned 31 that October. Mead's maternal contentment fueled Landes's uncertainties about her own future, as she wrote Mead: "I wonder when my day will come" (January 13, 1940, MMP, box C5). Would she ever be settled? Did settling involve a husband and children? Was this what she wanted? She was especially vulnerable to these musings when her career prospects looked so grim. These were the concerns foremost on her mind in this letter to Benedict: "I have a fierce ambition to work, to lose myself in the world of my work. It springs from a number of things, but the one I am most conscious of is a terrible loneliness. . . . What I need now is to meet people whose work and ideas are related to ours, and I hardly know anyone . . . I have been out of everything too long. . . . Please don't take this paragraph as a complaint: it really implies the contrary, and the arousing of very professional interests" (RL to RB, August 20, 1939, RFBP).

Contract Researcher

Ruth Landes was hired from July 10 to November 10, 1939, at $200 a month by the Carnegie-funded project "The Negro in America" to "prepare a memorandum on the Ethos of the Negro in various cultures in the New World" (Guy Johnson to Melville Herskovits, January 4, 1940, MJHP box 14, folder C).

In the fall of 1938 the Carnegie Corporation of New York, a private philanthropic foundation, had recruited Swedish economist Gunnar Myrdal to conduct a broad survey of American race relations. The corporation had chosen a foreign scholar to increase impartiality. Myrdal was also well known as a social engineer in Sweden. According to historian of anthropology Lee Baker, Myrdal was recruited to "help reform racial policies and practices in order to alleviate the menacing Negro problem" (1998:276). The product of the two-year study would be the 1,400-page *An American Dilemma: The Negro Problem and Modern Democracy* in which Myrdal would argue that white Americans faced a moral dilemma and psychological conflict between their egalitarian beliefs and their racist practices. Unlike most American social scientists who wrote about race relations in the 1920s and 1930s and who maintained that social science should be value neutral, Myrdal confidently applied scientific research to make policy recommendations.

As Myrdal's biographer Walter Jackson writes in *Gunnar Myrdal and America's Conscience: Social Engineering and Racial Liberalism, 1938–1987*, "Myrdal turned the conventional wisdom of white Americans on its head by arguing that the 'Negro problem' was really a 'white man's problem,' a massive social problem of national dimensions caused by white racial discrimination" (1990:xi). Published in 1944, *An American Dilemma* documented "the effects of white racism on Afro-American life" and established what Jackson calls "a liberal orthodoxy" around the ideas of integration, equal economic opportunity, and educational campaigns to reduce prejudice. The book emerged as "the dominant discourse on Negro and White race relations" and remained the most important study in the field until the 1960s (Baker 1998:168–169; Jackson 1990:xi).

Although Myrdal would canvas a wide and diverse range of scholarship on American race relations, he himself supported an assimilation model. In *From Savage to Negro: Anthropology and the Construction of Race, 1896–1954*, Lee Baker describes American social science research on race relations in the 1930s as polarized between the "cultural legitimacy" approach of sociologists influenced by Robert Park and the "cultural specificity" of Boasianists. The cultural legitimacy thesis was most clearly represented to Myrdal by African American sociologist E. Franklin Frazier, then teaching at Howard University. Frazier had received his doctorate under Park at the University of Chicago. Like Park, he argued that the problem African Americans faced was the problem of assimilation into dominant American society and the high rates of "deviation" from "American cultural and behavioral standards" (Baker 1998:178). In this view, due to the history of slavery, African Americans effectively had "lost" any specific or unique cultural attributes. This approach followed Park's evolutionary model, which proposed four universal stages in assimilation: competition, conflict, accommodation, assimilation. Boasianists, on the other hand, stressed the idea that unique historical and cultural continuities shaped African American cultures, which amalgamated African and European cultures. This "cultural specificity" approach was represented to Myrdal by Melville Herskovits. Herskovits directly critiqued Frazier. He documented and compared the survival of African cultural traits in different regions and under different historical conditions throughout the Americas and developed a continuum that measured the relative "intensity of Africanisms" (1990:16; Jackson 1986). The idea of African continuities was important to intellectuals of the Harlem New Negro Movement but was strongly criticized by Frazier, who argued that emphasizing the survival of Africanisms could be used to explain African Americans' "failure to assimilate" and detract from recognition of what Frazier said were the central reasons: "deleterious environmental conditions, racial discrimination, and the heritage of slavery" (Baker 1998:178). Myrdal, for his part, criticized Herskovits's approach as "excessive" and as "glorifying" African culture. In *An American Dilemma*, he would support Frazier's presentation of the African American problem.[2]

With funding of a quarter-million dollars from the Carnegie Corporation, Myrdal assembled a staff of collaborators representing the diverse and conflicting schools of thought on race relations in American social science as well as the major civil rights and reform organizations. By the spring of 1939, Myrdal had selected his chief of staff, a white southern sociologist, Guy Johnson. The other key staff members were Ralph Bunche, the African American political scientist who was part of a radical group at Howard University and was to become Myrdal's closest American advisor;[3] Dorothy S. Thomas, a sociologist who had worked with him in Sweden; and Richard Sterner, the Swedish social statistician and Myrdal's colleague. In the summer and fall of 1939 he hired additional staff and researchers, including physical anthropologist M. F. Ashley Montagu; Afro-American sociologists St. Clair Drake, E. Franklin Frazier, and Charles S. Johnson; psychologist Otto Klineberg; and anthropologists Ruth Landes and Melville Herskovits (Myrdal 1962: l:iii). By the end of the project, Myrdal's retinue included 6 top staff members, 36 assistants to the staff, 31 independent researchers and workers, and a corps of secretaries and typists.

In his first memorandum to the staff Myrdal outlined his general goals for the study (which became known as "The Negro in

America" Inquiry): "to examine the opinions of blacks and whites about racial questions as well as the Negro's actual social, political, and economic status"; "to study race relations in terms of 'the total American picture'"; and to "consider what changes are being or can be induced by education, legislation, interracial efforts, concerted action by Negro groups, etc." (Jackson 1990:114). Beyond these broad parameters Myrdal set no guidelines for researchers, claiming that he did not want to prejudice the results and hoped to receive a wide and diverse range of data and recommendations from his American collaborators.

Jackson depicts relations among staff and researchers as "a battleground in miniature, a microcosm of the larger intellectual and political struggles among American social scientists and reformers" (1990:xvii). Staff relations were chaotic, and bickering was endemic. There was little sense of a shared enterprise. Myrdal did not hold staff meetings or collective planning sessions. Instead, he assigned projects on an individual basis and met with staff and other researchers in an informal, one-to-one setting. Guy Johnson supervised the day-to-day work of the staff while Myrdal traveled extensively. Myrdal imposed strict deadlines, often requiring that reports be researched and written within a few months — as in the case of Ruth Landes's assignment. According to Jackson, "Myrdal had always driven himself at a ferocious pace and subordinated family and personal concerns to his work, and he expected the same kind of workaholic dedication from his associates," who found him "bombastic" and "difficult as could be" (117). He was a "bold creative and iconoclastic scholar" (xix), "an independent thinker with extraordinary energy and fierce determination" (xiv), and he challenged his research staff to be bold, original, and iconoclastic as well. He did not want it said that, in the end, this was "just another study of the Negro." Each of the collaborators wrote a summary of the literature in his or her area of research or a monograph on a more limited particular topic and was then free to publish the work independently. Myrdal read the reports and then produced his own.

Myrdal's love of argument and debate, his emphasis on individual research, and his appreciation for bold and original thinking, needless to say, attracted Ruth Landes. When she met with

Myrdal and Johnson to discuss her assignment, Myrdal stated simply that he was interested in having an anthropological perspective because the other academic collaborators were sociologists, economists, statisticians, and psychologists. He vaguely imagined this perspective to mean identifying patterns of cultural traits, and he contracted Landes to review the available literature on African cultures in the Americas. Landes was one of the few American scholars with firsthand comparative experience of race relations elsewhere in the Americas. According to Landes, it was Guy Johnson, a sociologist, not Myrdal or herself, who introduced the notion of ethos and titled her assignment "The Ethos of the Negro in the New World." No more specific questions or guidelines were given. As Landes put it, "nobody, not even Myrdal, had formulated the form the inquiries would take" (RL to RB, February 13, 1940, RFBP).

Unfortunately Landes did not question Johnson's title or ask him to define what he meant by the term ethos. Instead she tackled the amorphous project and tried to summarize an unwieldy body of literature. In her compliance to Johnson at this stage, she opened herself to the criticism that would later come from all quarters.

Memorandum on African Cultures in the Americas

Landes's Carnegie memorandum entitled "The Ethos of the Negro in the New World" was a 68-page report, including a 6-page bibliography of sources on African American cultures and societies in the New World. In the introduction she explained that the data were drawn principally from the available literature as well as from her own fieldwork in Brazil and Harlem. She concentrated on the six regions for which the most information was available: Jamaica, Haiti, Dutch Guiana, Brazil, the United States, and West Africa. In the Boasian tradition, she itemized "traits and trait complexes." She expressed her concern that the data were not comparable because they came from different sources, had been collected for different reasons, and had been collected without attention to "ethos" (1939:4). She did not herself define the term *ethos* in her report, but she told Melville Herskovits that she was working with Gregory Bateson's notion of ethos as "standardized affect" (RL to MH, September 30, 1939, MJHP, box 12, folder 13). The problem for her was that in her own field research she always stressed local diversity. In the Myrdal study she was forced to lump and generalize African cultures. The armchair speculation went against the grain of her personal commitment to firsthand observation through fieldwork. Her report, as a result, is speculative and superficial. It was also a superhuman task, and a four-month contract was not enough time.

She listed traits under what she called "Intra-cultural phenomena," by which she meant behavior traits widely observed across diverse Afro-American populations throughout the Americas. The headings she used were (1) slavery; (2) "caste-feeling"; (3) "easy assimilation" into the dominant Christian religion; (4) preservation of African religious traits; (5) political life; (6) economic cooperation; (7) the superior position of women; (8) the frequency of common-law marriages; (9) homosexuality and transvestism; (10) persistence of "African-like" styles of braiding the hair; (11) singing at work; (12) folk songs; (13) "Negro ceremoniousness"; (14) belief in "superstitions, dreams and magical charms"; (15) "a distinct emotional tone that is usually called extroverted"; and (16) the widespread use of kinship terms. She then listed various African traits that had been lost (such as languages), traits that had been retained only in particular local instances (such as *capoeira* in Brazil), and traits that had emerged under particular local conditions (such as transvestite priests in Bahia). The second part of the memorandum discussed and contrasted the behavior of whites toward blacks in four of the regions: the United States, Brazil, Haiti, and Jamaica. The third part contrasted interracial relations between the southern Catholic countries and the Protestant United States. In her conclusion, Landes pointed out that she had only been able to "indicate problems that can be followed through in field studies" (1939:60). She had provided a survey of some of the background information that would be needed for a study of ethos as none of the available literature specifically addressed *ethos*.

She then summarized key observations that she thought should direct future research. First, and again following Boas, she stressed that although institutions may appear identical, they may incorporate different meanings and behaviors and thus require firsthand investigation in each specific context. She contrasted, for example, the different forms of leadership in Afro-Brazilian possession religions in different specific contexts. Second, she emphasized that entirely new cultural practices have been innovated by African Americans in the New World — candomblé, for example. Third, she observed that Catholicism in Latin America and Protestantism in the United States contributed to the development of different local Afro-American cultures. Fourth, she argued that social class differences among blacks and changing class relations in the wider society have implications for cultural behavior. Fifth, she highlighted a "maternal focus," for example, in family and kinship relations in some contexts in the United States and in the women-led candomblé centers of Bahia. She observed that a predisposition to designate pivotal figures in domestic, community, and ritual life as "mother" was a continuity between African and African American cultures.

Finally, in her "bullheadedness," as she later told Benedict (February 13, 1940, RFBP), she presented a theoretical argument of her own: "[The] behavior of a local group of Negroes must be [understood as] the resultant of at least three forces: 1) the dominant African tradition (for example, Dahomey culture is dominant in Haitian peasant life; Ashanti in Saramacca . . . Yoruba in Bahia . . .); 2) the dominant European traditions; and 3) *local sociological conditions*" (1939:54–55; emphasis added). It is clear that what especially interested Landes were the innovations of African Americans in different parts of the Americas. Unlike Herskovits and Ramos, she was not concerned with identifying African survivals and measuring their authenticity. Nor was she, like Frazier, treating diverse African American cultures as representing different stages of assimilation. She had developed her knowledge and understanding of Afro-Brazilian cultural life and local conditions in situ through her personal experience of fieldwork. Rather than using existing analytical frameworks in American social science she used her experiential knowledge as the starting point for her analysis.

Landes submitted the memorandum to Guy Johnson on November 10, 1939, exactly four months from her starting date, thus fulfilling the terms of her contract. She wrote to Benedict: "The Report is really quite nice, my handling of the data being all original, and I discovered a number of interesting and useful and maybe important things" (October 17, 1939, RFBP). As possible reviewers for her report she suggested Margaret Mead, Ruth Benedict, Otto Klineberg (who had "been generous in his estimate of a draft" of the memorandum), Ralph Linton, and Melville Herskovits ("with whom I have been in most courteous correspondence") (RL to RB, November 11, 1939, RFBP). Over the next few months Johnson sent her memorandum to all of these scholars for comment and to Arthur Ramos as well. If the covering letter he sent to Herskovits is a model of the one he sent to the others, he asked simply: "If you could find the time to read through this memorandum and send me whatever critical comments you might like to make I shall be very grateful" (GJ to MH, January 4, 1940, MJHP).[4] Otto Klineberg would favorably cite Landes in his own report for Myrdal, which was published in his 1943 book, *Characteristics of the American Negro*. Ralph Linton's reply to Johnson was not located. All other readers were critical.

Ruth Benedict suggested that Landes dispense altogether with the concept of *ethos*, replace it with *culture*, and change the title to "A Survey of Negro Cultural Traits in the New World": "Calling it 'ethos' lays you open to Mel Herskovits' criticism" (RB to RL February 8, 1940, RFBP). Landes replied that she had kept ethos in the title because "they want a report purporting to be about 'ethos.'" She continued: "However Myrdal's views are a mystery to me . . . he wanted what he termed 'wooden data', hence the space devoted to surveying the cultural traits. If all this sounds ill-digested, do not lay the blame exclusively at my door. I was doing a short-term job with practically unformulated objectives, except that they wanted to play with 'ethos'" (RL to RB, February 13, 1940, RFBP).

Meanwhile, Margaret Mead, who had developed the notion of ethos with her husband, Gregory Bateson, wrote Benedict that she found Landes's treatment "pretty poor, I think. Most of the points she's considered haven't the foggiest relationship to ethos" (January 12, 1940, MMP, box B1). In her efforts to reintegrate into the discipline, Landes had attended the culture and personality seminar Ralph Linton and Abram Kardiner had directed at Columbia in the fall of 1939. In doing so, she had inadvertently trapped herself in Mead's rivalries. Mead objected that Landes was using what Mead called "the old definition of ethos . . . without any reference to *Naven*. . . . It seems a pity to go on using those vague, undefined definitions of ethos, instead of a systematic one" (MM to RB, October 2, 1939, MMP, box B1). By "systematic," Mead meant following the approach she and Bateson used, and not Linton and Kardiner's approach. After discussions with Landes about her report for Myrdal, Mead had protested to Benedict: "I think to have a Linton-Kardiner school vs. a Benedict-Mead school right here in NY city is too much to bear" (October 7, 1939, MMP, box B1).

Mead reported to Johnson that the conceptual framework of Landes's report was vague. Landes wrote to Mead: "No 'conceptual scheme' was wanted, nor indeed possible . . . in the time allotted. . . . Dr. Myrdal's constant point was to block out obvious background conditions" (January 13, 1940, MMP, box C5).

Melville Herskovits: African Survivals and Academic Protocols

Melville Herskovits responded to Landes's report by writing to both Johnson and Landes that he did not "see how the concept of ethos helps in such a study" and that "methodologically I cannot see that the approach had been any different from what the most conventional student of trait-distribution might have employed." To Landes, he said, "I have the feeling that the materials in the body of the work are quite useful, though my impression is that there are some serious misinterpretations due, probably, to the fact that you did not have the opportunity you desired to go into the requisite African literature" (MH to RL, January 16, 1940, MJHP, box 12, folder 13). To Johnson, he wrote: "I have been so terribly busy with preliminary work on the memorandum I am doing for Gunnar [Myrdal], and with routine tasks, that I am afraid I must return Miss [sic] Landes' paper . . . without having done more than to page through it." Despite his rushed reading, Herskovits did not hesitate to write: "My impression is that it needs more background than she has to do the job she has attempted, though I feel that the central part of her study brings together from the literature some facts that are useful" (MH to GJ, January 16, 1940, MJHP, box 14, folder 2).

Landes responded to Herskovits that she agreed that her report was not a study of ethos because, as she had stated in the report, the data for such a study was not yet available. Instead, she explained, she had surveyed the available background data on "Negro cultural traits in the New World." She told Herskovits: "It is a survey planned to raise questions about ethological behavior of the Negro, it is general and introductory, and should lead to plans for future research" (RL to MH, February 13, 1940, MJHP, box 12, folder 13). She had retained the term *ethos*, she said, because it had been the title of her research contract. She hoped that Herskovits might "sometime . . . have the leisure to look at the report again."

This exchange between Herskovits and Landes needs to be considered in light of correspondence Landes had initiated with him earlier in the fall of 1939. Landes had been frank and solicitous in her first letter to Melville Herskovits, then professor of anthropology at Northwestern University, on September 30, 1939. She wrote to tell him of her research in Bahia. She had, she said, reread his 1937 book, *Life in a Haitian Valley*, since her return from Brazil and noted remarkable similarities with her Bahian data. But there were also

some very large differences, which are chiefly in affect and this is associated with differences in the structuring of administration. I mean principally that Bahia is governed by a matriarchate completer than Bachofen ever imagined: not a matriliny, nor women functioning as transfer agents for men's powers; but everything that is the negation of the patriarchate, with men there in the actual position that women were among ourselves a century ago. Associated with this is a newly appearing phenomenon that you might expect: male priestly transvestites who are passive homosexuals, women-men who are trying to rival the priestesses who govern the community. (RL to MH, MJHP, box 12, folder 13)

She hoped to discuss her comparative data with him when he next came to New York.

Landes went on to describe her Carnegie contract as a "hair-raising proposition": "This Inquiry thing has been very difficult because I have had to work quite alone, and anthropological and psychological concepts are not especially welcomed." She said that she was using Bateson's notion of *ethos* and had consulted with Margaret Mead, "which has been a great help," but that her own thinking on this was preliminary. "Now I am reporting to you, as the master of Negro ethnology," she announced.

Herskovits's reply on October 17 was polite and brief: "Your findings concerning the social organization and cult practices of the Brazilian Negroes are very interesting, particularly since these diverge so strikingly from practice elsewhere that they must represent an unusually intensive form of local development." He raised three issues: first, he wanted to know if Landes had "checked [her] findings concerning the male priestly transvestites with Dr. Ramos"; second, he said that he could understand the difficulty she was having with the *ethos* concept and indicated that "I find it a little difficult to think in concepts which are as methodologically involved as this one"; and third, he reminded her that he regarded the problem of identifying African survival traits as "the single most difficult problem in New World Negro studies" (MJHP, box 12, folder 13).

Landes replied on October 26:

the precise data on priestly transvestites I got from Edison Carneiro. I put it in this way because of the fact that I got the hunch, and then went after the data hammer and tongs. I could not have got the case material otherwise, for a number of special reasons that you can imagine. And no one else had got the hunch, not even Dr. Ramos, so no one else had relevant data. . . . In long talks with Dr. Ramos at the beginning of my stay . . . he never touched on kindred matters, though I put questions about what looked like the androgynous character of some of the conceptions he reported in O Negro brasileiro, etc. I should remark that he knew only one cult group well, and this was one of the most intensely matriarchal of the region. (MJHP, box 12, folder 13)

She concluded her letter by stating her own theoretical position: "This is all a virile situation — no mere survival or crumbling character. The blacks are citizens of the country, in the main stream of local civilization, and all they do is taken very seriously."

Rather at cross-purposes, they continued their correspondence for another month, she noting "small, locally significant" differences in meaning between the ostensibly similar practices of different terreiros and he maintaining the importance of establishing continuity with the African origins of these practices. The differences between them are deep and theoretical.

Part of the problem was that Landes talked of *ethos*, which Herskovits rejected outright as too psychological and methodologically unwieldy. Herskovits had written: "I must confess that I am quite baffled when I try to envisage the difference between Bahia and Rio as one of disparity in 'ethos orientation'" (MH to RL, October 31, 1939, MJHP, box 12, folder 13). Landes had replied: "This is what I mean when I speak of different 'ethos orientations' in Rio and Bahia. I mean that the same institutions and details are found in both places, but that they are used with different affect and intended to provoke different affective reactions" (RL to MH, November 2, 1939, MJHP, box 12, folder 13). This is a classical Boasian view of culture. Landes could be citing Boas's 1896 "Limitations of the Comparative Method in Anthropology" in which he describes cultures as "local historical products" and reminds ethnologists that when similar cultural forms and practices are recorded in different geographical spaces and historical times, similarity of cultural meaning cannot be assumed. Meanings and interpretations can only be determined with reference to specific and local contexts of time and space. Where Herskovits worked with a generalizing model of African survivals in the Americas, Landes employed Boasian ethnographic particularism to observe and record local meanings and practices in Bahia. If Landes had used the theoretical concept of culture — not ethos — in her first reports on her Bahian research, the significance of the theoretical basis of the differences between Herskovits and Landes would have been clearer. As it was, Herskovits could dismiss Landes's work just as he rejected *ethos* and Mead and Benedict's psychological approach.

In their correspondence Landes had approached Herskovits as she had also initially approached Ramos: with the expected deference of a junior female scholar to a more senior male scholar. She understated her own knowledge and expertise. She asked Herskovits for references on recent Yoruban ethnology, saying, "I hate to start writing the book with the little comparative knowledge I have at hand" (November 2, 1939, MJHP, box 12, folder 13). She neglected to mention the extensive library research she had conducted both prior to going to Brazil at Fisk University with Robert Park and Donald Pierson and in Rio under Ramos's guidance. Herskovits, in any event, replied, "I'm afraid there is none in print that would be available" (December 11, 1939, MJHP, box 12, folder 13). She had also described to Herskovits how "Negro men have quite an important

place in Bahia's economic life" and wrote that she had been interested in studying the strong stevedores' union, which she thought
"might well be an outgrowth of the organizations of freed slaves,"
but she told him: "I had no time to learn more about this during my
visit, what with the time consumed in learning Portuguese, being
a woman in a very anti-woman country, and being put out by the
police. This is primarily a man's study" (November 2, 1939, MJHP,
box 12, folder 13).

Despite his acknowledgment that "since I have never worked in
Brazil I can say little about [your material] except to agree with you
fully as to the complexity of the data" (MH to RL, December 11, 1939,
MJHP, box 12, folder 13), Herskovits would unfavorably review her
Carnegie report and later critique her book *The City of Women* precisely in the two areas on which she had consulted him. He would
criticize what he called her "lack of preparation and inadequate
training in African ethnology" and what he saw as her neglect of
the masculine world (1948).

Ramos Weighs In

The final, and most damning, reader's report—that of Arthur
Ramos—arrived on Johnson's desk in late March 1940. Ramos also
sent a copy of his six-page critique to Herskovits for him "to evalu-
ate the criteria employed by Dr. Landes in her research and some of
the absurd conclusions she reached."[5]

Ramos began by stating a number of both general and specific
criticisms challenging Landes's knowledge of the literature and,
thus, her scholarly authority. For example, Landes had said that the
candomblé centers of Bahia were identified with particular African "nations" or "tribes" (notably, Yoruba) (Landes 1939:16). Ramos
took this to mean that Landes was suggesting there were African
tribes in Brazil although it is clear from her memorandum that she
was using the concept "nation" to refer to ethnic identification (see
Butler 1998). Ramos also disputed her reference to sorcery and the
use of poison and pointed to a single factual error: she had incorrectly identified Ogun as the orixá of trouble instead of the orixá
of war, whom she incorrectly identified as Xangô.

Ramos devoted the rest of his report to his main points of disagreement with Landes: her descriptions of the roles of women and of male transvestism and homosexuality in candomblé. Landes had written:

The status of women is very interesting, and deserves a long section to itself. It is curious that it has been little discussed. . . . It strikes me that nowhere except among the Negro people are women on the whole so nearly equal to men in status. In Africa this is practically axiomatic in the economic spheres, especially in west and central Africa . . . throughout the length and breadth of Africa are encountered "queen's courts" and priestesses. . . . In the new world, slavery sanctioned the Negro women as head of the family[.] This sort of matriarchate continues to the present among the Negro cotton tenants of the United states, and among the poor in Harlem, New York. (Landes 1939:19–20)

She had cited Herskovits on the important role of women in the markets in Surinam and his statement that "women are the carriers of the culture" (29). And she cited African American sociologist Charles Johnson on the matriarchal role of women in African American families in the southern United States. She outlined the roles of Afro-American women in religious movements in the United States and the Caribbean and concluded: "The climax of female power is reached in Bahia, Brazil, where women have absolute control of the religious, and therefore of the political life. . . . This is precedented nowhere in history" (20–21). Here, Landes cited her own fieldwork and her forthcoming article (Landes 1940a).

Ruth Landes was the first scholar to highlight the role of women in Afro-Brazilian culture, and Ramos strongly disagreed with her: "This is absolutely not the case," he wrote in his report to Myrdal. "In Bahia women do not exactly hold control over the Negro cults. The *mães de santo* are as renowned as the *pais de santo*, as has been demonstrated in the works of Brazilian researchers from Nina Rodrigues until the present. The most well-known cult leaders in Bahia, as elsewhere in Brazil, have been men, as was evident in the two Afro-Brazilian congresses." Here Ramos cited his own book *O Negro brasileiro* and two of his articles. In direct opposition to Landes, Ramos stated that "in the old Bahian cult houses of Yoruban tradition, it is the *pai de santo* who has all the prestige and control of the cult; his roles are inherited directly from cultural organizations of

the Gulf of Guinea with its patrilineal traditions, its totemic origins, etc. Priestly duties are masculine attributes. . . . The woman
is an associate; her position is secondary as in Africa, and it is only
later, with new social conditions, that her role has come to acquire
a certain relevance in the cult houses as today one observes in Bahia
and in other places in Brazil, not, however, that we can talk of a typical matriarchy!" (Ramos 1940:3; 1942:187). These "new social conditions" and their cultural products and practices were, of course,
precisely what interested Ruth Landes. Ramos, however, was concerned with defining "authenticity." He placed Ruth Landes's work
outside the long tradition of Brazilian scholarship. It did not concern him that all the other published studies were by male observers who had given little or no attention to the experience and
knowledge of Afro-Brazilian women. And he did not acknowledge
that Ruth Landes's observations were based on firsthand field experience that he did not have.

In her memorandum Landes had also identified homosexuality
and transvestism in all six regions in her survey. She wrote: "However they are never described in any detail; presumably it is difficult
to surmount the barriers that the people impose, and that exist
among ourselves" (30). The lack of documentation of homosexuality was, she said, due both to prejudice on the part of scholars as
well as stigmas within local populations in the 1930s. Landes had
observed similar silences surrounding the berdache in research on
Native American societies. Citing her own research, she wrote: "I
have examined the phenomena in Bahia. . . . Transvestism is ritual
in Brazil in ceremonial religious and secular settings, and in Bahia
it is linked with erotic change of sex, and priestly ambitions" (30).
Landes described the candomblé terreiros as fluid, creative, and
innovative cultural contexts: "The male homosexual transvestite
priests (see my article to appear in *Journal of Abnormal and Social Psychology*) are breaking in through the new *caboclo* groups" (56).

This statement incited Ramos's most strenuous objections. In
his report to Johnson, he wrote:

*I have left 'til last the boldest assertion of the author, this being that there
is ritual homosexuality among the blacks of Bahia! . . . The observations
and research of Brazilian scholars challenge this conclusion. There is no
ritual or religious homosexuality among blacks in Brazil. What [Landes]*

observed were a few homosexual individuals in Bahia who by coincidence held religious offices. But this is purely an individual phenomenon and has nothing to do with religious practices; it has no ritual or cultural signifi-cance. . . . The isolated cases the author observed do not have, then, ethnic or cultural significance; they are not linked to any African tradition. (Ramos 1940:6; 1942:188)

Again, Ramos's concern was to measure "authenticity" (by which he meant "Africanness"); he asserted the inauthenticity of the gen-dered practices, behaviors, and meanings that Landes recorded be-cause, he said, "they are not linked to any African tradition." He acknowledged that Edison Carneiro had noted the existence of homosexual *pais de santo* in his 1937 book, *Negro Bantus*, but Ramos dismissed these as "pure cases of individual sexual deviants . . . [they] do not have any relation to the cult and black religious prac-tices" (Ramos 1940:6; 1942:188). Ramos concluded his report by say-ing that Landes's work contained "errors of observation, hasty as-sertions and false or distorted conclusions. . . . It is lamentable that some of her conclusions, for example, about Afro-Brazilian matriarchy and the control of religion by women in Bahia and of ritual homosexuality among Afro-Brazilians, are already circulat-ing in scientific circles and are to be published in technical journals. These assertions, if published with the appearance of being based on extended observation through fieldwork, will bring regrettable confusion to honest and carefully controlled studies of the person-ality of the negro in the New World" (Ramos 1940:6; 1942:189–90). Ramos was disingenuous to contrast Landes's work with "honest and carefully controlled studies." His own research was conducted at arm's length, and he had no firsthand experience or data on the questions that concerned Landes. He also misrepresented her ar-gument. Landes had not asserted that transvestism had religious meaning. She saw the candomblé centers as providing a social space for transvestism in Afro-Brazilian culture. For Landes candomblé terreiros represented new and transgressive social spaces. Much as the terreiros offered poor women leadership roles and mutual sup-port associations, she suggested they offered male transvestites so-cial spaces in which they could inhabit an otherwise stigmatized gender identity in patriarchal Brazilian society. Ritual trance re-quired femininity because it was understood that to be a vessel for powerful orixás and the act of servitude were incompatible with masculinity. Her point was that some male transvestites found that the possession religions offered them a social space of belonging — not that the religious rituals required transvestism or homosexuality.[6]

Sometime during the spring of 1940, Gunnar Myrdal apparently showed Ramos's critical report to Landes. As a lover of intellectual debate and a critic of orthodoxy, she saw Ramos's criticisms as stemming from different methods and different theoretical interpretations, and it did not then occur to her that his report might contribute to her ostracization from the field of Afro-American studies or from anthropology itself.[7] The Myrdal Commission would, however, catalogue and shelve her memorandum as "unsatisfactory," and Ramos would publish his report in his 1942 book, *A Aculturação negra no Brasil*, in a chapter devoted exclusively to a critique of her and her work.

Meanwhile, Melville Herskovits completed his one-year contract and submitted his report to the Myrdal Commission in August 1940. It was accepted and published as *The Myth of the Negro Past* by Beacon Press in the fall of 1941.[8] In the book Herskovits argued that Afro-American descendants of slaves in the New World retain elements of the social, political, and religious life of the African societies from which they came, that African cultural elements survived the violence of slavery and persisted among contemporary Afro-Americans, and that Afro-Americans are not following a course toward assimilation to mainstream American society. It is a mammoth undertaking. In two chapters, Herskovits outlined the tribal origins and African cultural heritage of the slaves who were sent to the Americas in various waves over three centuries. In the next two chapters, he provided a history of slavery and discussed forced acculturation. In the remaining three chapters, he identified the "Africanisms" that survived in contemporary Afro-American life. Throughout, his discussion relied on historical sources, on his own field experiences in Africa and the Caribbean, and on the available secondary literature for the places for which he did not have firsthand knowledge. For Brazil, he drew extensively on the writings of Arthur Ramos but also cited Gilberto Freyre, Edison Carneiro, and Donald Pierson.

Herskovits did not cite Landes's memorandum or refer to her Bahian work. This is significant because one of the surviving "Africanisms" that Herskovits described in *The Myth of the Negro Past* was the "maternal" or "matriarchal" family and the high economic status of women in West African societies due to their agricultural work, their market trading of agricultural produce, and their autonomous control over the consumption and investment of their market earnings (1990:168–181). He also noted that women had "perfected disciplined organizations to protect their interests in the markets" (62) and that these organizations acted as price-fixing agencies that took into consideration factors such as supply and demand and the cost of transporting goods to market. He clearly outlined the strong social, political, and economic importance of women in West African societies and identified their legacies in the social roles of Afro-American women in the New World. Why did he not cite Ruth Landes's observations of women's roles in Bahia? His own understanding of the status of women lent credibility to her argument, and he did not have counterevidence to develop an argument against her portrait of the Bahian women ritual leaders.

There seem to be at least two sets of reasons (and a third if we want to consider the idea that Herskovits simply wanted to keep this academic terrain for himself in the United States). The first reason was instrumental: Landes was a nobody. She had no power and was of no use to Herskovits's career. It was more important for him to remain in the good favor of Arthur Ramos, on whom he was dependent to help him develop his own future plans for research in Brazil (which he would first visit in 1941). The second reason was Herskovits's conservative androcentrism. He resisted Landes's women-centered portrait in which men—although present as *ogans*, diviners, stevedores, union organizers, scholars, journalists, and poets—were ultimately subordinate to women in the ritual world of candomblé in 1930s Bahia. He also rejected Landes's observations on the emergence of male homosexual and transvestite candomblé specialists.

The clinching factor in silencing Ruth Landes was the alliance of Melville Herskovits and Arthur Ramos. Herskovits was planning his first trip to Brazil, and Ramos was the gatekeeper of Afro-Brazilian anthropology. Landes was unessential. More than this, she did not adopt a submissive daughterly comportment. Although she initially had approached both Ramos and Herskovits with deference as senior scholars and potential patrons, once she had collected her own data she wanted to discuss and debate her interpretations with them as their equal. They responded by closing ranks and refusing to listen. Instead Ramos complained to Herskovits: "As to my impression of Miss [sic] Ruth Landes and the work she did in Bahia, I am sorry to say that it is not favorable. She only sought me out two or three times in Rio before proceeding to Bahia. She did not keep me informed on the progress of her research and, when in Rio on her way back to the United States, she did not contact me" (March 14, 1940, MJHP, box 19, folder 14).

Matriarchs, Passive Homosexuals, and Margaret Mead

Ruth Landes did publish the results of her Bahian research in scientific journals. "A Cult Matriarchate and Male Homosexuality" appeared in July 1940 in the *Journal of Abnormal and Social Psychology*, edited by Gordon Allport of Harvard University for the American Psychological Association. And in November 1940 she published "Fetish Worship in Brazil" in the *Journal of American Folklore*, edited by Ruth Benedict.

In "A Cult Matriarchate and Male Homosexuality" Landes described how, in the context of rapid social, economic, and political change of early-20th-century Brazil, candomblé had come to offer some poor Afro-Brazilian women a social milieu of power and influence. It is in this sense that Landes casts the candomblé terreiros as matriarchal institutions. Under the wider social conditions of flux and in the everyday lives of grinding poverty, the terreiros represented archives of ancient cultural knowledge, havens from abuse and powerlessness, and hopes of transformation metaphorically represented in the theatrical trance possession of the spirits by the women.

Landes described the proliferation of new candomblé terreiros in Bahia in the early decades of the 20th century as "the way in which an outcaste group has made a new adaptation by taking advantage of changed circumstances" (1940a:386).[9] She cast the homosexual "fathers" as "the voice of a hitherto voiceless group . . . pathbreakers to new institutions" (393). As has been the pattern in her work, Landes legitimated social marginality by giving voice to subaltern experience.

Landes's analysis is, at the same time, consistent with the prevailing model of Brazilian society as patriarchal. When she portrays the candomblé terreiros as "matriarchal" she is not suggesting that Afro-Brazilian women have absolute power. She is fully aware that they have developed this supportive women-centered institution in response to their extreme poverty and marginalization in the wider Brazilian society.

In her discussion of male homosexuality she distinguished between the passive, "feminine" role in intercourse, which is stigmatized in Brazil, and the active, penetrator role, which is culturally constructed as "masculine," not homosexual, and is not stigmatized but, in fact, is often held by respected community leaders and heads of patriarchal households (see Kulick 1997). The stigma, she said, derived from adopting feminine roles and comportment in a patriarchal society, not from same-sex relations. The stigma of passive homosexuality mirrored the subordination of women. For passive homosexuals outside the terreiros, street prostitution was the most common way of life.

Landes portrayed the terreiros and the ritual culture as matriarchal even as she described ritual work as "service." She wrote that women performed the major ritual roles in candomblé because "only women are suited by their sex to nurse the deities, and that the service of men is blasphemous and unsexing." The role of medium was culturally understood as one of service (in this instance, to the spirits) and, therefore, feminine. Men were discouraged from taking the "unseemly" feminine postures of going into trances and possession. She noted a sign on the center post of the ceremonial room in one candomblé terreiro that read: "Gentlemen will kindly refrain from disturbing the rites or dancing in the space reserved for women."

Landes described how the wider social and political context both increased demands for conformity and created spaces for creative experimentation. The context of social change led some temple leaders to advocate greater conformity to African-based traditions to seek to solidify their own positions through claims of "authenticity." But it led others to innovate and open up candomblé practices by relaxing restrictions, thus gaining flexibility, which allowed them to expand their positions of power and the base for a new clientele. The most visible innovations Landes described were those of the *caboclo* temples—those that merged Amerindian beliefs, visions, and symbols with established candomblé practices.

It was in the caboclo temples that some men achieved positions as ritual leaders. These men were all under 45 years of age, suggesting to Landes that the acceptance of men was relatively recent, and they were all passive homosexuals "drawn from the outcaste homosexual solicitors of the Bahia underworld." The fundamental tenet that "femininity alone could nurse the gods" (1940a:393) was thus maintained. Heterosexual men and men who assumed the penetrator role in same-sex relations did not move into positions of ritual leadership in the new caboclo terreiros. Landes argued that, for passive homosexuals who do not "reflect the masculinity of the patriarchal culture in whose heart they live," candomblé provided them with the social space "to insist upon their womanliness and ritualize it in priestly trance" (394; cf. Fry 1995). Once they were located in a terreiro, they were no longer subject to the abuses of street life soliciting and having casual sex.

Mead and Benedict carried on an odd debate on the interpretation of Landes's data. Benedict asked Landes what factors explained the emergence of the "socially accredited" role of caboclo priest, to what extent this "allow[ed] for rehabilitation" of some passive homosexuals from street prostitution, and "the difference the role has made in their responsible conduct." "Obviously in many of your cases this rehabilitation has gone very far," she observed (RB to RL, September 24, 1939, RFBP).

Mead, once again, found Ruth Landes "trying" and her analysis erratic (MM to RB, September 26, 1939, MMP, box B1). Landes had tried to explain to Mead that the frame of reference for her analysis of Afro-Brazilian culture was "not tribal but national. I mean, that the blacks are considered 'Afro-Brazilians', nationals who happened to be colored and who are a vital part of the mainstream of Brazilian life" (RL to MM, August 4, 1939, MMP, box C3). Landes argued that candomblé produced alternative social and cultural opportunities and enabled new and fluid gender identities.

Mead, however, insisted on framing the analysis within romantic primitivist notions of "genuine culture" (see Sapir 1924; Stocking 1992). She rejected what she called Landes's "urban, complex, disorganized picture with prostitution" and "the reversal of the more usual picture" (MM to RB, September 26, 1939, MMP, box B1). Mead urged an analysis that was consistent with "the more typical primitive picture of integrated socially accepted transvestism" and wrote Benedict that "the male prostitutes [Landes] describes don't sound like people who would yearn for respectability and social rehabilitation." Finally, in exasperation she wrote to Benedict on October 2, 1939: "Ruth Landes really does wear me down. . . . If there were some way of teaching her to be either (a) a lady or (b) an ordinary academic female who would behave in a routine way in academic situations, it would be a help. I don't dislike her . . . but I find her hard to plan for" (MMP, box B1).

Benedict eventually guided Mead to appreciate Landes's ethnographic portrait:

My comment wasn't at all to the point that the explanation lay in those prostitutes longing for social rehabilitation; it was that when the caboclo cult introduced less exigent standards the only men who could qualify in Brazil were passive homosexuals — because passivity was the fundamental symbol associated with women whose place the men were stepping into; but it happens that in that society passive male homosexuality was contemptible, and that the only exponents possible were the male prostitutes. Which however didn't prevent the thing from happening, and, having happened, some of these men by virtue of their new role became even decent. Some of course didn't. But the point depends on differentiating passive from active homosexuality; it seems to me in her [Landes's] sexual material that they were differentiated in Brazil. (RB to MM, October 5, 1939, MMP, box B1)

Mead then conceded that she thought Landes "has enough material at least to offer the hypothesis (MM to RB, October 7, 1939, MMP, box B1).

It is unclear whether the "respectability" here discussed by Benedict and Mead had to do with homosexuality or prostitution or deviant behavior in general. If the first, it is quite hypocritical as both had lesbian leanings and experience. If they are discussing prostitution as deviant, they are reflecting the moral standards of the times and of the Anglo-American elite to which they both belonged. If they are referring to deviant and anomalous behavior generally as "in need of rehabilitation," their discussion then subsumes homosexuality and prostitution and includes Ruth Landes as well. Landes was neither submissive and plain like an "ordinary academic female" nor "a lady," for she had "gone native" in the field by taking a local lover. In puritanical Anglo-American culture Landes was exotic. For Margaret Mead, as for Arthur Ramos and Melville Herskovits, she was "the other" and "matter out of place" (Douglas 1966) in American anthropology.

CHAPTER EIGHT

The Early Ethnography of Race and Gender

So I went to Bahia and I was consciously uneasy for the first time in this exploration through different worlds of ideas. I was uneasy now because I had already learned enough to realize that I had no point of reference, no theory or belief to support or explode. – Ruth Landes, The City of Women

RUTH LANDES completed *The City of Women* in the spring of 1940 and sent the manuscript out to several trade publishers for review. She was unemployed again after the Carnegie contract ended, and she was depressed about opportunities in anthropology. She hoped that the book might sell commercially and that she might be able to launch a career as a writer. "If the book sells, I'll quit worrying," she wrote Benedict (February 13, 1940, RFBP). But later she continued, discouraged: "There are no jobs. I just hate to get out of anthropology. Things look so black for me, I mean, that I can only suppose that I've got to learn a technique of playing the game. . . . I suppose one's got to be quite pedestrian or quite extraordinary, and I'm neither. It seems so silly and wasteful to equip an eager and intelligent person with something that can't be marketed. And, in the case of anthropology, the "world situation" isn't to blame. I've been trying to get somewhere for several years" (June 11, 1940, RFBP). By August, the manuscript had been returned from four publishers (Little, Brown; Harcourt Brace; Vanguard; and Doubleday), and she sent it out to a fifth, Whittlesey House. "The general feeling," she wrote to Benedict, "is that it is 'good but too scholarly'" (August 19, 1940, RFBP). Whittlesey House also returned the manuscript, and in the summer of 1941 Landes rewrote the entire book.

Landes regarded *The City of Women*, published finally in 1947, as the high point of her career. For years afterward she tried again to "write a thing of beauty like my *City of Women*" (Notebook 7,

RLP). Edison Carneiro wrote to her after receiving the copy she sent him: "I read your book and was amazed to see how 'undying' are indeed the memories of that time—those beautiful and glorious days of Bahia. Even the simplest things—like the song of Master Domingos and the name Aydano and the others called me, Mestre Antigo,—were not forgotten by you. It's wonderful . . . I can not accustom myself with the idea that you could not make the book you would have written—a scientific one. But I am grateful to you for not letting that year die, for reviving those incidents of our daily life among the blacks of Bahia, for upholding the dreamy, the one-thousand-nighty tale of our friendly partnership" (EC to RL, July 28, 1947, RLP, box 4).

The book is written in a deceptively simple style intended to draw in the general reader. Its themes are those that have always intrigued Landes: the flow, flux, and lustiness of the cultural production of people who seize the cracks and contradictions in acculturation processes as opportunities to create new cultural experiences and new interpretations, and the possibilities of alternative gender relations and transgressive gender identities. Through description and dialogue, Landes also addressed theoretical issues at the heart of the discipline: scientific objectivity; race, class, and gender; romantic primitivism, tradition, and modernity; ethnography and the representation of experience.

Science, Race, and Class: Experience or Objectivity?

When she went to Brazil, Ruth Landes held a then-conventional American view of science as a language of rationality and objectivity. Like her teacher Franz Boas and like her labor Zionist family she also saw science as an instrument of progress and accepted her responsibility as a scientist to address issues of social concern. In her previous studies of Ojibwa, Sioux, and Potawatomi groups, she had assumed a scientific stance both in her comportment in the field and in her ethnographic writing. The legal and social separation of Indian reservations from mainstream American society and their constitution in anthropology as natural "laboratories" (Benedict 1934) for the study of human behavior had the effect of encapsulating anthropological knowledge and enabling anthropologists to maintain what they thought of as an objective perspective vis-à-vis Native Americans. The knowledge so produced was seen as existing independently of historical relations of conquest and colonialism and of contemporary experiences of relocation, confiscation of land, disease, poverty, and the trauma of loss of economic, political, and sociocultural autonomy. Landes had developed close relations with outstanding individuals such as Maggie Wilson, Will Rogers, Tom Topash, and Joe Masquat. In the Boasian tradition she had "collected" their oral texts, but she had gone beyond the norms of scientific writing and identified them by name and as friends. She described her relationships with them. In *The City of Women* she would further experiment with this ethnographic practice that late-20th-century feminist scholars would call "giving voice." And she would introduce herself as a central character in the field setting and explore her own experience as a source of knowledge. Through her innovations in ethnographic writing she implicitly recognized the intersubjective nature of anthropological knowledge.

Landes's treatment of race relations in *The City of Women* illustrates her experiential approach to knowledge. From the moment of her arrival in Bahia she had felt herself bombarded by contradictory images and worldviews. The noticeable separation of social classes and of the Brazilian elite from the predominantly poor black population especially unnerved her. Despite these structures of constraint, she also observed how, in a striking contradiction, the Afro-Bahian culture was central to the Brazilian national imagination: "What the Negroes do in Bahia is 'typical' of Brazil. The lyrics and melodies they compose and inspire, the manner of singing, the types of orchestration, the dances, sports, amusements, foods, drinks, dress, literature, the Carnival that lasts for months, the forms of religious worship, even the personality and physical beauty of the women are a dear part of Brazil. Out of Bahia come forms and symbols for national chauvinism to cling to. . . . Brazil's social scientists devote themselves to these Negro citizens . . . in a . . . mood of gallant appreciation and of expiation for the past" (1947:7).

In comparison to race relations in segregated Nashville, Landes saw an absence of racial conflict in Brazil that led her rather recklessly to write: "This book about Brazil does not discuss race problems there because there were none" (1947:vi). In this passage she repeated then widely held notions of racial harmony in Brazil that were supported nationally and internationally by activists, writers, and intellectuals (Fry 2002). In this statement she also signaled that she was changing her focus from the study of race relations as a "social problem" to a study of cultural production and gender relations within the racialized context of Afro-Brazilian Bahia.

Describing her first visit to Engenho Velho, the oldest candomblé terreiro in Bahia, Landes ensures that readers appreciate from the outset that her subjects—candomblé practitioners and their followers—are members of the poorest underclass of Brazilian life. She assumes the stance of the uninformed American reader and gives to Edison the voice of authority:

"They are poor people, Edison?"

"Poor! You will never understand how poor. You see how rough their skins are, how decayed their teeth? They have not had enough to eat for decades. The average earnings of a candomblé woman, if much, are a hundred milreis [five American dollars] a month. That has to take care of the woman and her children and also of her obligations to the temple." His tone became drier and quieter, as though he had to throttle his indignation.

"But their husbands, Edison?"

He lit a cigarette and shrugged faintly. "Husbands?" There aren't many of those, not reliable ones anyway. This is not a comfortable bourgeois society, dona. Nowadays there isn't enough work to go around among the men. They don't earn enough to support themselves, let alone a family." (1947:40)

She set her study against the stage of Brazil in the 1930s: "This well intentioned study of race relations could not avoid the rumblings of the times . . . fascist ideologies were only newer versions of the widespread motivations that had crystallized out in our country as race bitterness" (1947:8). She critiqued the "drawn but stilled battle of the races" in the United States by describing the fluidity of race relations in Brazil. She suggested that the differing character of race relations in the two countries required different methods of field research. Recording the complex social interactions she found herself engaged in, working as a foreign scientist, a woman

—"women were as handicapped in their movements as political opponents" (9)—and a Jew in Catholic Brazil under military dictatorship during the prelude to the Second World War, she decided: "My training in pure science had left me unprepared for such events." Once she had, as she said, "stripped" her anthropological inquiry "of the safety, of the sanctity of the ivory tower" (9), what constituted scientific procedure was no longer obvious.

Far from being an authoritative scientist, Landes describes in *The City of Women* feeling instead "disoriented and helpless as in a jungle" (9). To try to grasp the meanings of the "jungle" of conflicting images and social relations of which she found herself part, Landes decided to adopt instead an experiential, participatory approach: "I felt it was fine just to be among them, and I wanted to be of them" (15). She wrote: "I knew I could not study Bahia as . . . I could certain Indian tribes on our reservations where it is possible to hire individuals to sit in a chair for months at a time and tell about themselves. I should have to persuade the Bahians to take me into their life. I should have to force my way into the flow and become part of it. To study the people I should have to live with them, to like them, and I should have to try assiduously to make them like me" (16).

She described being driven around Bahia by a noted medical doctor who had taken it as his task "to show the 'Africans' to me" (17). The doctor would stop and give a coin to a woman street vendor and then interrogate the woman about candomblé ritual. "I was dissatisfied. . . . Possibly I was mistaken, but I felt that these Negro Bahians should be approached in a more personal manner, in a manner that conveyed clearer evidence of my regard. Actually, I wanted to see them live their own lives instead of merely hearing them answer my questions. Indeed, I myself could not ask questions before I knew about their lives" (18). Just as she objected to the constraints she found imposed on her own person in Brazil, Landes's strong notions of democratic social relations led her to try to reduce hierarchy in her relations with the Afro-Brazilians whose lives she hoped to record. There was no "mystery" to the method, she later wrote: "To study the humanness of customary behavior, and feel it bounce in one's own reactions, one had to brave the field" (1973:45). She recognized that, although the anthropological method of participant observation in the field did not produce objective facts, it was also not purely subjective. One's identity in the field is constructed through interactions with individuals and in local contexts of gender, class, and race.

The chief obstacle to carrying out this new research strategy was her lack of freedom of movement. She was required to live in an expensive hotel. She was advised by Brazilian colleagues and American expatriates against going alone to the poor, black neighborhoods and certainly not at night, which was when spirit possession rituals took place. She rejected the sensational stories the Americans told of "black magic" and "sex orgies" in the candomblé temples, but she soon recognized that she would be "unable to move about unless escorted by a reputable man" (1947:14). Landes thus accepted local protocols when she established a working relationship with Edison Carneiro, who would accompany her during her fieldwork, but she did so on her own terms. The American expatriates "scorned me for going around with a colored man" (129), she writes. That Carneiro and his circle were communists and that the terreiros were frequently raided by police would also draw her to the attention of authorities and eventually lead to her expulsion from Bahia. "I should never have disturbed the police if I had continued sightseeing with Jorge [the American consul's secretary with whom she had visited countless of Bahia's legendary 365 Catholic churches]," she observed (137).

Unlike her anthropological contemporaries, Landes was ahead of her times in describing field research as a reciprocal relationship. She understood that she was both observer and observed: "I realized soon enough that my study of Bahia was not a one-way arrangement, which I could limit as I chose, or begin and end at will. I had been instrumental chiefly in bringing myself to Bahia, and after that I was more or less driftwood on the tides of public opinion. Very few people there, I am sure, had faith in my simple intentions" (1947:20). She described instances when people expressed suspicion of her and of her motives (83). She also acknowledged that she often could not understand the meaning of the behavior she was observing. Sometimes she attributed her failure to her scientific allegiances: "Scientific generalizations don't give one much feeling for the nature of faith or fate," she wrote (90). "The philosophy, the mysticism and emotionality of candomblé always puzzled me. I learned to know it by rote, the way one learns a new language in school . . . but my reactions were as remote as those of an adding machine to numbers" (88).

At other times she attributed her lack of emotional engagement to her lack of familiarity with the Catholic ritual that so infused candomblé or, for that matter, her lack of experience with *any* religious ritual, since she had been raised in a firmly secular setting. Outside of anthropological fieldwork, she had no personal experience with religion. She did understand candomblé as lending an enchanted dimension to workaday life as well as an outlet for creativity, as a leisure pursuit, and as a fundamental institution of social support for an oppressed population. "They touched me with their qualities of devotion and tenderness" (1947:236). "The outpouring of energy, the hallelujah of living was overwhelming" (243). "I almost wished I could join them" (241). At the same time, she could not refrain from asking: "What *were* they so happy about?" (243), a question she knows is answered by the same enchanted, emotional states that candomblé allowed and that she found herself unable to experience: "Why, I thought pettishly, don't they throw all this energy into work? Why don't they move faster in health and social programs? Why does so much of it go into fun and god-imaginings? Why? Well, I answered myself, one reason naturally was that they were not instructed in these other saner pursuits. Another was that they were very, very poor, very, very little educated. And another was that they found something real in the [festivals], deep personal satisfactions they could discover nowhere else" (67).

The idea of a racial democracy that had been irresistible to Landes in the United States was assailed and ruptured by the racism of white expatriates and by many members of the Brazilian elite as well as by her observations of the poverty and obvious social and political inequality of the black population. She reported on her meeting with a prominent minister in the Vargas regime who wanted to ensure that she correctly understood Brazil's political situation: "Since you are going to study Negroes, I must tell you that our political backwardness, which has made this dictatorship necessary, is due entirely to our Negro blood. Unfortunate. So we are trying to breed the blood out, making one nation of all the people, 'whitening the Brazilian race'" (1947:6). But Landes also observed relations of mutual respect between elite scholars and candomblé practitioners. Describing a conversation between Mãe Menininha and a professor at the medical faculty outside Menininha's terreiro, Gantois, Landes wrote: "I watched them with great interest, one the picture of a ruler of the land, the other the picture of a humble Negro. Yet they treated each other with the courtesy of equals" (79). When Carneiro's friend, the poet Aydano de Couto Ferraz, made the statement "African traditions are now Brazilian — and we call them Afro-Brazilian" (101), Landes contrasted this with

white friends in Nashville and New Orleans. . . . I had an actual physical awareness at the moment of the opposition between the convictions I had left at home and the convictions I was encountering here. The difference between them was terrible. And, thinking only this, I sighed: "My Southern acquaintances would be horrified. They would think you had lost your 'pride'." Even I, because I am used to them, have to strain myself to follow you.

"Really?" demanded Edison, and the others slowed up to listen. "What can be so difficult?"

"Well, North Americans think in terms of race. A black man is inferior to a white man because of his race."

"What about the black man's culture?"

"That doesn't matter. A black man isn't supposed to have any of his own, only what he gets from whites, and that he is supposed to hide."

It was very embarrassing to explain these matters, especially in the face of their incredulity. (101–102)

Always, however, she was acutely aware of how social class consciousness intersected racial discourse in Brazil: "The class sentiment of Brazilian society is something to which I never grew accustomed," she wrote (1947:58). "[Edison] viewed the candomblé people as from across a gap. To him they were specimens, although of course human beings with an inalienable right to live as they chose. . . . Somehow this distant, patronizing attitude, passionate as it can become, is distasteful to an American reared 'north of the line'; it quite denies the common humanity proclaimed in the beliefs of Jeffersonian democracy. However, the people understood

Edison's attitude, which was their own, and not mine, which came out of another scheme of living. And they respected Edison... while they merely tolerated the good intentions that Edison told them I had" (60–61).

If, in *The City of Women*, she chooses to highlight the cultural creativity rather than the social problems of poor stevedores and laundresses, bricklayers and prostitutes, she also never loses sight of the ways that race relations intersected with class in the discrimination they faced everyday: "I knew... that I should never be as naïve about the language of 'racial equality' as when I arrived in Nashville. In Nashville a man could be tortured and killed because of his color. In Brazil that could happen only because of his political color. But it could happen, and so there was no question of 'safety' or 'freedom' despite the difference in phrasing. In Nashville a Negro could go to college, but his soul was always sick. In Bahia every Negro could hold up his head, people said, but in Rio they laughed ... over his African ways" (1947:7–8). In her conclusion to *The City of Women* Landes both anticipated the theoretical emphasis on social class that would dominate subsequent decades of scholarship on race relations in Brazil (Wagley 1952; Reichmann 1999) and offered her own explanation of the meaning of candomblé:

I was sent to Bahia to learn how people behave when the Negroes among them are not oppressed. I found that they were oppressed by political and economic tyrannies, although not by racial ones. In that sense the Negroes were free, and at liberty to cultivate their African heritage. But they were sick, undernourished, illiterate, and uninformed. ... It was their complete poverty that cut them off from modern thought and obliged them to make up their own secure universe. They lived in the only world that was allowed them, and they made it intimate and friendly through the institution of candomblé, whose vigor and pageantry and promises of security lured others too in Bahia, and were a matter of excitement and pride to the rest of Brazil also." (1947:248)

Romantic Primitivism, Tradition, and Modernity

Despite her critical observations on the intersections of race and class in Bahia, Landes also retained romantic primitivist sentiments that resembled those of many of her contemporaries in interwar anthropology (Healey 1996; Stocking 1992). "In retrospect, the life there seems remote and timeless," she wrote. She retained a romantic optimism about the possibility of a racial democracy, and she focused her observations on the cultural creativity rather than the structural constraints of the poor and marginalized. As social institution and cultural practice, candomblé offered her a prism to explore both the creative possibilities and the contradictions in acculturation processes—a theme that always guided her work. She saw in candomblé the contest between tradition and modernity, a stage on which the people dramatized their knowledge of the past, their present-day disenfranchisement, and their fears and hopes for the future. She placed candomblé at the center of her analysis and presented contesting local interpretations of its meaning and purpose for individuals who were differently situated in Bahian society. Landes treated candomblé as a system of knowledge—in late-20th-century poststructuralist terms, a discourse—and recognized that the debates surrounding it revealed the conflicting experiences of different social groups living under conditions of rapid change. She presented women as key players who through their trance performances dramatized the contradictions of history and through spirit possession metaphorically represented hopes of transformation. Landes underscored that it is women who "serve" the spirits and women who also serve the material needs of their communities by creating in the candomblé terreiros neighborhood institutions of social and economic support. Her analysis is intuitive: as she had with Maggie Wilson at Manitou Rapids, in Salvador she recorded her observations on women's work, their relationships, and their responses to social change. Her analysis of women's ritual work in candomblé anticipates late-20th-century scholarship that describes spirit possession as women's "moral historical work" in marginalized communities that are experiencing rapid social change (see Mageo 1996).

The writing style Landes adopted in The City of Women allowed her to reproduce the internal debates among Afro-Brazilians who through candomblé reinterpret the past and explore possibilities for change. In her text Landes developed profiles of particular individuals who were differently situated in terms of race, color, class, gender, occupation, and education and who serve in the text to represent different positions in these internal debates.

Martiniano, the 80-year old *babalão* (seer, diviner) with jet-black skin, who was born under slavery and had been sent by his parents to Nigeria at the age of 14 to study tribal lore and ritual, represents the voice of tradition. He had worked closely with Dr. Nina Rodrigues and was the first person to whom Edison Carneiro introduced Landes. Martiniano deplored the people's general ignorance of African traditions, the innovations some women ritual leaders had made in their terreiros to include male transvestites — "They are all pretenders!" (1947:31) — and the preoccupation with "whitening" as the route to social mobility in the wider Brazilian society. All were tendencies he observed and regretted, not least because they had bypassed him, leaving him without any followers: "I'm out of everything now," he observed. Landes, who herself supported integration, declared: "He could not appreciate that it was an inevitable consequence of the emancipation of the slaves, when the opportunities and the urge for assimilation increased immensely" (23). But her portrait of Martiniano is also compassionate: we learn that he experiences his responsibility as curator of tradition as a burden, that as social changes have passed him by he is overwhelmed by loneliness, and that he cannot resist expressing feelings of sexual desire toward the young, fairer-skinned Rosita, whom Landes had brought to him for a divining session (215). Describing Martiniano's world of tradition, Landes powerfully captures the aura of stagnation that contrasts with the vibrancy, excitement, and innovation of the emergent caboclo rituals that Martiniano critiques:

The room was windowless and stuffy, and held a jumbled assortment of candomblé paraphernalia such as I had never seen before. There were wooden and bronze statuettes of gods, with their sacred beads, fans, and swords, all made by Negro artisans of Bahia, now dead. . . . There were fetish stones, containing the very power of the gods, and they were swimming in oil, blood, and alcohol which they had been fed and in which they had been bathed several times. Dust lay like a blanket . . . and the room stank with an old mild odor. . . . He examined a dish of cooked chicken that lay in an alcove, so old a sacrifice that it had molded, and then he bent over a small dish of coagulated blood. . . . Suddenly he straightened up. *"That'll do, that'll do,"* he said hurriedly, shooing us out and locking the door. *". . . I wish I didn't have to take care of it, but my parents left it."* He smiled and turned to Rosita. *"Stay out of these things. You're too fair for that life."* (215–216)

If Martiniano represents "tradition," it is Edison Carneiro who carries the romantic primitivist voice in the text. Much of the book takes the form of constructed conversations between Landes and Carneiro. Edison's voice evaluates the rituals and events they observe against a generalized standard of "the 'true' African style" (1947:108) Although Landes gives his voice a dominant place in the text, she also presents the positions of others whose words contest or nuance those of Carneiro. Carneiro later wrote Landes that he was not "always satisfied with my portrait, as in the case of my aristocracy" (July 28, 1947, RLP).

"'This is samba!' Edison tapped me enthusiastically on the arm. 'This is the real thing, not the tripping about you see in the ballroom! This is genius! The blacks forget everything when they use their feet!' Edison, whose literacy and light skin privileged him in the local racial hierarchy, romanticized an Afro-Brazilian 'essence': 'The people are good, all of them are poets. . . . They always sing and dance and play, and create colorful designs and never allow each other to feel lonely or poor'" (1947:110). Of the new caboclo rituals and terreiros, he does not hesitate to pronounce: "By the high standards of Yoruba tradition, the caboclos are blasphemous because they are ignorant and undisciplined, because they have created new gods at will, and because they welcome men into the mysteries" (37). Of women's experimentation with modern dance steps and hair straightening and wearing rouge, uplift brassieres, and tight dresses, Edison is patronizing and does not contextualize their aspirations within their experiences of racial inequality and social exclusion: "The old Africans are losing out to the beauticians. . . . Here you see them learning to become sophisticated . . . leaving Africa for the western world and the twentieth century. They are trying to think as we do. If they had the opportunity, they would be just as conventional as any white person, or as any educated black. They are playing at breaking away from their poverty, even if it means offending the gods. But of course they show their true character anyway: it's the women who aren't afraid to dance, and they keep that bahian walk of theirs even though the dresses are wrong for it" (197).

Significantly, it is women who transgress. It is the women who are more adventurous and willing to explore novelty. The attention Landes gives to them suggests her implicit theoretical understanding that women serve as a metaphor for community desires and vulnerabilities. But she ultimately fails to analyze the larger contexts of Brazil's racial and gender hierarchies within which these experiments with modernity take place. Her focus on individual experience prevents her from stating generalizations in the ways that Edison did and that the discipline of anthropology also required. Instead she simply commented that in contrast to Martiniano and Edison, who deplored modern dancing in the terreiro, Flaviana, the 90-year old "mother "of the temple, accepted it. Flaviana, Landes suggests, recognized the people's need and right to experiment in order both to integrate in a world that was rapidly and irrevocably changing and to negotiate racial discrimination.

Landes's theoretical approach is also implicit in her rejection of a rigid opposition between "tradition" and "modernity." She did not catalogue "African survivals" and "Catholic" elements. She describes candomblé practices as imaginative and innovative: "The people speak of God 'in the Catholic life,' and of Oxalá 'in the African'; and this means that they believe they are practicing only one religion, although they are using two languages in doing it" (1947:89). Landes understood that candomblé represented a new religion in a changing sociocultural universe.

The character of Sabina, the leader of a breakaway caboclo temple, in *The City of Women* represents the "blasphemy" that concerned Martiniano and Carneiro. Sabina catered to the middle-class residents of the Barra neighborhood and rejected the long Bahian skirts and dress in favor of modern, tailored, white skirts and jackets. Landes and Carneiro attended her festival to the sea spirit, Iemanjá, and accompanied the procession of people dressed in immaculate white and bearing flowers and gifts for Iemanjá. They boarded one of the small fishing boats to go out to sea to deposit the gifts on the water and to receive Iemanjá's blessing for the coming year. During ecstatic singing and drumming, several of the women, including Sabina, fell into trance and rocked with the motion of the boats. As

Landes is caught "in the wave of feeling" and overwhelmed by the beauty and enchantment of "the Middle Ages" (1947:163), Edison grumbled that "he was inclined to underrate these ready trances" (165): "I admire this enormously . . . but I can't take it seriously. Sabina has such control over her gods! She can turn them on and off. . . . Just look at Sabina. She gives me the impression merely of working hard. In the Yoruba temples a woman in honest trance moves like a sleepwalker, sweeping and sure, and her eye is glazed. I don't believe the women here could stand the needles Dr. Nina used to jab into Mother Pulcheria's priestesses to test their state!" (168–169).

Less concerned with measuring "authenticity" and orthodoxy, Landes was interested in what the people were thinking and experiencing. She replied to Carneiro: "But they believe they're doing the right thing, don't they?" Carneiro, whose concern was with African tradition, responded: "Surely. But I hate to see the classic tradition corrupted." Landes persisted: "Still, now they know that they will have enough to eat next year, and that their personal affairs will go well?" "Yes," he agreed" (1947:169).

Landes described how the concerns the candomblé practitioners expressed differed from Martiniano and Edison's fears for the loss of African tradition. Alone, Landes visited Sabina at her home one afternoon during the week following the festival. Sabina explained that other people criticized her: "Everybody is jealous of me. They don't like me because I am modern and clean, and they are old-fashioned and filthy" (1947:180). Later Landes asked Mãe Menininha, the respected leader of the classical Yoruban terreiro, Gantois, about Sabina. Menininha expressed concern not for African tradition but because she said Sabina was guided by individual ambition rather than by the sense of communal obligation that in Menininha's view was fundamental to the terreiro as a mutual aid society and neighborhood association (147). "She wants men around her! She wants money too, she doesn't care really about helping people!" (158). By contrast, Menininha respected Bernardino, the transvestite pai who had started his own terreiro, because she said he possessed this sense of obligation to community that Sabina seemed to lack.

When Landes does turn to so-called African standards to critique a "modern" practice, she does so less from concern for the survival of African practices than to critique the "modern" gendered behaviors the people seemed to be embracing. Reflecting on the dancing couples she and Edison had observed at Flaviana's birthday party, she expressed her distress: "There was no idea behind the dance except courtship, no display of virtuosity, no summoning of the gods" (147:200). The people seemed to be abandoning Bahian skills and knowledge in favor of adopting the romantic notions and gender roles that Landes herself had rejected in American society. "I discovered that I had become African in my prejudices" is how she rather lamely chose to phrase this observation (200). This statement might be interpreted as deference to Edison's romantic perspective and to the idealization of Afro-Brazilian culture that was so central to the Brazilian nationalist imagination in the 1930s. But, in thus reproducing national Brazilian discourse, Landes subordinated her own gendered, experiential frame of reference.

Gender and the Body

The race, class, and gender relations that defined the conditions under which she was able to conduct fieldwork framed Ruth Landes's analysis of Afro-Brazilian culture. Landes encountered these when she arrived and tried to find a place to live in Bahia. There were no houses or apartments to rent so "I took a room in the best hotel in town" (12). She soon learned that living alone as a woman was a provocative act, that a woman would live alone only in order to establish privacy for sexual intimacy, and that women who lived alone were usually prostitutes. She also soon discovered the constraints upon her as a single woman in Brazil that made it impossible for her to visit the black neighborhoods unaccompanied. However, once she had allied herself with Edison in order to study candomblé, she then became subject to his notions of feminine respectability. As she succinctly put it, "An aristocrat never allows his womenfolk to walk alone after sunset" (59). Edison would always find someone to replace him as an escort on the occasions when he was unable to accompany her. Nor would he allow her to dance or drink in public, that is, when conducting field research.

Landes critiques the constraints on elite white women in Brazil by pointing to the power and authority commanded by the Afro-Brazilian "matriarchs" of the candomblé terreiros. As with Maggie Wilson's Ojibwa women, she was especially impressed that the women had redefined the institution of marriage: "Children and husbands are welcomed by a woman of the temple. They are her family, and she takes care of them as willingly as she takes care of her god. In return, she demands freedom for herself. Most of the women dream of a lover who can offer financial support at least to the extent of relieving her of continuous economic worry; but they do not think of legal marriage. Marriage means another world, something like being a white person. It brings prestige but not necessarily joy in living" (1947:148). Common-law husbands — who were often respected citizens — would visit the terreiro, where they might maintain a sleeping hut for themselves on the temple grounds and would serve as financial patrons, often *ogans*, of the terreiro, but each would remain subordinate to his wife, who would be unwilling to marry either civilly or religiously and who would live permanently in the temple.

Landes offers vivid descriptions of the bodies of the women. The images strike the reader powerfully both because they are so evocative of the place and the people and because we realize they have been so absent from the writing of scientific monographs.

The body for Landes was a critical vehicle of self-expression. It established one's identity and one's social place. It was simultaneously a place of potential power and subordination, of subversion and convention. She carefully cared for her own body throughout her life and was "something of an athlete" (Richard Slobodin, personal communication, October 13, 1993). She swam several times a week and died at the age of 83 while doing her morning sit-ups beside her bed. She had three abortions, not only because she had decided not to be a mother, but because she resisted the modification of her body through pregnancy. After a hysterectomy in 1955, she took hormones, increased her exercise regime, and became obsessed with using petroleum jelly on her face to help control the aging of her skin. In letters and conversations, when referring to others, she always described their physical appearance ("handsome," "unattractive," "glowing"), which was an endless source of fascination and entertainment to her. When she was involved in an abusive relationship, her students remember her coming to class to teach in a backless sundress that fully displayed the bruises on her upper back and neck. Far from hiding these signs of violence, it was typical of Landes to display them as bodily evidence of social and gendered relations.

When we read her descriptions of the Bahian women she met, we can see them as fully consistent with her interest in the body and her understanding of the body as a mirror of the self. "I smiled to see these women who did not care about being dainty," she wrote. "Their concern was to lay claim to where they sat" (1947:83).

She described one Sunday afternoon at the terreiro of Engenho Velho that was her first meeting with one of the candomblé leaders, "a big impressive woman named Luzía":

She talked and moved majestically, strolling over to a low curved bench which was painted white and encircled a white pillar in the center of the room. . . . She sat down on the bench, spreading her thighs like an eastern potentate and leaning her elbows on them. Her flowing skirts made a huge circle on the floor. She began to intone the chants, and the old women near her got up and danced in bare feet. She intoned further, and they lifted up offerings of oil, rum, and popcorn, offerings which were to buy the good will of Exu. . . .

Watching Luzía, I would have said she was not the least interested in this routine, for her deep monotone pulled the songs lazily and her sad eyes were shut. But I cannot know, for they had roused her from her nap, and after all she knew her gods so well, as had her mother and aunt and sisters before her. How many numberless times had she chanted the Padê, bargaining with the docile demon to leave the gods in peace and carry mischief to the crossroads? (1947:43–44)

She described the ceremony later that night: "The men began to beat the drums and a few old daughters straggled out to dance in honor of the god of the evening; they were dressed in his prescribed lace, and danced in a wide circular path before the drummers. The women were black-skinned, strong and big, and had none of the mincing ways that the upper class considers feminine and alluring. In fact, they seemed to me like men dressed in the skirts of the Bahian women" (1947:48).

Meeting Menininha, considered by Brazilian ethnologists the

greatest living priestess, wrapped in a black shawl sitting in the shade at the entrance to her house selling sweets, Landes "wondered if any outsider could have suspected her position":

She was about five feet tall, fat and dark, with kinky hair, and a large tooth missing in the front of her mouth. Her clothes were not pretty or neat. But I felt dignity in her, diffident at the moment yet pervasive, accustomed to authority. I noticed her full, heart-shaped face, her small full nose and lips, her cool bronze skin. . . .

"Come in, my lady," the priestess urged listlessly, "let us sit down and have a little visit." She lowered herself heavily into a flimsy chair, placing her palms on her thighs. Suddenly she was remote and obscure as a Stone Age Venus. Her shawl gone, sitting in a loose cotton dress, her great breasts flowed over a great stomach which bulged over tremendous thighs supported by powerful legs tapering to small ankles and feet. Her brief sleeves exposed large arms, masses of firm smooth flesh that dimpled hugely at the elbows and ended in seemingly fragile wrists and hands. "My lady", she said quietly . . . "you wanted to see me?" (1947:79–80)

Landes described the priestess Flaviana on her 90th birthday: "On the cot, she held herself rigidly erect, balancing with back-thrust buttocks in the manner of the bahianas, and her old eyes, rimmed red in her black face, looked at things unreal above and beyond us. Her bones and face were dainty, thin, and broad, and her thick hair was snow-white, cropped and curling becomingly in the mannish style favored by the priestesses who bind their heads for carrying loads. She wore a lovely blouse of white drawn work, cut so low and wide that it slipped off a shoulder, and its texture dimly bared her thin breasts" (194–195).

These testimonials are full of admiration for women's bodies and reveal a fascination with the diversity of their bodies and their ability through movement and posture to communicate the authority of ordinary women in a particular place and time.

Ethnography and the Representation of Experience

When Landes returned from Brazil, several newspapers interviewed her and sensationalized descriptions of her work under headlines such as "Girl Explorer Tells Jungle Cult Secrets" (Hearst Syndicate,

August 6, 1939) and "Magic Powers of Jungle Priestesses who Rule 40,000 Men — Ruth Landes Brings Back Weird Tales of Brazilian Matriarchs" in an article by Hazel Canning in the *Boston Sunday Post* (August 6, 1939). Landes had lamented to Benedict that interviewers were "vulture-ish": they "insisted that all Negroes have orgies" or that "I was a reincarnated goddess of Love" (July 17, 1939, RFBP). *The City of Women* was marketed by Macmillan as a popular account and was widely reviewed in the book pages of major newspapers. The book arrived on the scene at the end of the Second World War and at the height of the popularity of the music of Carmen Miranda and Vila Lobos in New York. Some reviewers objected to the "sensational" title (Mishnun 1947), the focus on women, the descriptions of what they called "sisterhood" and "free love," and that "marriage is considered a luxury hardly worth the expense and inconvenience it causes women" (Hughes 1947). "Apparently the women of Bahia are dominant, but to what worthwhile end does this dominance lead?" complained J. F. Santee in *Social Studies*. Another reviewer pointed to the "insecure" position men found themselves in due to women's dominance (Honigmann 1947). Gitel Poznanski in the *New York Times* praised the "gratifying" absence of "jargon" and the "brilliant passages" describing "matriarchal authority" (August 3, 1947). Some reviewers charged that Landes had de-emphasized the political and economic disenfranchisement of Afro-Brazilians in order to critique American race relations. Some lamented "that she chose the topic of witch doctors instead of a more profound topic" (Anonymous 1947). Others recognized her empathy for acculturation and women's experience and her appreciation of religious syncretism. They situated her work alongside that of Zora Neale Hurston and Katherine Dunham, who had also recently written popular accounts of syncretic African American religions (Chapin 1947; Schuyler 1947). Many commented on the book's rich descriptions (Wolfe 1947). Anthropologist John Honigmann, writing in *Social Forces*, said: "By her informal style Landes has richly captured the spirit of Brazilian Negro life . . . the book reads far more like a very intelligent travel work than the technical record of an experienced anthropologist's observations." Others compared her work to that of Melville Herskovits, finding his work "much more thorough and systematic" (Chapin 1947) and describing her work as "a local Cook's tour with a guide more discerning than usual" (Krogman 1947). One reviewer commented, "There is a little too much of those velvet tropical nights in it" (Gannett n.d.).

American Anthropologist asked Melville Herskovits to review *The City of Women*. In his lengthy review, Herskovits charged that Landes had a "false perspective on the role of men and women in the culture that gives the book its misleading title" (1948:124). He continued:

What Miss [sic] Landes does not realize is that men have places that are quite as important as those of the women; that the African counterparts of the Bahian cults have priestesses as well as priests. . . . The basic thesis is also wrong because of the misreading of an economic cause — that is, few men are initiates, in Bahia no less than in Africa, because they cannot afford the time its takes, because in Africa it is easier to support a woman in the culthouse than to withdraw a man from productive labor for months on end. Miss Landes overstresses the homosexuality of male priests — there are many "orthodox" as well as caboclo priests in Bahia who have no tendency toward inversion. (124)

Herskovits asserted that Landes had misinterpreted the relations of men and women in candomblé because she had not been adequately trained "in the Africanist field" and that she had been "ill prepared" to conduct research in Bahia because "she knew so little of the African background of the material she was to study that she had no perspective" (1948:124). Landes, as we know, had prepared herself through library research at both Fisk University and in Rio under Arthur Ramos's direction before going to Bahia. Abundant subsequent research furthermore has also supported Landes's interpretation of gender roles and relations in the terreiros (Birman 1988; Fry 1995; Murray 2000; Wafer 1991) and of spirit possession as "a local way of thinking about the past" and a kind of "moral historical work" that women do for traumatized communities (Mageo 1996; see also Constantinides 1982; Kendall 1985; McCarthy Brown 1991).

In the 1930s and 1940s, however, anthropologists who conducted research on African American culture envisioned only two possible analytical frameworks: one was to measure degrees of assimilation to white American society; the other, as Herskovits did, was to look to Africa for explanations for cultural differences of African Americans. "In either case, African-American culture was largely examined in terms of something or somewhere else" (Fraser 1991:407). Instead, Ruth Landes worked to develop a third framework: to observe Afro-Brazilian religion on its own terms and in light of her own experience. She believed that she was studying a new, living Brazilian religion and wanted to portray candomblé as fully integrated in the way of life of the urban poor blacks of Bahia. Landes also wanted to understand the ways that candomblé met the needs of women and the meanings it held for them. She sought to achieve this understanding by "entering deeply into the field culture, joining it twenty-four hours a day, each day, all the months or years of research" (1970b:121). In her writing she was ahead of her time in exploring the link between experience in the field and ethnographic understanding of culture: "Field work serves an idiosyncrasy of perception that cannot separate the sensuousness of life from its abstractions, nor the researcher's personality from his experiences. The culture a field worker reports is the one he experiences, filtered through trained observations. . . . Through field work at the pleasure of the host culture one learns one's place there and that it is one's only vantage point for penetrating the culture" (121, 138).

Landes's field methods contrasted with those of Brazilian scholars such as Ramos who conducted formal interviews in their university offices or relied on secondhand reports. Nor did she focus, as they had, on obtaining technical descriptions of the physiological characteristics of spirit possession or on dissecting the Catholic and African origins. Her field methods were Herskovits's major criticism. He wrote that her training on American Indian reservations had not prepared her for "what might be called the diplomatic aspects of fieldwork. . . . Students of acculturated societies must be . . . taught how to conduct themselves in the capital as well as in the bush, told how to turn the corners of calling cards, when to leave them, and how to 'sign the book.'" Landes had chosen not to spend her time socializing with the elite of Bahian society and instead to devote her energies to getting to know people for whom the beliefs and practices of the terreiros held profound meaning. The City of Women is filled with the names and stories of these people, descendants of African slaves, who worked as stevedores, bricklayers, fishermen, seamstresses, laundresses, and street vendors. As Landes wrote, "I felt it was fine just to be among them, and I wanted to be of them" (1947:15).

Herskovits's criticism of Ruth Landes's field methods was a veiled attack on her personal comportment in the field — of her love affair and research alliance with Edison Carneiro — and reproduced the complaints Ramos had expressed in his 1940 report to Myrdal. Landes had considered that Carneiro's companionship as an escort had given her intimate access to life in the candomblé terreiros. Once again, criticism focused on her manners, finding her behavior unladylike and charging that her anthropology was, as a result, compromised.

Rereading The City of Women

Scientific ethnography was characterized by a style of writing that Jonathan Spencer called "ethnographic naturalism": "the creation of a taken-for-granted representation of reality through the use of certain standard devices such as free indirect speech and the absence of any tangible point of view. . . . Ethnographic naturalism, while working with ostensibly unproblematic literary devices, in fact constructs a kind of object — a world robbed of its idiosyncrasies and foibles — which is foreign to the experience of its readers" (1989:152–154). Following postmodernist and feminist critiques in the late 20th century, the discipline has come to accept that the emergence of scientific ethnography was not inevitable but was the product of hegemonic processes of canon making by influential individuals and powerful institutions. Scientific ethnography came to dominate the field by marginalizing other types of writing. Rethinking ethnography has encouraged a fresh reading of the history of anthropology.

The City of Women, marginalized during the making of the disciplinary canon, rewards rereading as an early ethnography of race, gender, and acculturation. Landes refused to produce a portrait of candomblé (and Afro-Brazilian culture) as a homogeneous, integrated whole, as a "genuine culture" (Sapir 1924). Instead, she described internal contestations of meaning in a context of racialization and economic marginalization. Through her focus on gender and the alternative gender roles and identities that candomblé produced, she portrayed the people's hopes for change and transformation. In Landes's analysis, the possibility for change emerges in the contradictions that the processes of acculturation create. It is this fluidity that Landes tries to represent through her various textual strategies: multivocality, dialogue, the stories and words of particular and differently situated individuals, the naming of friends, and reflexive writing about her subjective experience in the field and her situated position as an author. Landes did not escape the exoticization of cultural difference—the romantic primitivism—of her day, but she did try to reject the discipline's rhetorical strategies of "othering." She refused the scientific writing style of ethnographic naturalism to assert textual authority; she did not remove culture from its social, political, and economic contexts; and she did not write out of her texts the contradictions of history and of "unruly experience" (Clifford 1988:25). She insisted on situating herself as an American and a woman in her writing—a practice of self-identification that, although increasingly current in present-day anthropology, was anathema to the rhetorical assertions of ethnographic authority in her day. She defined race and gender as topics for scientific research, and she found the prevalent scientific theories inadequate to address them. She thus let go of academic reference points and scientific theories of culture and endeavored to let Bahian women speak to her on their own terms, a process she describes in *The City of Women*. In making this decision, she could have been a pathbreaker. Instead she was assigned a position on the borders of a discipline that was seeking to legitimize its professional status as the "science of the study of man."

In *The City of Women* Landes had inserted her voice into the text to illustrate the intersubjective nature of anthropological method and knowledge. Instead of editing incongruities out of the text, she had tried to show the fluid and divergent local interpretations of events and experiences. And she had endeavored to let Bahia speak to her "on its own terms." She was proud of the book, but within the discipline it was harshly judged and soon forgotten. Her world of powerful, authoritative women, of hybridity, ambiguity, and contradiction, was not easily tolerated by an academic discipline bent on explanation and pattern. But anthropology—"this exploration through different worlds of ideas" — was Ruth Landes's lifeline. Despite her marginalization she continued to cling to the lifeline of anthropology in order to keep from falling or being washed away into the world of the mundane, the orthodox, the conventional.

Life and Career

A whole library of theorizing can't give half the real conviction that comes from adventuring through the life of one restless, highly endowed woman. – Ruth Benedict in Margaret Mead, An Anthropologist at Work

Evidently, one can't be an individual, even if harmlessly. – Ruth Landes, October 21, 1950, Notebook 1, RLP)

DURING THE YEARS when Landes was trying to find a publisher for *The City of Women*, she was also trying to find employment. The Carnegie Commission contract was only the beginning of what would be 25 years living an itinerant lifestyle, working as a contract researcher and part-time instructor. On December 12, 1939, a few weeks after the Carnegie contract had ended, she wrote to Benedict: "Can you help me with ideas about future work? A 'position' seems out of the question, so much so that I don't even inquire. I was wondering about another period of work in Brazil—since now I have the language, literature, experience and real interest. I'd like to have another field trip anyway, before I retire; and I probably will have to retire, what with age, chronic sinusitis and the feeling that I ought to be doing something about getting a husband and children" (RFBP).

Eight months later, on August 19, 1940, she wrote again about finding employment: "I suppose I might as well come out now with the horrible facts as later. I'm stymied. Everything I touch turns to paralysis. People look at me with open and admiring eyes and say, 'I'm *confident* that you will be successful', and I am insofar as rousing their 'sympathies' . . . is concerned, but never in re a job. I have displayed wondrous amounts of what you dubbed 'initiative', but 'it really do not matter' as my Fisk brightlings liked to say." She reported on her efforts to work on the Sioux, Potawatomi, and Ojibwa manuscripts. She wondered if Benedict thought there might be interest at Columbia in a course that she would like to develop on Latin American and inter-American problems, and she asked, "Do you think that a book about the matter could be subsidized?" She also asked why Benedict hadn't replied to her various research proposals for a Guggenheim application, and she concluded forlornly: "But I suppose it does not matter overly. I feel so dead. I've tried and am trying, and have stayed in the damn city for it, and have also been subsidizing the doctor twice weekly in order to get rid of the ailment [anemia, chronic fatigue, and sinusitis] I absorbed in Brazil. And now fall is approaching." She continued in this depressed state, working on her various manuscripts for the next year.

When the United States declared war on Japan in December 1941 and anthropologists flocked to Washington to work on various wartime assignments, Ruth Landes was among them. She worked first, briefly, on the "Brazil Desk" for the United States coordinator for inter-American affairs and then from 1942 to 1944 as a consultant on various contracts for President Roosevelt's Fair Employment Practices Committee FEPC, first on African American affairs and later on Mexican American cases. With the FEPC she traveled on assignments to Louisiana, Arizona, New Mexico, Colorado, and California. She tried to keep her ethnographer's eye engaged during these bureaucratic years by recording her observations on race relations in New Orleans and on Mexican Americans in the Southwest (see Landes 1965), but she would later describe this as a time of professional boredom and restlessness.

With her career stagnating, Landes was receptive to the idea of marriage. In the spring of 1944 she became engaged to Salvador Lopez Lima, a Mexican lawyer whom she had met through her work on FEPC hearings on anti-Mexican discrimination and who was in the United States working for the protection of the rights of migrant Mexican farm workers. In anticipation of marriage, she quit her Washington job and traveled with her fiancé to Mexico City in June. On her return she spent several months in New Orleans waiting for Lima to free himself from his work. During this time she conducted an informal study of the French shrimp fisheries and wrote to Benedict on August 13 that she was "learning about caste, class, race, science, politics, industry and the South" and was hoping to sell some articles based on the work. By October she was back in New York, living with her parents and again looking for work. The marriage had been postponed indefinitely. Lima was traveling constantly between Mexico and his law practice in Denver. Landes applied for a government job in Denver. She wrote to Benedict that she had been "planning to return to anthropology" once she was married and living in Mexico, but now she needed to consider government work although she did not enjoy it and found "the enforced reorientation extraordinarily difficult." She would "appreciate whatever suggestion" Benedict could offer (October 16, 1944, RFBP). By December the prospect of the marriage ever materializing was remote.

She wrote two articles that were based on her experiences during the war years, and these were published in 1945: "A Northerner Views the South" in *Social Forces* and "What about this Bureaucracy?" in *The Nation*. She became optimistic again about her career. She applied to the American Jewish Congress for work as a researcher in January 1945. Before receiving a response from this application, she was hired for several months "to direct a small FEPC-type program in New York" created by Pearl S. Buck and a group of interdenominational clergy to analyze pending New York anti-discrimination legislation (Landes 1965:6). Unemployed again in July 1946, she wrote Benedict that she was borrowing "money from family" to go out to Los Angeles. "I have no idea at all about jobs, but I'll bend an ear to the winds when I arrive" (July 10, 1946, RFBP).

By September 1946, Landes was settled in California working for the Los Angeles Metropolitan Welfare Council on a research contract to conduct a study of race and youth gangs. She wrote Benedict: "It's a community-supported program which strives to re-educate Mexican and Negro adolescent gangs. It is social work, of course, and the salary is modest, but I imagine it will bring me exactly the material I want, so I have accepted . . . actually I regard it as a windfall, like a good fellowship grant" (September 13, 1946, RFBP). She asked Benedict to recommend some relevant anthropological readings. A few months later she wrote that the youth gang material was "better and better," and she was planning a book on the subject. Collecting data in a new field site, she was at her happiest, writing effusively to Benedict: "I wish you could know how I love you for setting me on this path—the many times that you did and the steadiness of the doing" (December 9, 1946, RFBP). While in Los Angeles she met journalist Ignacio Lutero Lopez, whom she would eventually marry—briefly—ten years later.

The contract came to an end in May 1947, and Landes, unemployed again, returned to New York to live with her parents and to launch *The City of Women*, which was published in August 1947. After a brief flurry of radio interviews and reviews in newspapers, interest in the book apparently dissipated. With her father's help she was hired as a contract researcher with the American Jewish Congress, where she worked from 1948 to 1950. She was depressed to be living again with her parents, and her refusal to settle into a marriage continued to create conflict with her mother. She also found it stifling to live and work in the heart of the American Jewish community, which she described as "small and provincial." She found New York after the war radically different than it had been during her youth:

I was brought up so neutrally and in the last few years lived without "segregation" as a Jew—especially in Brazil and Louisiana. Nobody knew or cared, and I didn't either. I felt AMERICAN. Returning north to New York suddenly plunged me into a world that seemed fevered actually over these distractions. I was shocked. I was shocked to hear people use "race" widely here with what strikes me are the fixed ranked meanings in Nazi usage. And Jews are now calling themselves a "race"! To me, and I should think to all other Jews, America is such a generous, continuing experience that it goes "against nature" to particularize as Jewish or not. Yet I am constrained to so label myself on Federal forms. Being "American," I can't let myself deny it. (RL to RB, March 4, 1944, RFBP)

Margaret Mead asked Landes to write a report on "the Jewish family" for the "national character" studies she was coordinating for Columbia University's Research in Contemporary Cultures project. This is the study that resulted in the article Landes coauthored with Mark Zborowski, "Hypotheses concerning the Eastern European Jewish Family," discussed in chapter 1.

Ruth Benedict died in September 1948, and Ruth Landes found, strangely, that she felt stronger and more independent. She was now clearly on her own to define her future. Benedict had supported her during her student apprenticeship and had appreciated her intellect and energy for fieldwork, but she had done little to integrate Landes into the institutions of academia. She had helped Landes find short-term funding for field research, but how was Landes to support herself back in New York? Benedict did not find a single teaching position for Landes (temporary or permanent) and never invited Landes to join her at the American Anthropological Association meetings, which Benedict attended each year and then reported on after the fact. Landes had been on her own to create employment during the war years, and she alone had found a publisher for *The City of Women*. Benedict had not read Landes's Sioux, Potawatomi, and Ojibwa book manuscripts as she had said she would. They languished among Benedict's papers and would remain unpublished until Landes herself—years later—could arrange a publisher. Benedict had, it seemed, disengaged from Landes after her Brazil research. There is no record of any correspondence between them concerning *The City of Women*. Landes, however, was thrilled with *The City of Women*. Its publication gave her confidence, and she imagined that she might make a living as a writer. On September 30, 1950, she started a diary that she also used as a writing log to record reflections on her life as a "woman in mid-life at mid-century" and that she thought might provide material for a novel.

She even became hopeful again of an academic career. In the fall of 1950, she applied for a Fulbright fellowship to study Caribbean migration to Britain. Pursuing academic opportunities, however, required academic patrons. She asked anthropologist Kenneth Little at the University of Edinburgh (whom she had met at Fisk) and Charles Johnson (still at Fisk) to write letters in support of her application to the Fulbright Foundation. With hesitation, but because Boas and Benedict were both dead, she turned to Margaret Mead for a third letter of reference. In 1950 Mead was virtually the only woman who wielded any influence in American anthropology. At a symposium on anthropology sponsored by the Viking Fund in 1950, of 89 invited participants, only 2 were women: Mary R. Haas and Margaret Mead. Mead played an important role in defining the places other women would occupy in the discipline in the United States in the postwar period.

Landes had previously written and asked Mead to keep her "in mind for anything pertinent that might come your way." She had updated Mead on her various work assignments during the war, saying, "These took me far from academic work, though to my eyes they look like applied anthropology," and explained that when the war ended "I felt I had to return to anthropology. My way was to write *The City of Women*." She wrote Mead: "I always felt that Ruth Benedict was my life-line to anthropological developments — as she had been, in fact. So now I do not know where to turn. I prefer research above all, but having gone without a salary for over a year, my first need is for a job — not a temporary one. . . . Burdened as you are, I was reluctant to add my troubles — but where else would I turn for anthropological advice, if not to you?" (October 13, 1948, MMP, box C5).

Landes had reservations about approaching Mead for a letter of reference. Mead could be arbitrary in lending support, and from their discussions a few years earlier about Landes's "Cult Matriarchate" article, Landes knew that there were theoretical differences between them. She also recalled how, in Washington in 1944, when she had told Mead of her engagement to Salvador Lima, Mead had pronounced: "I don't know if that isn't the best thing for you! You've always had a yen to marry into the minority group. You'll toy with the aristocracy but you'll marry minority" (RL to RB, June 18, 1944, RFBP). Speaking from her established position in "aristocratic old America," Mead referred not only to Landes's affairs with minority men but also to Landes's own minority status in America. In her diary Landes described Mead as "obsessed with 'old American'" (October 21, 1950, Notebook 1, RLP).

On October 2, 1950, Mead wrote the following letter of reference in support of Ruth Landes's application for the Fulbright fellowship:

Dr. Ruth Landes . . . is thoroughly trained in anthropological field methods and untiring as a field worker. . . . During the years since she received her degree she has been unencumbered by economic responsibilities beyond her own support and therefore has been free to follow research opportunities rather than to seek any sort of steady professional advancement. This leaves her without a teaching record, but I believe that she would do a competent job of lecturing to advanced students. She has continued to grow intellectually, and has during the last year taken considerable steps ahead in integrating her work with current personality theory. She has serious professional interests and commitments and would take the responsibility of a grant from the Committee on International Exchange of Persons as something not to be handled lightly. I think I should add that Dr. Landes is considerably better looking and more attractive than many of her sex who seek academic careers and that this circumstance may be looked upon not without acrimony by both male and female colleagues." (MMP, box D4; emphasis added)

Landes was furious. After fuming for two weeks, she wrote Mead: "I have felt increasingly distressed and dismayed at the statements about me that you . . . sent to the Fulbright Board. I regret exceedingly that you felt it necessary to write as you did." (October 18, 1950, Notebook 1, RLP). Mead replied by telephone, telling Landes: "Why you've made a three-ringed circus out of life! . . . it's known all over the country . . . *you've lived your own life!* . . . and when you live dramatically, and look dramatic, and aren't married . . . why you've told me things that make one's hair stand on end . . . the things *you told Ruth!"* (October 21, 1950, Notebook 1, RLP).

Landes observed in her diary that Mead's words were an eye-opening revelation to her. Landes wrote that she would, once and for all, make a break from what she now perceived as her dependence on Benedict and, through Benedict, on Mead—a dependence perpetuated by her lack of a secure professional position in anthropology. She recalled "how venomous Ruth Benedict was over my efforts to write short stories based on Indian tales—Sad, not to have understood this all those years. . . . What I said could not have been much, but evidently she [Benedict] did gossip" (October 21, 1950, Notebook 1, RLP). Observing that in 1932 she had "transferred" her "former dependence on parents" to Benedict, she wrote on October 1, 1950: "Now I wonder why with her great beauty, and genius and personal effectiveness to true largeness—she was so cold emotionally, so lonely (not just alone, as she wept in poetry), so perhaps resentful of men (colleagues-competitors, my lovers), so eventually needing power, so unhappy and tense. My 'transference' to her was certainly a love-involvement like with a man, completed by authority—and parenting?—factors, and a great need to receive approval and give admiration—Now I want companionship, which is my notion of marriage, and to set it in the country among the permanent beauties of the seasons and live things like water, trees, crops, horses — and babies?" (Notebook 1, RLP).

Mead's arbitrary judgment reminded Landes of her outsider status, and she wavered again in setting a direction for her future. On October 22 she wrote: "It is obvious that I need marriage now for protection against the world and for companionship." But a few weeks later she was again focused on career possibilities and wrote hopefully: "the Fulbright will reinstate me academically." These conflicted musings were intensified by the aggravations of daily life in her parents' home. She desperately wanted to move into her own apartment, but she needed a secure job to "swing it financially." The only other route out would be marriage, which might "mean perhaps relaxation, play and support, as well as a conventional bulwark" (January 1, 1951, Notebook 5, RLP) — "but marriage for me has been the great 'closing-in' situation" (December 3, 1950, Notebook 1, RLP).

Landes was successful in obtaining the Fulbright fellowship and did go to England for a year's research (1951–52). The year in London was a happy experience. She made strong and lifelong friendships with women, especially historian Sally Chilvers (and her husband, Richard) and Chilvers's friends, anthropologist Phyllis Kaberry and poet Stevie Smith. Landes observed of her newfound collegial environment: "This is a long way from the Ghetto-tension shading most of my life, and yet also direct connections through tides of 'democracy', learning and social responsibility" (November 19, 1955, Notebook 2, RLP). Sally Chilvers, whom I interviewed in Oxford in 1997, described Ruth Landes during that year in London:

A terrific romantic. [She] was brought up to feel that the world could be made better. She was a mercurial, quicksilver personality. . . . Rebellious. She was curious about everything. . . . She was funny, pretty, had her own charm and at the same time was "her own man." . . . She was very comfortable with blacks. She swam through the English professional classes with great aplomb. She was not intimidated. Not patronized or patronizing. She was egalitarian in social interactions. She could draw anyone out. She treated children with great respect and was terrific at getting them to talk. . . . Forthright: she went down very well here! I remember when she presented a paper on her research to the RAI [Royal Anthropological Institute] in May 1952 old Edmund Leach, who was very hard to please, said:

"Good points and delivered with great charm." But in the U.S., she was too much of an individualist. No compromise. No political correctness.

In England she also established close professional friendships with male anthropologists, including Kenneth Little and Raymond Firth. Sir Raymond Firth explained to me in an interview in 1997 that the contrast between Ruth Landes's acceptance by colleagues in Britain and her censure by the American academy was because

at that time, Britain could handle high-mettled women like Ruth Landes better than America. At the LSE [London School of Economics] we always had women professors. We haven't had this diminution of women as in America. We had the sense that women anthropologists in the U.S. were not given as much credit as they might have been. American anthropology was very naive: it worked a lot in stereotypes . . . and Ruth Landes challenged those. . . . I was very fond of Margaret Mead, but it was unfortunate for women in the U.S. I think it would be fair to say that Margaret Mead may have been a difficult barrier for Ruth Landes because Ruth Landes was an individual — she wanted to be independent — and Margaret Mead required dependency, control. American anthropology works more on a model of mentor/dependent.

When the Fulbright fellowship ended, Landes was again unemployed.[1] Returning to New York in September 1952, she moved into the Hotel Paris at 96th Street West and Broadway ("at $148 per month for room, bath, kitchenette, terrace and swimming pool") and lived there for the next three years: "I have no luxury and 'love' at all — except my West End hotel flat on the 26th floor — and no job," she wrote in her diary (Notebook 7, RLP). During these years she taught part-time at the William Allanson White Psychiatric Institute, at the New School for Social Research, and at the University of Kansas (where she renewed her Potawatomi friendships). At the Hotel Paris "between library and swimming pool" she tried to make a go of it alone.

But on September 28, 1954, just days before her 46th birthday, she wrote in her diary: "I need a partner — there seems no one but ILL [Ignacio Lutero Lopez]. Now he also wants a companion, he says. This will be similar to a business deal, which neither of us will admit to the other. . . . If we marry, perhaps we can make something out of it, with caution" (Notebook 10, RLP). On November 1, 1955, she wrote in her diary: "I won't say I'm happy about the marriage I see ahead of me (I think) but I'll be glad to be settled in life emotionally and socially, and able to go ahead with my own writing" (Notebook 10, RLP). On April 2, 1956, Landes and Lopez married, and she moved into Lopez's home in Los Angeles. Little more than a year later, however, they separated, and she rented a small apartment near the University of Southern California where she was by then teaching in the School of Social Work. Landes spent the rest of her years in California living in a flat near the campus library and swimming pool until she moved to Canada in 1965.

In California Landes began a new phase of her career, one that excited her very much but that never yielded permanent employment: she developed a program at the Claremont Graduate School to teach social work and education students the importance of appreciating cross-cultural differences in values and family structure and relationships. This culminated in the publication of *Culture in American Education* (1965), of which Landes was extremely proud. In this book she describes the method of reflexivity that she taught her students in California and that she would bring with her to McMaster University, where she required students in her courses to undertake small, local, field research projects, each beginning with an autobiographical life history exercise. As she wrote to one friend, physical anthropologist Ruth Sawtell Wallis, after the publication of the book: "I think the turning of teachers (and other "service" professionals) to their own backgrounds . . . is absolutely vital to effective communication. I did not devise this for therapeutic purposes . . . but oddly it always had such consequence — not so odd since dignity went with it. It was a direct transfer from our habitual anthro. 'comparisons.' . . . You understand, I'm sure, that that's why I wrote my opening chapter about myself" (July 10, 1967, RLP, box 2).

When her contract position as director of the Claremont Anthropology and Education Program ended in 1962, Landes finished writing *Culture in American Education* and lived again on short-term teaching contracts: in 1963 she taught summer school at Columbia University, and in the summer of 1964 she taught at the University of Kansas. She was still without permanent employment when Margaret Mead wrote on February 2, 1965, to tell her that the

American Anthropological Association had started a job placement service and to suggest that Landes register her name: "There are jobs going everywhere, big, little and middle-sized. . . . Everyone who registered is getting showered with offers from the U.S. and Canada" (MMP, box C74). Landes registered with the AAA service.

McMaster University, Canada

In 1964 Richard Slobodin, a Columbia-trained anthropologist, had been hired in the Department of Sociology and Anthropology at McMaster University in Hamilton, Ontario, Canada, to help build up its nascent anthropology program, which, he said, the university "envisioned as a kind of native studies program."[2] The undergraduate program in sociology had started in 1955, and an M.A. in sociology had been offered since 1961. Slobodin learned through the AAA that Ruth Landes was looking for work. The possibility of hiring a senior scholar who had conducted fieldwork in Canada and whose intellectual lineage could be traced directly to Franz Boas and Ruth Benedict was attractive. The chair of the Sociology and Anthropology Department at McMaster, sociologist Frank Jones, contacted Ruth Landes's three references, Margaret Mead, Jules Henry, and Conrad Arensberg, and asked Landes to make arrangements to travel from California to Hamilton for an interview.

Margaret Mead sent this letter of reference to McMaster on April 2, 1965:

I am glad to write to you about Ruth Landes. I have known her since she was a young Ph.D. She worked with me when we were doing the Social Science Research Council study on Cooperation and Competition among Primitive Peoples, and I have been in intermittent touch with many phases of her later research and applied work. As you will know from her vitae, she has spent most of her life in a variety of inter-cultural projects, and less time in teaching. But she taught our Columbia University summer school a summer or so ago with great success, and arouses a great deal of enthusiasm in her students. She can bring to a new department what is so hard to find today, a sense of perspective and history, long experience, the standards of an earlier day, to combine with the innovations of younger members. I have had some experience recently in the problems of new departments who wish to expand their graduate offerings and they are very fortunate indeed if they can get someone as experienced as Dr. Landes. Her early fieldwork among the Ojibway gives her an entré into North American Indian materials, and her later work in Brazil, The United Kingdom, and the West Coast provide her with a wide perspective on modern anthropological problems.

Jules Henry, professor of anthropology and sociology at Washington University in St. Louis, wrote to Jones on March 31, 1965: "I consider her among the top people in the new field of cultural factors in education." And Conrad Arensberg, professor of anthropology at Columbia, wrote on March 25: "Dr. Ruth Landes . . . is a distinguished senior anthropologist, much published. . . . She is a specialist and authority on race relations in the United States, Great Britain and Brazil, in all three of which countries she has carried out anthropological and sociological research. . . . You can be assured that she is experienced in both graduate and undergraduate teaching, so much so that we brought her from the West Coast to summer school here at Columbia."

After negotiating to travel first-class rather than economy fare, Ruth Landes flew from California to Hamilton to be interviewed at McMaster University on April 1, 1965. She met with the president, the deans of arts and graduate studies, and department members the following day and then returned to California. Jones recalled that as part of the interview "my wife and I had a party. Ruth charmed all the movers and shakers."[3] On April 7, the university president wrote offering her an appointment as professor of anthropology at a salary of $15,000 and with moving expenses up to $500.

Landes "gladly" accepted the offer in a letter to Jones on April 11, and after negotiating an increase in the moving expense allowance to $1,000, she turned to the subject that was foremost on her mind: where to live and how to make a home on her own as a single, now mature, woman in a new city and country. She enlisted Jones's help not only to locate an apartment for her but also to assess the state of its carpets, wall paint, and window coverings: "I do have a dream of a flat already discovered by some one of you, to which I can direct the movers!" she wrote to him on April 11. "As you know, I would like a place within walking distance of the University and food shops. . . . If painting is to be done I like all-white or faintly eggshell white." She asked him for information about swimming pool hours, banks, public library. She confided: "I've just visited the storage vault where my furs have been in uninterrupted rest for 9 years. Remembering my natal eastern weather, I'm having them cleaned, remodelled, etc. at an estimated cost, so far, of over $350.00[.] It makes me feel quite bridal again!"[4] She was not marrying, but she was at the threshold of a new beginning. An accomplished anthropologist, she had finally obtained in midlife, what she earlier, in a letter to Ruth Benedict, called a "position" in the academy in anthropology — a world she had longed for all her life. The prospect was exciting, even romantic, making her look hopefully toward future years.

In this correspondence Landes initiated the relationship with the department that she would continue during her years at McMaster: she treated the department chair and administrative staff like a kind of family and expected them to serve some of the functions that family members, notably wives, provided male anthropologists. When preparing to return to Hamilton from summer research trips, she would contact the chair of the department and ask him to call the superintendent of her apartment building to ensure that the electricity and telephone would be connected on the day of her return. Once, when leaving for a research trip, she left her camera in the taxi she had taken to the airport; she called the chair of the department to track it down for her. When she broke her wrist one night falling over a bicycle rack on campus "that had been moved by vandals," she asked the chair to assign one of the department secretaries to help her finish typing a manuscript. Her requests of colleagues and staff for daily and domestic services created all of the ambivalences of family relationships.

Indeed, the period at McMaster is marked by contradictions and ambiguities. In a sense she now had no personal life — or at least no personal life separate from her professional life in anthropology. In a letter to Margaret Mead she would later describe her years in Canada as "curious — absolutely no personal aspects" (April 18, 1977, MMP, box D34). Anthropology was the sole context within which she now lived her life, all aspects of it. The years at McMaster were extremely productive, leading to numerous publications and recognition by peers. But Landes's initial enthusiasm for her first and only permanent appointment rapidly evaporated. She felt hemmed in and displaced in "drab" Canada. The prospect for stability resulted in her perennial restlessness. And she longed for her beloved America. She acutely experienced her life in Canada as a life in exile.

Frank Jones (with the help of his wife, Jean, and Richard Slobodin) did find an apartment for Ruth Landes in Camelot Towers at 981 Main Street, within walking distance of the university. She moved in during the first week of September 1965 and died in the same apartment 25 years later—the paint and window coverings untouched from when she moved in.

The tenure of Ruth Landes at McMaster receives mixed reviews from those who worked or studied with her. Landes was always engaged in research. She devoted long hours to her graduate students and imposed high standards of scholarship and expectations of originality. But she did not participate in the communal life of the department and remained uninvolved in its day-to-day operations. As Richard Slobodin observed: "At the age of 57 when most male academics are looking toward retirement, she was introduced to the world of tenured professor and university life—committees, etc. She never took to any of this."

Slobodin reflected that in her first years at the university Ruth Landes helped promote anthropology on campus: "No one at McMaster in the 1960s had the faintest idea what anthropology was about and that was one of our problems—one of our tasks was to establish that. On one occasion in the late 1960s, the then-Dean of Graduate Studies—a theoretical physicist—asked us to come over and talk about this. . . . Now he had evidently heard of Ruth, or somebody had apprised him, that she was somebody who had written books and so on. So you could see that he thought she was the one to talk to. . . . She certainly rose to the occasion. She told him about the four subdisciplines of anthropology and something of their relationship . . . and very, very well. And he was impressed."

Graduate students had many and varied responses to my questions about Ruth Landes. Many found her simply too harsh in her judgments and expectations and stayed away if they could. But for some she was inspirational.

Lynne Teskey-Denton, one of Ruth's favorite students, did remarkable doctoral research on a women's ascetic religion in India in the 1970s. In an interview on May 27, 1993, she remembered Ruth Landes as an inspirational "mentor": "I must frankly admit to you that my intellectual and emotional ties to Ruth Landes are strong and complex. She had a brilliant mind and powerful personality and would not countenance the separation of the two." Lynne recalled her first meeting with Landes in the classroom: "Hers was my 19th undergraduate course, the first taught by a woman. She gave an impassioned 20-minute introduction to anthropology. . . . A humanist, Ruth Landes represented the best of the anthropological tradition." Lynne also described Ruth's suffering from rheumatoid arthritis in her last years—and her loneliness. But, she said, Ruth maintained that "as to loneliness, it is the condition for all understanding."[5]

Another former student, sociologist Ellen Wall, saw Ruth almost daily during the last months of her life and regularly drove her on shopping errands and to the post office and bank. Ellen described Landes as "a daunting presence to be around. She drove herself relentlessly. She was a courageous and powerful intellect. The energy of the intellectual endeavor was an essential part of her passion to live life to the fullest." Ellen Wall remembered how Ruth, despite failing eyesight, continued to read incessantly and was reading Emma Goldman's *Living My Life* in the weeks prior to her death. She told Ellen that the world that Goldman described reminded her of her own childhood and family. Ellen remembered Ruth as "an exile of sorts." It was not only that she did not feel at home in Canada and felt herself to be exiled from her native America, Ellen said, but "she was never at home. She could never be at home anywhere so was in a form of exile. She would not allow herself to rest in comfort and so never settled and created a home."[6]

Whatever ambivalences she and others might have had, McMaster University provided Ruth Landes with the security and credibility to launch a new and final phase of her life and career. She immediately began two major initiatives: the first was to arrange funding to return to Brazil in the summer of 1966 to study "urbanization in an underdeveloped country." The second was finally to arrange publication of her three unpublished manuscripts from the 1930s as well as her M.A. thesis on the Harlem Jews.

When she arrived in Rio de Janeiro in May 1966, she was shocked by the changes: "This once gorgeous city is hellishly noisy, crowded, dirty, being rebuilt and torn down—it looks and sounds under blitz" she wrote to Frank Jones. "My strongest wish is to end this bloody enterprise and never see Latin America again." She stayed in Brazil until September, was often debilitated by the heat, and most of the time was ill with various flu-like symptoms and sinusitis. But there were also good tidings that summer. Ruth Landes met Edison Carneiro for the first time since 1939. In 1962 he had been appointed the first director of the Ministry of Education and Culture's new Special National Agency for the Protection of Folklore. One of the first projects he had undertaken was to commission a Portuguese translation of *The City of Women*. Landes devoted part of the time during her stay in Rio to reviewing the translation, and after she returned to Canada, Carneiro personally and painstakingly corrected the Portuguese translation—"a Herculean task," he wrote to Landes on December 22, 1966 (RLP, box 4). The book was published as *A cidade das mulheres* in Rio de Janeiro in August 1967, 20 years after its publication in English in the United States and almost 30 years after she had conducted the research. Landes wrote to her old friend Maria Julia Pourchet, a Rio anthropologist, on October 1, 1967: "With his faultless translation, our epoch of international, ethnological and humane friendship is extended a little longer. I very much wish that the spirit of our group, identified by specific names, will survive" (RLP, box 2).

When she was in Brazil that summer, both the University of Toronto and University of Wisconsin Presses offered contracts to publish her manuscript *Ojibwa Religion and the Midéwiwin*, based on the 1932–33 collaborations with Maggie Wilson and Will Rogers. "Now I am back in Indian country where Indian materials seem to be of both ethnological and civil rights interest," she had written prospective publishers that spring. Living in Ontario, she began to appreciate the intense and growing political issues of aboriginal self-determination and land claims in Canada. In September she accepted a contract from the University of Wisconsin Press to publish not only the Ojibwa manuscript but also *The Mystic Lake Sioux* and *The Prairie Potawatomi*.

Landes fearlessly undertook the necessary revisions of the three manuscripts. In a letter to anthropologist Fred Eggan on April 20, 1967, she described the experience of revisiting this old work: "It is a pleasure (though pressure-making!) to prepare finally these mss. that date from the start of my adult self. It's almost like a fairy tale, though then I thought it was drudgery. Real drudgery now is university business, at least up in (dreary) Canada. . . . I finished the Ojibwa Midéwiwin and Religion ms., as I may have told you, and after I finish [the Mystic Lake Sioux ms.], there will be the very lengthy Potawatomi taking certainly another year. This will not exhaust my unpublished book-length mss. but it will dispose of my 1930s self. How odd" (RLP, box 2). And to Ruth Sawtell Wallis she wrote on July 10, 1967: "I manage to harass myself with many pressures, like getting through these 3 books (I'm starting on the 3d now, and it's the biggest undertaking) so I can start to live again — elsewhere I hope" (RLP, box 2).

Once these three books were published, in 1970 she initiated a decade of research on comparative state bilingualism funded by the Canada Council that would take her to South Africa, Louisiana, New Mexico, Spain, Switzerland, and Quebec. Based on this research, she would complete a book manuscript entitled "Tongues That Defy the State."

Landes was forced, against her will, to retire in 1973 when she reached 65, the age of mandatory retirement by Ontario law. She continued teaching part-time until 1977, the maximum post-retirement teaching allowed at McMaster. She then reluctantly became professor emerita. When, in the spring of 1978, Richard Preston, then chair of the department, asked her to give up her office to make room for a new incoming full-time faculty member, she was both outraged and distraught and wrote back to him: "Am I to be dispossessed? I had always understood that I would have an office for the duration of my stay!" Not concerned with the allocation of space in the department — as was Preston — she was, rather, preoccupied again with the problem of "home": where was she to live out her retirement and how would she pack up her things and move? And, more immediately, how would she finish her manuscript on the bilingualism research if she was disrupted from her office and her routine? Preston then arranged for office space that she could share until she finished her book.

On November 16, 1978, the day after she received the news of Margaret Mead's death, Landes wrote to friend and Ojibwa scholar Keewaydinokwe Peschel that the news had "crushed" her: "[Margaret] had so much vitality, such a zest for combat, that she made Anthropology seem important! Her zest will survive longer than her ideas" (RLP, box 2). She then went on to describe her own retirement: "I stay on . . . unpaid, in order to clear up the remains of the past 12 years, and to do some emending on my latest ms. to be a book. They give me a shifting office and everyone likes me because I am no longer a threat. . . . McMaster hung my photo on the Library wall as a 'distinguished professor' (There were 15, of whom just 2 were women. How is that possible?). On Jan. 2d I go to Florida State Univ., Anthro Dept, for their Winter quarter; it's Tallahassee. I return here in March and prepare to leave for good by the end of August probably to Tallahassee. It's likely to be a dull place but I want the U.S. and warmth and at the moment see nothing else."

Landes did not, however, move to Florida. Over the next few years she continued to try to establish research affiliations with several different universities in hopes of finally retiring to the United States. But she could never make arrangements that completely met her needs and desires, and so she stayed on in Hamilton. She revised her manuscript "Tongues That Defy the State" and tried to find a publisher for it until she wrote, discouraged, to Thomas Vennum on October 10, 1985: "Nobody wants my long, scholarly book ms. on Tongues that Defy the State (bilingualism, culture, politics). They won't even agree to read it, saying it won't 'sell'. I'm sure the fault is Canada's drabness (as I know after 20 years here). I'm still hoping to repatriate" (RLP, box 3). In 1989 Landes applied for her last research grant from McMaster. She received $2,120 to assist her in preparing a final version of her autobiographical memoir based on her year at Fisk University. This, too, would not find a publisher. During this time, she also reread and annotated all her unpublished professional papers and correspondence and made arrangements for their eventual deposition in the National Anthropological Archives at the Smithsonian Institution.

In 1978 the University of Wisconsin–Green Bay gave Ruth Landes a Faculty Award of Merit, and in 1985 the AAA acknowledged Landes for her pioneering contributions in two fields of research: gender and race. First, at a reception hosted by the AAA Committee on the Status of Women in Anthropology, she was honored for her early ethnographies of women. Then, at an invited session entitled "Anthropological Study of the United States," sponsored by the AAA Program Committee, Landes and fifteen others who had contributed to a special 1955 issue of *American Anthropologist*, "The USA as Anthropologists See It," were recognized as pioneers in anthropological research "at home" in the United States. Landes's contribution to that 1955 volume was an article titled "Biracialism in American Society: A Comparative View."

After becoming established at McMaster University, Landes had published a reflective essay on her professional experience in Brazil in 1938–39, the now-much-cited "A Woman Anthropologist in Brazil" (1970b). As a result, she was often asked to give public lectures on her experiences as a woman in anthropology. In 1980, in a lecture to the Department of Anthropology at the University of Calgary titled "Women in Anthropology," she took the opportunity to say: "I hardly think it an accident that only I have ever described the Brazilian priestesses. Or for that matter, the Ojibwa women of Ontario's Rainy River. Male and female scholars preceded me and followed me in both places for decades. Neither set of women, Indian and Brazilian Black, gained me straight professional attention. In the last few years *The Ojibwa Woman* has been manhandled in our leading anthropological publications to the effect that I had followed some bias, either in selecting the women or in giving a warped picture. That is, my personality was focussed on, not theirs. As Boas had written decades before, in 1936, about a critique of Kroeber's: 'It was interesting to me to read . . . [the] analysis not only of my scientific work but also of my personality. . . . I wish to express my complete disagreement with his interpretation' (*American Anthropologist*, vol. 38, no. 1, p. 137). Boas's words and mine. But Boas was the world authority whom younger men hoped to dethrone, whereas I was the presuming woman" (1980). She went on to remind her audience: "Keep in mind that our women anthropologists are often depreciated as being emotionally prejudiced. It means they are not scientific; or intellectually as powerful as men; or even reliable. I was told this by no less an authority than Linton. Boas was dead" (1980).

On February 11, 1991, in the depths of the Canadian winter that she found so harsh, Ruth Landes died at the age of 82. She was frail and unable to go out in the cold and snow to walk to the campus to pick up her mail and enjoy a swim and sauna as she had almost every day since her move to Hamilton some 25 years before. But she was clear of mind and spirit and still at work revising her Fisk memoir.[7]

Ruth Landes and American Anthropology

Ruth Landes made little impact on the discipline during her lifetime. She was rarely cited, and because, as Margaret Mead observed, Landes did not hold a permanent teaching position, she did not train a cadre of graduate students to advance her vision of anthropology. Her major works—*The Ojibwa Woman* and *The City of Women*—were published to negative critical acclaim and were soon out-of-print. The extraordinary attacks of her critics, however, now direct our attention to the innovations she was making and to the raw nerves she was touching in the discipline. The negative criticism of her work acts as "a kind of radar that picks up the ping of the work's originality. The 'mistakes' and 'excesses' that early critics complain of are often precisely the innovations that have given the work its power" (Malcolm 2001:16)—and our current appreciation of its value.

In this book I have reviewed the ethnography of Ruth Landes and reconstructed the processes by which her work was marginalized and her career controlled. The book is a case study in the history of disciplinary professionalization. It reveals the erasure of early work on race and gender, the rejection of experimentation in fieldwork, and the silencing of personal experience in ethnographic writing. But more positively it also reveals continuity and the enduring interests that motivate the discipline itself. For the irony is that Ruth Landes's work has stood the test of time. The reasons she was chastised and her work denounced are the very reasons we have for reconsidering it today. A careful rereading of her work now places her at the very heart of anthropology, working with issues that define the most important debates in our discipline at the dawn of the 21st century. Landes's major concerns and contributions can now be easily recognized: her theory of culture, inclusive of gender, race, sexuality, and class; her concern for writing; and her belief in fieldwork.

Landes understood culture as a dynamic and contested process. While Margaret Mead generalized the "ethos" of a harmonious cultural whole, Edward Sapir theorized "genuine culture," Ruth Benedict identified "patterns," and Melville Herskovits looked for "survivals," Landes asked questions about internal diversity — especially about diversity based on social positions determined by race, class, gender, and sexuality. She derived insights from her own life experiences of acculturation, gender norms, and marginality that led her to recognize internal differences within cultural groups at a time when the convention in the discipline was to discover and report hegemonic cultural wholes or patterns. Ruth Landes rejected prevailing dogma and orthodoxy. She understood that her job as an anthropologist was not simply to record the dominant norms and prescriptions of a culture but to record the ways that particular individuals and groups of individuals make their lives meaningful in spite of divergent norms and prescriptions. Her focus on differentiation, and her delight in the contradictions she observed in the dynamics of culture, frustrated many of her contemporaries. However, Ruth Landes's perspective and focus clearly anticipated late-20th-century theorizing on the concept of culture in anthropology.

Ruth Landes's innovations in ethnographic writing were also prescient. From her very first fieldwork with Maggie Wilson she attempted to establish democratic relationships in the field and to reveal in her writing that the knowledge she obtained was neither objective nor subjective but the product of an intersubjective research process dependent upon the respective relationships with her informants and on the "situated position" of those informants. In her books and articles she sought to represent this process, her role in it, and the diverse roles of particular informants. She experimented with multivocality and self-reflexivity in her writing, peopling her books with lively descriptions of real individuals and personalities, informing the reader about her own empathies and crises of identity. *The Ojibwa Woman* was her first experiment. Relying largely on the voice and expertise of Maggie Wilson, Landes recorded testimonies of the subaltern experience of dozens of women whose lives challenged and creatively reinterpreted dominant norms and constraints. The analysis in *Ojibwa Religion and the Midé-wiwin* revolves around a moving description of her relationship with the elderly shaman Will Rogers and the context within which they had worked together. *The Mystic Lake Sioux* mixes conventional third-person narrative with personal anecdotes and reflections. In *The Prairie Potawatomi* Landes began to experiment with the approach she would fully develop in *The City of Women:* she organizes her narrative around several main characters ("informants") who are situated in the local social scene in terms of age, gender, class, religion, and color and whose words and experiences illustrate the different local interpretations of cultural practices and behavior. In *The City of Women,* she is most radical in motivating the narrative through her own experience and reflections on those experiences as she engages in social discourse with a series of individuals in Brazil. To utilize her anthropological training she used not only reason but also empathy and intuition to guide her thinking and understanding. As a result, far from treating research subjects as "museum specimens," the ethnography is filled with the sense of the "dense, teaming vitality" of a living culture (Bastide 1978:221).

Landes's ethnographic experiments with dialogue, multivocality, and reflexivity went against the tide of professionalization in American anthropology in the interwar years and the decade following the Second World War. Then, the discipline was seeking to establish its legitimacy in the academy, and one of its key strategies was the production of scientific monographs. Professional ethnography became associated with a style of scientific report writing that relied on an absent omniscient narrator using a distanced third-person voice to create the illusion of objectivity and scientific authority. Historians of anthropology now recognize that the emergence of scientific ethnography was not inevitable or natural but was the product of the hegemonic processes of canon making by influential individuals and powerful institutions. Marginalized in her day, Ruth Landes's ethnography can now be read as anticipating postmodernist and feminist critiques. Reconsidering Landes's work from such a perspective places her squarely in the center of the discipline, traces the lineage for late-20th-century experiments in ethnographic writing, and reminds us of the enduring concerns in the discipline.

Finally, rereading Ruth Landes's work, we are reminded that the integrity of the discipline depends on fieldwork. In her writing Landes is transparent about her field methods and relationships. Her approach is rooted in two principles: the value she gives to the personal friendships and relationships she establishes and the value she gives to her own experience in the field as a source of knowledge.

Landes rejected the cliché that fieldwork is an initiation rite for the novice scholar after which she or he becomes an anthropologist. "Fieldwork," she said, "is the lifeway of [the] anthropologist. It means attempting to enter the lives of those being observed, in order to sense how things look to *them*, as well as to me. The 'field' teaches the researcher" (1973:44). For Landes, fieldwork is the process through which anthropological knowledge is built. There can be no knowledge without it — for either novice or established practitioner.

She also rejected the notions of the "neutral observer" and "participant observation": "Has any seasoned field worker kidded himself about these? It takes little to learn that informants and others of the field-community assign the outside observer-visitor to this, that, and others of *their* factions . . . wielding power on [the] spot" (1973:44). She maintained that "through field work at the pleasure of the host culture one learns one's place there and that is one's only vantage point for penetrating the culture" (1970b:138).

"Participant observation," Landes said, was a phrase coined by sociology, but the method of anthropological fieldwork is far more sensual and the goal no less than human understanding. Landes believed that "special temperament moves an anthropologist into fieldwork" (1973:45) and that "the methods of an effective field worker are rooted in his personality" (1970b:122).

Landes also firmly believed that "highly practical results" can come from the new perspectives that field studies can generate (1973:45). Landes's first commitment was not to the ivory tower but to the real world of mixing, contradiction, and conflict, a world that she knew could be bettered only through increased human understanding. The first step to understanding cultural differences was knowledge obtained through firsthand experience. Landes's appreciation for cultural difference was based on her own experience and not in a simplistic code of cultural relativism. She thus did not depend upon a notion of culture as a harmonious, integrated whole. Rather, she acknowledged, even celebrated, the internal struggles and conflicting local interpretations of cultural meanings because she knew these contests were giving voice to marginal and subordinate social categories, to experiences with which she herself identified.

Landes advocated fieldwork as a source of self-knowledge. As she wrote in 1970, in the field "one's concept of self disintegrates because the accustomed responses have disappeared" (1970a:123). "Field work permits one to live further, beyond the ordered arrangements of one's origins, in a personality and a society with other borders. Briefly one lives two or three additional lives . . . the addicted fieldworker does not really care for ease any more than does the competitive athlete. The lure of another culture can never be discounted for it is the lure of self, dressed otherwise. Moving among the world's peoples, one sees that personalities here may resemble personalities there, underneath and despite the culture differences. So one comes home, again and again, to friends and kinsmen" (138). "The stance of field work" became for Landes "a private philosophy of living" (138). "Most jobs," she said "are paths to comfortable ends. But the solitary field work, whatever the eventual byproducts in books and academic promotions, remains unique, stirring the researcher's optimum sense of himself as he tests himself continually against environing strangeness" (123). "What counts in the field and after is that one glimpses, over and over, humanity creating" (138).

A nomad and a pilgrim, Ruth Landes, unlike the biblical Ruth, remained on the outside of the discipline, always gleaning in the fields of Boas. She found eventual stability in Canada, but far from the heartland of her anthropological apprenticeship under Boas and Benedict, she did not find a home.

Landes pioneered research on the intersections of gender, race, and class. She pointed the discipline toward reflexivity about fieldwork, the very process of the construction of anthropological knowledge. Her ethnographies document the adaptive strategies and cultural creativity of marginalized groups—women, African Americans, Native Americans, Afro-Brazilians—with whom she identified. Her interests, neglected in her day, are now legitimate fields of study, central to the discipline in the 21st century. In acknowledgment of this, second editions of *The City of Women* were published in English in 1994 and in Portuguese in Brazil as *A cidade das mulheres* in 2002. The third edition of *The Ojibwa Woman* was published in 1997. The questions Ruth Landes asked about the cultural integration of diversity remain, however, as urgent for anthropology now as they were then. There is much unfinished work to do.

Notes

INTRODUCTION

1. See also Alice Echols's *Scars of Sweet Paradise: The Life and Times of Janis Joplin*, a powerful study of how these contradictions played out in the tragic life of the rock singer who died of a heroin overdose in 1970 at the age of 27. A bright and creative adolescent, Joplin desperately sought to break out from the constraining femininity of 1950s America in order to live her own life. But she also longed to belong and wanted the eventual security of marriage and family, what she called "that white picket fence" (1999:86–87). Joplin's radical "bad girl" individuality so challenged not only conventional gender codes but also the "earth mother" ideal for women in the 1960s counterculture that she was left alone and isolated.

2. Richard Slobodin at the memorial service for Ruth Landes, McMaster University, April 25, 1991.

CHAPTER 1

1. This story is told in a short, undated, autobiographical memoir entitled "An American Education" (RLP, box 12). Other "Ruths" who studied anthropology with Boas included Ruth Benedict, Ruth Bunzel, and Ruth Underhill. I have been unable to identify who the other "Ruths" might be that Landes refers to here.

2. In her memoir *Notes from an Undirected Life*, Esther Schiff Goldfrank, Boas's secretary, reports that she gave him this nickname during the summer she accompanied him to Laguna Pueblo for a few weeks of fieldwork in 1920 (1978:39). It stuck, and many of his female students called him "Papa Franz" thereafter.

3. Bundism grew out of the Jewish labor movement in Russia and Poland during the 1870s and 1880s. In addition to being a movement of radical intellectuals based in Marxist ideology, Bundism was associated with devotion to Yiddish and to secular Jewish nationalism within Eastern Europe and was sharply opposed to Zionism and other conceptions of a global Jewish identity. The Bund (General Jewish Workers' Union in Lithuania, Poland, and Russia) was the Jewish socialist party officially

founded at a secret convention held in Vilna in October 1897 (*Encyclopedia Judaica*, 4:1497–1507).

4. "Bessie" and "Matthias" are Americanized names.

5. See the obituary for Joseph Schlossberg in the *New York Times*, January 16, 1971. See also the entry for him in *Encyclopedia Judaica*, 14:978.

6. David Ben-Gurion (1886–1973) was the first prime minister and defense minister of Israel (1948–53, 1955–63). Born in Plonsk, Poland, in 1886, he moved to Palestine in 1906 and for the next three decades headed the political mobilization to establish a Jewish socialist society in Palestine. Joseph Schlossberg met Ben-Gurion when he came to New York in 1915 to recruit young volunteers to settle in Palestine.

7. In a letter dated December 4, 1958, Anna informed Ruth that she "would not get a red cent of the inheritance due you when we depart" because Anna and Joe so strongly disapproved of her second marriage to Los Angeles journalist Ignacio Lopez. Concluding the list of everything she found wrong with Ruth's marriage choice, Anna wrote "The man . . . never contributed towards your support, why then must you continue your relationship with him[?] . . . How can a self-respecting person endure such a relationship[?] . . . In what way does such a married status enhance your prestige?" (RISM, n.d.).

8. In an undated letter Ruth's maternal cousin, Eleanor Sachs, wrote to Ruth: "From what I know she [Anna] was not a demonstrative mother and somehow caused the strange deficiency in your relationship" (RISM). This portrait of the Schlossberg marriage and family life is my interpretation based on my reading of Ruth's correspondence and diaries and on my discussions with Ruth's paternal cousin, Emily Sosnow.

9. Typical is a letter dated August 1959, in which Anna wrote to Ruth: "We are happy with your professional progress and hope that things will crystallize in the near future" (RISM).

CHAPTER 2

1. Historian Carroll Smith-Rosenberg makes a distinction between the New Women who emerged from Victorian society at the end of the 19th century and who organized for collective political and economic rights for women and the modern young women of the 1920s and 1930s who focused on individual self-realization and sexual expression. See also Barbara Caine (1997:134–147). Smith-Rosenberg described the first generation of New Women as

a cohort of middle and upper middle-class American women born between the late 1850s and the early 1900s, who were educated, ambitious, and most frequently, single. . . . Edu-

cation constituted their most salient characteristic and their first self-conscious demand. They linked college education to intellectual self-fulfillment, to autonomous roles outside the family, to glorious achievements. Graduating from college, the New Women more frequently than not refused to return to their mothers' worlds of reproduction and domesticity. Rather, boldly asserting their right to a public voice and visible power, they had laid claim to rights and privileges customarily accorded only to middle-class men. They moved into the public sphere, not as religious, reforming matrons but as independent women trained in the new professions. As lawyers, doctors, writers, or social reformers, they created new roles for themselves as experts in urban problems, as political lobbyists, union organizers, publishers, and creative artists. In radical flight from the patriarchal home and heterosexual marriage, they created a variety of alternative female institutions. Living with (frequently espousing love for) other women within the separatist environment of women's colleges, settlement houses, and reform organizations, dedicating their lives to securing social justice for middle-class and working-class women, the New Woman amassed greater political power and visibility than any other group of women in American experience. (1989:109)

2. Debates about the New Woman also reflected the emphasis on sexuality and sexual relations that accompanied the emergence of sexology and psychoanalysis. Havelock Ellis, in particular, argued that sexuality was the core of personal identity and that women's sexuality needed to be acknowledged. Feminist historians are divided in their interpretations of the impact of sexology. Some argue that it undermined feminism by making both celibacy and the female friendships that were so common among pre–World War I feminists seem abnormal, deviant, and perverse. Others point to the positive effect that accompanied a recognition of women's sexuality and that allowed it to be acknowledged in more open ways.

3. The lesbian relationship of Ruth Benedict and Margaret Mead, for example, although not public at the time, can be understood in this context (Bateson 1984; Lapsley 1999).

4. See Ryan 1983; Todd 1993; Ware 1993. Historians continue to debate the place of the 1920s in the history of feminism (see Freedman 1983; Caine 1997; Cott 1987; Scharf and Jenson 1983). There was tremendous diversity of opinion, and no unifying issue such as suffrage had provided earlier feminists. Women were divided: professional middle-class mothers were separated from working-class mothers; mothers were separated from single women; and ethnic and racial differences among women became increasingly visible due to high rates of immigration in the early decades of the century and to the migration of hundreds of thousands of African Americans from the southern states and the Caribbean. Cott writes:

Literally millions of women were organized into groups, competing with and opposing one another rather than gathering into one denomination. Advocates of sex-based legislation combatted equal rights amendment supporters. Women lined up on the political spectrum from left to right. Women were pro- and anti-Prohibitionists. Women professionals differentiated themselves from women volunteers and clients. Women had different ideological predispositions on questions of marriage and employment tangled up with their education and wealth, their class and race and ethnicity. . . . For decades after the 1920s, decentralization and diversification, competition and even sectarianism were the hallmarks of efforts to define women's interests and work toward parity between the sexes. The problems and promises made visible between 1910 and 1930 — persistent structures and ideologies of male dominance, women's assertions of their heterogeneous and conflicting interests — reverberated through the twentieth century. (1987:277, 282)

5. During the summer of 1933 when Ruth Landes was in the field in Minnesota, Ruth Benedict sent her article "Negro Jews in Harlem," based on Landes's master's thesis research, to *Social Forces* and *American Journal of Sociology*. Both turned it down. At Boas's suggestion Landes later sent a revised version to a German sociology journal; the manuscript was lost when the journal along with others was shut down as part of a prewar Nazi purge of libraries and publishing houses (Landes 1965:2–3). She later reconstructed a summary of her findings that was published as "Negro Jews of Harlem" in the *Jewish Journal of Sociology* (1967b).

6. Marcus Garvey started the Universal Negro Improvement Association (UNIA) in his native Jamaica in 1914. In 1916 he immigrated to the United States to organize a New York chapter. Unlike the intellectuals of the Harlem Renaissance and organizations such as the National Association for the Advancement of Colored People (NAACP) headed by W. E. B. DuBois, who appealed to the sympathies of liberal white society, Garvey taught that racial prejudice was endemic in American society and that the only future lay in emancipation through a return to Africa. He taught that Africans had a noble past, and he created a formal organization called the Empire of Africa, appointing himself as president and declaring others as deputies, knights, and dukes. His appeal to racial pride rapidly found him a huge following among the poorer classes and the recent rural migrants struggling in hostile northern cities. By some estimates the UNIA had more than half a million followers by 1923 when he went on trial for fraud. Garvey was pardoned and deported as an undesirable alien in 1927. He died in London in 1940 (Franklin 1974:365–366; Johnson 1968:251–259).

George Baker, or Father Divine, started a small group in Sayville, New York, in 1919, and by the 1930s he had an enormous following and was holding open house and feeding thousands in places that came to be known as "heavens" throughout the eastern and Midwestern states. The movement also attracted a large number of white followers, some of whom were wealthy (Franklin 1974:367).

The Beth B'nai Abraham black synagogue, like Garvey's UNIA, was a nationalist movement that organized the illiterate poor and recent migrants and rejected the social movements led by black intellectuals such as W. E. B. DuBois and the writers and artists of the Harlem Renaissance. For their part, black intellectuals denounced the religions as spurious and their leaders as charlatans and opportunists (Franklin 1974:365; Landes 1967b:175; Johnson 1968).

7. Sociologist Howard Brotz, who studied Black Jews in Harlem in the early 1960s, traces the movement to the African American leader Booker T. Washington, who, Brotz says, had provided a stimulus to this way of thinking around the beginning of the 20th century when he called attention to the Jews as a model for success that African Americans could emulate and pointed to Jews' pride in their history as a key to their success (Brotz 1964:8; see also Landes 1967b).

8. Howard Brotz in his doctoral research on another Black Jewish sect in Harlem, the Commandment Keepers Congregation of the Living God, speculated that Ford did not immigrate to Africa because funding during the depression would have made the costs prohibitive. He suggests instead that Ford moved to Detroit, where he became a Muslim, changed his name to Farrad, and founded an Islamic congregation (1964:12). The idea that African American slaves were Hebrews—the lost sheep of the Biblical House of Israel—continued to be a theme for black preachers, and throughout the 1920s and 1930s small Black Jewish sects appeared in Philadelphia, Washington, and New York as well as in smaller eastern cities. With the disappearance of Ford, the Commandment Keepers Congregation in Harlem (also known as the Royal Order of Ethiopian Hebrews), with a following of about one thousand (of whom almost 70 percent were women), became the largest Black Jewish congregation under its leader, Wentworth A. Matthew (see Brotz 1964).

9. In anthropology, the classic revitalization movements are the late-19th-century Melanesian "cargo cults" that arose in response to European colonial domination and whose religious belief system focused on the acquisition of material goods ("cargo") through ritual means. The Native American Ghost Dance and Peyote religions are other revitalization movements associated with experiences of colonialism and social and economic deprivation and marginalization. These politico-religious movements are creative efforts of subordinate groups to imagine a

brighter future and re-establish control over their lives. See Hobsbawm 1959; Wallace 1956; Worsley 1968; Wilson 1973.

10. Landes wrote several versions of this fictionalized autobiographical memoir, the first in the 1950s. She revised the manuscript again in the 1980s but never found a publisher. The version quoted here was titled "Now at Athens." Earlier titles were "Color Cancer" and "A Chronicle of Bloods." All versions are deposited in the Ruth Landes Papers at the National Anthropological Archives. The memoir was inspired by the year 1937–38 when she taught at Fisk University.

11. They were not officially divorced until the fall of 1935.

CHAPTER 3

1. Mead wrote, "in Boas's eye [Ruth Benedict] was a wife, amply supported and with obligations of a wife . . . someone . . . for whom he need not be responsible" (1959:343). Esther Goldfrank, at one time Boas's secretary and later his student, also recorded his views (widely held in American society at the time) that married women were financially protected by husbands: "To judge from my relations with him and his with [Erna] Gunther, [Gladys] Reichard, [Ruth] Benedict, [Ruth] Bunzel, and [Margaret] Mead as well, he clearly put no roadblocks in the path of a woman student because she was a woman, but he believed marriage and a family came first in a woman's life; and however promising a woman student might be, he never encouraged her to limit or forsake familial duties in order to further her academic career" (1978:93).

2. These students included Alfred Kroeber, Ph.D. in 1901; Robert Lowie in Ph.D. in 1907; Edward Sapir, Ph.D. in 1907; Alexander Goldenweiser, Ph.D. in 1910; Paul Radin, Ph.D. in 1911; Melville Herskovits, Ph.D. in 1923. The teaching and legacy of Franz Boas is a huge topic impossible to treat adequately here. According to historian of anthropology Regna Darnell: "The central historiographic question in twentieth century North American anthropology has been the formidable presence of Franz Boas at center stage" (2001:33).

3. Boas officially remained department chair until Ralph Linton was brought in from Wisconsin in 1937 to succeed him. According to Robert McMillan (1986), Linton was chosen over Ruth Benedict or other possible successors because the administration "did not want a Jew or a woman."

4. Regna Darnell has described William Hallowell's 1926 University of Pennsylvania Ph.D. thesis, "Bear Ceremonialism in the Northern Hemisphere," as making a transition between trait distribution and culture pattern/psychological integration studies. Darnell calls his thesis "the last

of the major distributional studies . . . [and] a precursor of the future in which cultural integration . . . would be the major theme" (1977:14).

5. The anthropology department was in the Faculty of Philosophy; sociology was administered in the Faculty of Political Science. This was unlike the University of Chicago where, until 1929, anthropology had been part of the sociology department and where, after their separation, the two disciplines maintained close intellectual ties through the work of anthropologists such as Robert Redfield and Lloyd Warner. Historian of anthropology Robert McMillan attributes the antipathy between sociology and anthropology at Columbia to Franklin H. Giddings, who headed the Department of Sociology for more than three decades at the beginning of the 20th century. According to McMillan, Giddings blocked anthropology from finding a place in the Faculty of Political Science; he objected to Franz Boas as a Jew and described anthropology as "either a natural science having no proper place in a school of Political Science, or an amateurish sociology we could not afford to recognize" (quoted in McMillan 1986).

6. During the 1930s six major schools produced 111 Ph.D.'s in the four subfields of anthropology: Harvard, 25 doctorates; Columbia, 22; Chicago, 19; Berkeley, 19; Yale, 15;, and Pennsylvania, 11. In addition, one or two Ph.D.'s each were also awarded at Wisconsin, Michigan, Duke, and Northwestern during this decade. In the years 1930–40 all of the degrees awarded at Harvard and Yale and all but one degree at Chicago were granted to men. At Columbia, 50 percent of doctorates (11 of 22) were awarded to women. The University of California at Berkeley (under Boas's former students Alfred Kroeber and Robert Lowie) was also active in the training of women anthropologists at the time: 40 percent of its doctorates (8 of 19) were awarded to women. The majority of Harvard's degrees were in the fields of archaeology and physical anthropology. Adjusting the figures to record only those Ph.D.'s in ethnology or cultural anthropology gives the following results: Berkeley, 17; Columbia, 14; Chicago, 13; Harvard, 11; Yale, 9; Pennsylvania, 8. By the end of the 1930s there were more than 20 separate departments of anthropology and another dozen or so combined departments of sociology and anthropology; the number of professional and amateur ethnologists in the United States numbered about 300 in 1940 (Frantz 1985). Between 1921 and 1940, a total of 19 women and 20 men received Ph.D.'s in anthropology at Columbia University. Not until the 1980s would women again begin to enter the discipline in such proportionate numbers. The history of women in 20th-century anthropology parallels that of women in other disciplines: their numbers reached a peak in 1930 when 15.8 percent of full professors in social science

departments at American universities were women and plummeted to an all-time low in 1960, when only 3 percent of full social science professors were women (Parezo 1993; Rossiter 1982).

7. Although it is true that in the 1930s equal numbers of women and men were trained at Columbia, few of these women secured permanent employment in anthropology after receiving their Ph.D.'s. Parezo agrees with Aisenberg and Harrington that "for the academic profession there is such a thing as *women's* experience" (1988:xii). Parezo points to the barriers to women and the accommodation strategies women have adopted in order to find intellectual and social spaces within the discipline. Women's experience, she says, is the experience of devising gender-specific strategies to overcome barriers. Barriers have included higher IQ requirements for women for acceptance into some universities; perpetual employment in untenured, contractual positions and at non-elite institutions; required reliance upon a male patron; repeated employment as field and lab assistants without advancement to the status of co-researcher; and less-frequent citation of women's scholarship — citation being critical to the establishment of scholarly careers and reputations (see also Lutz 1995). Furthermore, Parezo notes, "rarely were professional women able to organize groups of like-minded women. To succeed, women had to align themselves with men, especially those in positions of power. . . . The lack of support networks . . . was a common theme for all women. It required that women strive for self-sufficiency" (1993:342).

8. This was not the case in psychology, however, where male scholars such as Erik Erikson (1950) and Abram Kardiner (1939) used cross-cultural anthropological data to build on Freudian theory, taking into consideration a much broader spectrum of conditioning factors than Freud had envisioned, including the effects of cultural variables. They explored cultural diversity in such early childhood experiences as toilet training, nursing, weaning, sibling rivalry, and sexual play and the implications for the formation of adult personality in a given society. They worked with anthropologists and supported the development of culture-and-personality studies in the discipline in the 1930s, notably by Mead and Benedict. In 1936 Abram Kardiner, a practicing analyst, organized a seminar at the New York Psychoanalytic Institute in which Edward Sapir, Ruth Benedict, and Ruth Bunzel participated. In 1937 the seminar moved to Columbia University, where Ralph Linton (then head of the department) and Cora DuBois joined the discussions. DuBois, who had received a Ph.D. in 1932 under the supervision of Alfred Kroeber and Robert Lowie at the University of California at Berkeley, undertook two years of psychocultural research in Indonesia at Kardiner's suggestion and as a National Re-

search Council postdoctoral fellow. She published the results in 1944 in *The People of Alor: A Social Psychological Study of an East-Indian Island*. Ruth Landes attended the seminar on several occasions but in letters to Benedict expressed skepticism about the speculative method and results of Kardiner's psychocultural analysis (see their fall 1939 correspondence, RFBP).

9. Not all students shared Ruth Landes's enthusiasm for Benedict. Henry Elkin, who began graduate study in anthropology in 1935, remembers with irritation what he described as Benedict's "blank stare" signifying deafness and her "seraphically sweet and condescending loving smile" that she bestowed on the circle of students who surrounded her, whom Elkin describes as "her favorites" (quoted in McMillan 1986:75). For many, her lectures were tests of endurance. Landes recognized that Benedict "had the reputation for being a miserable lecturer . . . whomever you talk to will tell you that. . . . It was like being in a furnace when you were working the bellows because she would . . . stammer and stutter and repeat herself and go back and forth. . . . If you were absorbed in her as I was, it was this mind at work . . . I was absolutely mesmerized" (quoted in McMillan 1986:198). Another student, Irving Goldman, contrasted Benedict's lectures with Boas's. Where the latter based his lectures on library research, Ruth Benedict "offered her own point of view: We need to penetrate these societies — discover patterns." Describing her lectures as "repetitive, ruminative," Goldman remarked, "I happen to like that. . . . I particularly enjoyed in her . . . a certain hesitancy . . . uncertainty . . . she was thinking . . . she was an honest woman" (quoted in McMillan 1986:203; see also Barnouw 1980:506). Sidney Mintz (1981:156) unequivocally states: "I decided to become an anthropologist because I heard Ruth Benedict give a lecture."

10. Like Boas, Benedict critiqued the ethnocentrism by which Americans used their own society as a measure or standard evaluating other cultures and peoples. She pointed out that it was only because of "fortuitous historical circumstances" that Western society had "standardized itself over most of the globe" and "protected us as man has never been protected before from having to take seriously the civilizations of other peoples; it has given to our culture a massive universality that we have long ceased to account for historically, and which we read off rather as necessary and inevitable" (1934:5–6). She argued: "We need to turn to a wider survey in order to check the conclusions we hastily base upon this near-universality of familiar customs. Most of the simpler cultures did not gain the wide currency of the one which, out of our experience, we identify with human nature, but this was for various historical reasons

and certainly not for any that gives us as its carriers a monopoly of social good or of social sanity. Modern civilization, from this point of view, becomes not a necessary pinnacle of human achievement but one entry in a long series of possible adjustments" (1966:262). Not incidental to her critique were her observations on American norms of masculinity: "Western civilization allows and culturally honors gratifications of the ego which according to any absolute category would be regarded as abnormal. The portrayal of unbridled and arrogant egoists as family men, as officers of the law, and in business has been a favorite topic of novelists, and they are familiar in every community. Such individuals are probably mentally warped to a greater degree than many inmates of our institutions who are nevertheless socially unavailable. They are extreme types of those personality configurations which our civilization fosters" (279).

11. Benedict was privately confronting a growing ambivalence toward anthropology. In her diary in 1934, the same year she published her landmark *Patterns of Culture*, Benedict, then in her late 40s, confided that her longings for intimacy and her pleasure in the companionship she had found with a younger woman, Nathalie Raymond, prevailed over anthropology: "I ought to have enough self-knowledge to know what would make life meaningful to me. Not my work in anthropology, much as I owe to it. Like eating and drinking it has a necessary place in my life and adds to it, but the role it plays in Margaret [Mead]'s life or Boas' is impossible. Companionship comes close to the core of the matter, and loving Nat and taking such delight in her I have the happiest conditions for living that I've ever known" (quoted in Modell 1983:214). For accounts of Ruth Benedict's life and her experience of social marginality, see Babcock 1995; Caffrey 1989; Mintz 1981; Modell 1983. Benedict had left her husband in 1930 after sixteen years of marriage. During the years that Ruth Landes knew her, she lived with women partners: Nathalie Raymond from 1931 to 1938 and Ruth Valentine from 1939 until Benedict died in 1948.

12. In her doctoral dissertation, "The Concept of the Guardian Spirit in North America" (1923), Benedict had relied exclusively on published sources on Guardian Spirit belief systems in Native North America and found the only descriptions of Ojibwa beliefs and practices in John Long's 1791 *Voyages and Travels of an Indian Interpreter and Trader* and in the 19th-century writings of George Copway (1852), Peter Jones (1861), Johann Kohl (1860), and W. J. Hoffman (1891).

13. The correspondence between Benedict and Jenness, in addition to illustrating the patron-client character of teacher-student relations, also shows the legacy of colonialism. Community members at Manitou Rapids were not consulted; instead, Landes was introduced to administrators

in the Canadian Department of Indian Affairs. In a letter to Jenness on June 2, 1932, Benedict wrote: "The Department has money for a summer field trip for one of our students, a married woman whom I can recommend as intelligent and of good judgment. She is anxious to go to the Ojibwa, and those of this country are so Siouan-hybrid that I have suggested to her that she go to a group in Canada. I am writing as to whether this would meet with your approval and if so whether you will send me some specific suggestions. Has anyone been among these groups recently? Is there a pretty uniform acceptance of white conditions among them, or are some of them still comparatively uninfluenced? . . . The student's name is Ruth Landes" (RFBP, box 31:317). Jenness wrote to Benedict on June 22 enclosing a copy of the letter he had sent to the deputy superintendent-general of the Department of Indian Affairs (DIA) and adding in a postscript: "Our DIA — like yours? — is very sensitive to anthropologists and their ways, but Mrs. Landes will surely have no difficulty, whether the Indian Department acknowledges this letter or not." To the deputy superintendent-general, Jenness had written: "Mrs. Ruth Landes, who is on the staff of the Department of Anthropology, Columbia University, New York, is planning to visit and study the Ojibwa Indians either on the Manitou Indian reserve or on the reserve at Lake of the Woods. Her Department has asked me to approach the proper official to give her such papers as will facilitate her work. I am therefore forwarding you a copy of its letter, for such action as you may consider advisable."

PART II. PROLOGUE

1. Back in Montreal, I contacted various Native women's organizations (regional and provincial) in Thunder Bay and Toronto as well as Ojibwa feminist writers to try to find women who would be willing to read and discuss *The Ojibwa Woman* with me. I hoped to find women who might see the collaboration of Ruth Landes and Maggie Wilson as I did — as a political act. They might see that "gossip" and "women's stories" can tell truths. Understandably, however, First Nations women activists were busy with more current pressing concerns — poverty, unemployment, youth, housing, health, and political organizing and funding.

CHAPTER 4

1. Ruth Landes's letters have been preserved with Ruth Benedict's papers at the Vassar Archives whereas many of Ruth Benedict's letters to Ruth Landes have been lost due to the latter's constant change of residence.

2. In the 1940s another Columbia University doctoral student, Ernes-

tine Friedl, followed up Landes's study. In her dissertation, "An Attempt at Directed Culture Change: Leadership among the Chippewa, 1640–1948" (1951), Friedl developed an argument concerning long-term continuity in Ojibwa character and personality that supported Ruth Landes's interpretation. Ralph Linton, who had succeeded Franz Boas as chair of the Department of Anthropology at Columbia University (1938–46) had been intrigued by Landes's portrait of Ojibwa individualism and social "atomism." He had directed Friedl to the topic and suggested that she undertake a study of culture change and patterns of leadership and interpersonal relations among the Ojibwa for her Ph.D. research (Friedl 1995:10). She conducted both ethnohistorical research for the period 1640–1948 and fieldwork in 1942 and 1943 with the Wisconsin Chippewa and documented the persistence of individualism and atomism despite large-scale political and economic changes. She argued that individualistic behavior and personality were adaptive for survival under the conditions of frequent and unpredictable change that the Chippewa had experienced through colonial history and under subsequent Indian administrations. Friedl suggested that disruptive historical changes reproduced the social behavior that the unpredictability of game resources had produced in an aboriginal foraging economy: "The all-pervasive condition of change" was the constant in Chippewa life that maintained persistence in personality traits (1956:823). Hallowell similarly argued in his work with the Ojibwa of Berens River, Manitoba, that "considerable acculturation can occur without any profound effect upon the 'modal' or 'communal' aspects of personality" (Hallowell 1953:613).

3. This account is from a letter Maggie Wilson sent to Ruth Landes around 1934, which begins 'Dear Ruth, This is the story of my mother, Mrs. Bunyan." It is catalogued as story 119, box 38, RLP. According to Maggie, her Scottish maternal grandfather was "named Simpson." I have, however, found no archival sources to confirm the name.

4. I obtained the dates of Maggie Wilson's marriages and the births of her children from copies of the Treaty 3 annuity pay lists that are in the Ruth Landes Papers. In the last decade of her life, Landes had conducted research in Ottawa at the Public Archives of Canada and the Department of Indian Affairs and compiled handwritten notes for a biographical sketch that Landes titled "Maggie Spence Wilson" (n.d.). These notes are among her papers in the National Anthropological Archives.

5. Personal communication, July 10, 1996. Shaganash was devoted to Maggie Wilson and much saddened by her death, after which he left Manitou Rapids permanently in 1942 to marry and to work in a pulp and paper mill near Thunder Bay. He and his wife, Eva, had 13 children, 12

of whom lived to adulthood. When he was seven years old, he accompanied Maggie Wilson when she went to Red Lake, Minnesota, to work with Ruth Landes in the summer of 1933: "I don't remember much about that trip to the States. They talked and talked and wrote things down. I just played."

6. Maggie Wilson had given the Star Dance for the first time in the fall of 1918. It was probably because of her dance and songs that she became known to ethnologists, the first of whom was Frances Densmore, who visited Manitou Rapids the following summer, in July 1919, to record Ojibwa music (see Densmore 1979). In addition to her spiritual knowledge, Maggie's bilingual and bicultural competence also made her a good informant. For other collaborations between bicultural Native Americans and anthropologists, see Black-Rogers 1989; J. Brown 1989; Cannizzo 1983.

7. See Joan Mark's biography of Alice Cunningham Fletcher, whom she describes as "Mother to the Indians" (1988). But see also Alice Kehoe's analysis of the unpublished stories the Blackfoot woman elder Insima told to another of Benedict's graduate students, Sylvia Sue Sommers, in the summer of 1939 (Kehoe 1996). Sommers, like Landes, was the daughter of Russian Jewish immigrants and had worked as a social worker in Harlem. Also like Landes, she was interested in the experiences of acculturation. Sommers noted a difference between the stories men told, which were nostalgic about past battles, origin myths, and bison hunting, and the stories women told, which focused on actual reservation life and told of who married whom and how good or bad husbands were. According to Kehoe, "Insima, who had listened for too many years to men's stories of war and prescriptions of correct ritual, wanted young Long Braids [Sommers] to hear and record the affairs of real life, how Blackfoot people lived" (398). Kehoe cites Clark Wissler's observation that "so far as I could see, the morale of the women was far less shattered [by reservation life] and it is they who saved tribal life from complete collapse" (399). It is interesting to speculate that women's storytelling, by enabling women to turn the stuff of their everyday lives into history, may have assisted women therapeutically in overcoming the humiliations of reservation life.

8. Maggie Wilson dictated this story to her daughter Janet and mailed it to Landes. It is 30 handwritten pages catalogued as story 74 in the Ruth Landes Papers. It is typical of the more than 100 stories Wilson told Landes, some recorded by Landes in the field and others mailed to her in New York. Other than making minor editorial and punctuation changes, I have reproduced it here as Wilson dictated it.

9. The letters Maggie Wilson wrote to Ruth Landes during the 1930s

are deposited with the Ruth Landes Papers in the National Anthropological Archives at the Smithsonian Institution. Most recount the lives of women known to Maggie Wilson, a few are mythical stories, and some bear a strong resemblance to European fairy tales. The letters apparently remained in Columbia University files and were found in the papers of William Duncan Strong in the 1990s by a Smithsonian archivist who reunited them with Ruth Landes's papers (personal communication: James Glenn, November 1994).

10. The way that Maggie told other women's stories as a metaphor for her own is similar to the storytelling practices of Yukon Athapaskan women described by Julie Cruikshank in *Life Lived Like a Story: Life Stories of Three Yukon Native Elders.* Cruikshank recalls: "When I asked women to talk about the past, they used traditional stories — particularly stories having a strong competent woman as the central protagonist — to explain events in their lives" (1990:347). The Yukon women repeatedly told Cruikshank that young girls should be learning from the stories. Also similar is the way the Yukon women's stories, like Maggie's, tell of women who have been captured and escaped or who were lost or abandoned and survived through their resourcefulness and practice of a range of skills taught to women at puberty. The stories teach that "women who rely on learned, shared, 'practical' knowledge to achieve their ends eventually succeed" (342–343).

11. But see J. Cole (1979) and Van Kirk (1980).

12. On January 27, 1936, Benedict wrote to Landes, who was then in the field in Kansas: "The money for *Ojibwa Sociology* came through last week. That means it will be published in the Columbia University series with you to pay about $150 for the chapters the Department accepts as the 'thesis.'" In a letter later that spring, April 11, 1936, Benedict wrote: "I can't tell 'til the printer estimates costs just how much of the total can be published. $1250 is appropriated for the part exclusive of the thesis, that is 50 or 60 pages will have to be paid for extra. The usual cost per page, bound and distributed, is about $3.50 . . . so you can calculate roughly."

13. On November 4, 1935, Benedict wrote to Landes in Kansas: "Will you drop me a line right away whether you have a carbon of the Ojibwa Woman? I'm having some editorial work done on it, and if there's a carbon, I'll have this pasted up at certain points and sent to you before copying for the publishers." On February 4, 1936, Benedict wrote: "I'm sending along the first chapter of the Ojibwa Woman tomorrow . . . the rest will follow in less than a week. For this kind of book all diacritical marks are a stumbling block and any native names you use should be simplified. Nor is there any advantage in keeping the correct names of

individuals mentioned—rather the reverse. You can run a note somewhere saying that actual names are on file here. But select short names and pronounceable ones. Nat [Nathalie Raymond, Benedict's companion] has written questions out too, which show what an attentive and uninstructed reader might have to ask. Take time to go over this soon, as I have a typist on hand to do it for the printer." Landes did follow Benedict's advice and changed most of the Ojibwa names to short, "pronounceable" ones. She did not change the names of individuals who used anglicized names. On February 13, 1936, Landes wrote to Benedict from Kansas, "I am sending the Ojibwa [Woman] now—carefully gone over and every alteration made—thank you inexpressibly for your kindness and Nat's." On March 16 she wrote: "Am still working over the Ojibwa Woman of Nat's." And on March 20 Landes wrote, "I am wending my way to the close of the Ojibwa Woman. Sorry it takes so long: but there is lots to do on it; and I have been a-flu-ing or something."

CHAPTER 5

1. In her letters during the summer of 1933, Ruth Benedict also reported that "the tales from [Manitou] keep coming in great style." Wilson and Bombay were sending stories in letters to Ruth Landes c/o Benedict at Columbia, and Benedict was sending money orders back to Manitou to pay the women for their work. She also discussed her attempts to find a publisher for Landes's "Negro Jews in Harlem."

2. See Jules Henry's 1941 ethnography, *Jungle People*. Henry conducted fieldwork with the Kaingáng from December 1932 to January 1934.

3. Landes would receive six credits in the Ph.D. program for her field report on the 1933 research (RB to Dean McBain, Columbia University, April 13, 1934, RFBP).

4. See Devereux 1937. Walter Williams observes:

Given the masses of detail that anthropologists have churned out about Native American cultures, what is surprising is that no more has been written about the berdache tradition than there has been. Part of the reason for anthropologists' avoidance of this topic is that few of them have felt genuinely comfortable in writing about sexual variance. Indeed, it sometimes seems that the first generations of anthropologists who associated on a personal level with berdache (most of those who come to mind are women: Matilda Coxe Stevenson, Elsie Clews Parsons, Ruth Underhill, Margaret Mead, Ruth Landes), were an iconoclastic bunch who would dispassionately describe whatever they saw. They seemed more likely to be sympathetic than more recent scholars. . . . Despite their claims to objectivity, most anthropologists have been raised in Western cultural traditions. . . . With Western aversions to the discussion of homosexuality, and the assumption—con-

trary to all the scientific data — that this behavior is relatively rare, many have avoided discussion of the topic." (1992:11–12)

5. Stephen O. Murray (2000:348–349) suggests that berdache remains useful as an etic term but that "good emic analysis" uses the local term in the local language.

PART III. PROLOGUE

1. The Department of Social Science at Fisk was developing three programs of specialization: Southern Rural Life, Race and Culture, and African Studies. It offered courses such as The Negro in America, Culture Conflicts, Personality and Culture, and Race and Culture, as well as courses on Africa and the Caribbean. E. Franklin Frazier (*The Negro Family in the United States*, 1939), James Weldon Johnson (*Black Manhattan*, 1930), Horace Cayton (*Black Metropolis*, 1945), and John Hope Franklin (*From Slavery to Freedom*, 1948) all taught at Fisk during the 1930s. White scholars Robert Park, Donald Pierson, and Hortense Powdermaker (*After Freedom*, 1939) were among those who also taught at Fisk in the 1930s.

2. The memoir describes the attempts of her female protagonist, Adele Howard, to redress the stereotypes of "sex, misery, violence, hunger, hate" she had read about southern blacks before coming to the South (n.d., "Athens":84, RLP). What emerges from the description of Howard's affair with the black professor, Ethan Quarles — besides great confusion regarding age and racial differences — was that he "was a good man, kind, thoughtful, generous. . . . He was the sole one to show that she, Adele Howard, was a person, an individual woman, likable . . . he took her seriously enough to care to appraise her. . . . It was wonderful how this man roused in her a belief that she had special worth. . . . Until now, she thought, she had been handled like a child, considered obedient here, disobedient there, never reckoned with as a creature of purpose. Ethan Quarles reckoned with her" (142).

CHAPTER 6

1. Arthur Ramos signed his correspondence and publications "Arthur," but some scholars since have referred to him as "Artur"; both forms are now current in the literature. Ramos was later appointed to head the new Department of Social Sciences at the UNESCO office in Paris but died suddenly a few months after his arrival in October 1949. Ramos's contribution to the development of anthropology in Brazil is a subject of some debate among contemporary Brazilian historians of anthropology (Corrêa 1988, 1997, 2000; Cunha 1999). See Stolcke (1998) for discussion of the rivalry between Freyre and Ramos.

2. Vargas was reelected president in 1950 by a popular vote but did not complete his mandate. He committed suicide in 1954 on the eve of a military coup that would have ousted him from power. See Fausto (1999:198–236).

3. Cunha (1999:278) cites a 1935 criminology study of "recalcitrant criminals": 33 blacks and mestizos charged with homicide, alcoholism, and vagrancy and 195 passive homosexuals.

4. See Kim Butler (1998) for a useful history of the development of candomblé in Salvador, Bahia. Butler divides the history into four phases. In the first phase religious expression was an integral part of the formation of Afro-Brazilian community life around different African ethnic groups (nações, lit. "nations") in post-abolition Salvador. The second phase is the period of consolidation of the major features of candomblé ritual and secular life, the proliferation of new terreiros, and the growing prestige of the Nagô (Yoruba-based) terreiros. The third stage is the adaptive response to increasing police repression at the beginning of the 20th century, and the fourth phase is the absorption of candomblé into the general popular culture of Brazil in the last half of the 20th century (190).

5. Landes kept Carneiro's very personal love letters with her professional papers, and they are filed together at the National Anthropological Archives. Landes's letters to Carneiro have not been located. It is significant that she kept these letters, because she later destroyed the letters she had received from Elmer Imes throughout the year she was in Brazil.

After October 1940 Carneiro and Landes lost contact until 1946. Carneiro, then working as editor-in-chief of the Rio de Janeiro office of the Associated Press, wrote Landes on February 22, 1946, to ask if she had published her "book on the Bahian negro" and to tell her that he had translated parts of her "Cult Matriarchate" article to appear in a forthcoming book that he said he planned to dedicate to her as "My friend and my companion of so many beautiful days in the candomblés of Bahia" (RLP, box 4). This anthology, Antologia do Negro Brasileiro (Carneiro 1950), contains excerpts from more than 150 sources in Afro-Brazilian studies. All, except the two excerpts from Ruth Landes's article ("Mães e filhas-de-santo na Bahia" and "Os deuses africanos"), are written by men. Writing again on March 14, 1946, Carneiro updated Landes on the lives of their Bahian friends and on events in the candomblé world (RLP, box 4). Carneiro would be instrumental in establishing the Campanha de Defesa do Folclore Brasileira in 1958 (which, in 1978, became the Instituto Nacional do Folclore). He was its executive director from 1961 to 1964, during which time he inaugurated the Biblioteca Amadeu Amaral and helped initiate plans for the national museum of folklore, which was established in 1968 and has been known as the Museu Folclorico Edison Carneiro since 1976. Carneiro died in 1972.

6. Charles Wagley's experience provides a contrast to theirs and highlights the gender, class, and race codes that worked to position Ruth Landes both in Brazilian society and in Brazilian anthropology. A handsome and affable Anglo-American male scholar and Amerindian expert, Wagley was recruited by Dona Heloisa for the position at the Museu Nacional to develop a training program in anthropology in Rio. There he met his future wife, a white Brazilian, Cecilia Roxo, and he continued to work in Brazil for several years. He eventually received a permanent academic appointment at Columbia University and was able to build a lifelong career as the North American authority on Brazilian anthropology. He was also able to marry Cecilia and bring her to the United States. The affective relationship he contracted while working in Brazil thus supported respectable conventions whereas Landes's relationship with Carneiro would be fodder for corridor talk for years to come. São Paulo anthropologist Herbert Baldus, who visited Landes in New York several times between 1949 and 1951, told her that Ramos had continued his slanders against her for years after she left Brazil (October 11, 1950, Notebook 4, RLP).

7. The reasons for Buell Quain's suicide on August 2, 1939, are not known. He left a suicide note addressed to the captain of the Maranhão state police saying that he was dying of a terminal and contagious illness and asking that his death not be investigated. He also left detailed instructions for the disinfection of his fieldnotes and their deposition at the Museu Nacional and for the distribution of specific amounts of his remaining monies to Dona Heloisa and to particular Indians who had worked with him (Buell Quain to Sr. Manoel Perna (copy), RLP, box 7). Letters from Ruth Landes to Ruth Benedict refer to Quain at various times as "nervous," "mournful," "hurt." On May 27, 1939, Quain wrote his last letter to Landes: "I am having metaphysical troubles about which I need your advice. Benedict is either too gullible or too busy to help much. I would like to talk to Lesser. On the other hand — Al is too well disciplined in philosophy and loses patience with muddleheadedness" (RLP, box 7).

CHAPTER 7

1. Physical anthropologist M. F. Ashley Montagu was hired to research and write a memorandum entitled "Origin, Composition and Physical Characteristics of the American Negro Population." Myrdal used Montagu's work along with Herskovits's anthropometric studies, Otto Klineberg's work on IQ scores, and W. Montague Cobb's applied anthropology

to establish that African Americans were not mentally or physically inferior to whites (Baker 1998:182).

2. See Baker (1998:276–277) for discussion of Myrdal's critique of Hers-
kovits. Baker discusses the approaches of Park (at Chicago and Howard
Universities) and Boas as the dominant frameworks, but he also notes the
work of numerous other social scientists writing on race relations in the
1930s: "Donald Young's comparative analysis of minority groups, Howard
Odum's southern sociology, John Dollard's 'caste and class' approach,
W. E. B. DuBois's interdisciplinary studies of Black society and culture,
Carter G. Woodson's Negro history movement, Charles S. Johnson's more
liberal variant of Chicago sociology . . . Otto Klineberg's social-cultural
psychology approach to studying racial differences and Hortense Pow-
dermaker's functional-structural studies of southern culture" (1998:182).
Baker argues, however, that Myrdal was most strongly influenced by the
Howard University circle, especially Ralph Bunche and Franklin Frazier.
Their "failure to assimilate" model supported Myrdal's social engineering
program.

3. After his work with Myrdal, Ralph Bunche (1904–71) left Howard
University and joined the civil service in 1941. He was a chief research analyst in the Office of Strategic Services and the first African American to be a
division head in the Department of State. He was the first African American to work for the United Nations, beginning in 1946. In 1947 he became
principal secretary of the UN Palestine Commission for which work he
was awarded the 1950 Nobel Peace Prize.

4. Mead pointed out "the vagueness of criticism when the context and
purposes of the report were unknown" and apparently asked Johnson to
clarify the questions the commission had asked Ruth Landes to address.
The commission had not provided any direction to Landes in the form of
specific research questions at the time she was hired. She did not see those
that Johnson later sent to Mead (and to Benedict), but she told Benedict
that, whatever they were, they were "a seven-month-later after-thought"
(RL to RB, February 13, 1940, RFBP).

5. All quotations from Ramos's report are my translations from the
Portuguese. It is not known who translated the report for Johnson and
Myrdal. Ramos later published the full contents of his report in 1942. I
have noted the page numbers in both sources. In the accompanying letter to Herskovits, Ramos first thanked him for his support of Ramos's
application for a Guggenheim fellowship and reported that he expected
it to be successful. Ramos planned to combine the fellowship with an
invitation to be a visiting scholar at the University of Louisiana. He then
discussed recent research by various of Herskovits's "disciples and col-

laborators" on Hausa and Yoruba cultures and commended Herskovits on his recent book, *The Economic Life of Primitive Peoples*, which Ramos was reviewing enthusiastically for a Brazilian journal.

6. For further discussion see Fry (1995:201; 2002) and Murray (2000: 342–347). Fry notes that part of the problem arises because both Landes and Ramos "used the term 'homosexual' without ethnographic information about the classificatory scheme of the people concerned." Thus, "when Landes wrote of 'passive homosexuals' it is not possible to know whether she referred to persons who always assume the 'passive role' in sexual intercourse, those who assume certain 'effeminate' mannerisms, or those who are merely imputed to indulge in one of these" (1995:201). Both Fry and Murray also note that Ramos misrepresented Landes.

7. It is likely that Ramos's report to Myrdal on Landes's "Negro Ethos" memorandum is the "letter" Landes refers to in her 1970 essay "A Woman Anthropologist in Brazil." A thorough search of archival sources has not yielded any other document that resembles the letter Landes describes. It is important to appreciate that Landes's 1970 reflexive memoir was written with the knowledge of hindsight and of her lived experience of marginality and the many years of itinerancy in anthropology that she entered into after the Brazilian fieldwork. The 1970 memoir does not necessarily describe her feelings and knowledge in 1940, when she seemed to be more concerned with her employment status and personal well-being than she was with what Herskovits and Ramos thought of her. At that earlier time she does not seem to have worried that their critique might jeopardize her career.

8. In putting together a staff that would represent the major schools of thought on race relations in American social science, Myrdal also hoped to placate those who might have been slighted by the appointment of a foreign scientist to head the project, those who might be predisposed to be critical of its findings, and those who were well situated within the American academy to have their criticisms taken seriously. Thus, although Myrdal found Herskovits's focus on African origins "excessive," he nonetheless contracted him to contribute an entire monograph on African cultural influences (Mintz 1990:xv; Herskovits 1990). According to Guy Johnson, for Myrdal "it was much more important just to feel that he had got this man [Herskovits] to participate than to get what he was actually going to contribute to the study" (quoted in Jackson 1990:110). Herskovits, who had originally hoped to become the director of the Carnegie project, instead found himself preparing a manuscript for Myrdal and given a one-year deadline.

In *The Myth of the Negro Past* Herskovits revoked the assimilationist views he had held in the 1920s (Mintz 1990:xii–xiii) and declared his commitment to documenting the survival of African cultures among contemporary Afro-Americans. He would devote the rest of his career to mapping African survivals throughout the New World. Melville Herskovits was extremely productive, publishing over 400 articles and almost 20 books over the course of his career (Merriam 1964). Unlike Ruth Landes, Herskovits had the advantages of the stability of a long career at one institution, Northwestern University, from 1927 until his death on February 25, 1963. Many of his publications were coauthored by his wife, Frances, who served as his research assistant and typist from the date of their marriage in 1924, the year after he completed his doctorate, until his death in 1963. After her husband's death, Frances Herskovits brought together a selection of his published and unpublished writings in a book titled The New World Negro (1966).

9. According to a survey conducted by Edison Carneiro in Bahia in 1938–39, 20 Yoruban candomblé terreiros were led by women and 3 by men, whereas 10 of the caboclo centers were led by women and 34 by men (see Landes 1940a:393).

CONCLUSION

1. Ruth Landes submitted a 310-page manuscript entitled "Color in Britain" to Oxford University Press in 1952, but it was not published.

2. The quotations from Richard Slobodin in this chapter are from my interview with him on October 13, 1993.

3. Frank Jones, speaking at the memorial service for Ruth Landes held at McMaster University on April 25, 1991.

4. This correspondence and subsequent correspondence between Ruth Landes and the various chairs of the department is held at the Department of Anthropology, McMaster University.

5. Lynne Teskey-Denton also spoke at the memorial service for Ruth Landes on April 25, 1991. Lynne died of a rare form of leukemia in 1994, the year after our interview.

6. Ellen Wall, speaking at the memorial service for Ruth Landes on April 25, 1991. I also interviewed Ellen on May 27, 1993, and have maintained steady contact with her since.

7. Landes bequeathed a substantial estate, accumulated through shrewd investment and frugality, to the Research Institute for the Study of Man (RISM) in her native New York. The funds now support the annually awarded RISM Landes Awards for doctoral and postdoctoral interdisciplinary research in her fields of interest: race and ethnic relations, comparative aspects of education, gender issues, and problems of aging.

Bibliography

PRIMARY SOURCES

The Franz Boas Papers (FBP), American Philosophical Society, on microfilm
The Margaret Mead Papers (MMP), Library of Congress
The Melville J. Herskovits Papers (MJHP), Northwestern University
Research Institute for the Study of Man (RISM), New York
The Ruth Fulton Benedict Papers (RFBP), Vassar College
The Ruth Landes Papers (RLP), National Anthropological Archives, Smithsonian Institution

SELECTED WRITINGS OF RUTH LANDES

Landes, Ruth. 1937a. The Ojibwa of Canada. In *Cooperation and Competition among Primitive Peoples*. Margaret Mead, ed. Pp. 87–127. New York: McGraw Hill.

———. 1937b. *Ojibwa Sociology*. New York: Columbia University Press.

———. 1937c. The Personality of the Ojibwa. *Culture and Personality* 6:51–60.

———. 1938a. The Abnormal among the Ojibwa. *Journal of Abnormal and Social Psychology* 33:14–33.

———. 1938b. *The Ojibwa Woman*. New York: Columbia University Press. 2nd ed., New York: W. W. Norton, 1971. 3rd ed., Lincoln: University of Nebraska Press, 1997.

———. 1939. The Ethos of the Negro in the New World: A Research Memorandum. Carnegie-Myrdal Study. Unpublished paper.

———. 1940a. A Cult Matriarchate and Male Homosexuality. *Journal of Abnormal and Social Psychology* 35:386–397.

———. 1940b. Fetish Worship in Brazil. *Journal of American Folklore* 53(210): 261–270.

———. 1945a. A Northerner Views the South. *Social Forces* 23:275–279.

———. 1945b. What About This Bureaucracy? *The Nation* 161:365–366.

———. 1947. *The City of Women*. New York: Macmillan. 2nd ed., Albuquerque: University of New Mexico Press, 1994.

———. 1953. Negro Slavery and Female Status. *Journal of African Affairs* 52 (206):54–57.

———. 1955. Biracialism in American Society: A Comparative View. *American Anthropologist* 57(6):1253–1264.

———. 1965. *Culture in American Education: Anthropological Approaches to Minority and Dominant Groups in the Schools.* New York: John Wiley and Sons.

———. 1966. The Ojibwa and Their Observers. Unpublished paper.

———. 1967a. *A cidade das mulheres.* (Portuguese translation of *The City of Women.*) Rio de Janeiro: Editora Universidade Federal de Rio de Janeiro.

———. 1967b. Negro Jews in Harlem. *Jewish Journal of Sociology* 9(2):175–189.

———. 1968a. *The Mystic Lake Sioux: Sociology of the Mdewakantonwan Sioux.* Madison: University of Wisconsin Press.

———. 1968b. *Ojibwa Religion and the Midéwiwin.* Madison: University of Wisconsin Press.

———. 1970a. *The Prairie Potawatomi: Tradition and Ritual in the Twentieth Century.* Madison: University of Wisconsin Press.

———. 1970b. A Woman Anthropologist in Brazil. In *Women in the Field.* Peggy Golde, ed. Pp. 119–142. Chicago: Aldine.

———. 1971. *The Ojibwa Woman.* 2nd ed. Preface by Ruth Landes. New York: W. W. Norton.

———. 1973. Comment. *Western Canadian Journal of Anthropology* 3(3): 44–46.

———. 1976a. Ojibwa lecture. Thunder Bay, Ontario, July 23, 1976. Unpublished. RLP.

———. 1976b. Response to Alexander's Review of *The Ojibwa Woman. American Anthropologist* 78:348–349.

———. 1980. Women in Anthropology. Paper delivered to the Department of Anthropology, University of Calgary. Unpublished. RLP.

———. 1994. *The City of Women.* 2nd ed. Introduction by Sally Cole. Albuquerque: University of New Mexico Press.

———. 1997. *The Ojibwa Woman.* 3rd ed. Introduction by Sally Cole. Lincoln: University of Nebraska Press.

———. 2002. *A cidade das mulheres.* 2nd ed. Preface by Mariza Corrêa; introduction by Peter Fry. Rio de Janeiro: Editora Universidade Federal de Rio de Janeiro.

———. n.d. An American Education. Unpublished. RLP.

———. n.d. Maggie Spence Wilson. Unpublished notes. RLP.

———. n.d. Now at Athens. Unpublished. RLP.

———. n.d. Remembering the Ojibwa after 50 Years. Unpublished. RLP.

———. n.d. Ruth Benedict, Teacher. Unpublished. RLP.

———. n.d. Tongues That Defy the State. Unpublished. RLP.

Landes, Ruth, and Marc Zborowski. 1950. Hypotheses concerning the Eastern European Jewish Family. *Psychiatry* 13:447–464.

SECONDARY SOURCES

Abu-Lughod, Lila. 1990. Can There Be a Feminist Ethnography? *Women and Performance* 5(1):7–27.

Aisenberg, Nadya, and Mona Harrington. 1988. *Women of Academe: Outsiders in the Sacred Grove*. Amherst: University of Massachusetts Press.

Albers, Patricia C. 1989. From Illusion to Illumination: Anthropological Studies of American Indian Women. In *Gender and Anthropology: Critical Reviews for Research and Teaching*. Sandra Morgen, ed. Pp. 132–170. Washington DC: American Anthropological Association.

Alexander, Herbert. 1975. Review of *The Ojibwa Woman*. *American Anthropologist* 77:110–111.

Anonymous. 1947. Review of *The City of Women*. *Columbia Missourian*, July 18. Photocopy.

Anonymous. 1999. Review of *The Ojibwa Woman*. *European Review of Native American Studies* 12(2).

Antler, Joyce. 1998. Introduction. *Talking Back: Images of Jewish Women in American Popular Culture*. Hanover NH: Brandeis University Press/University Press of New England.

Babcock, Barbara. 1993. Feminisms/Pretexts: Fragments, Questions, and Reflections. *Anthropological Quarterly* 66(2):59–66.

———. 1995. "Not in the Absolute Singular": Rereading Ruth Benedict. In *Women Writing Culture*. Ruth Behar and Deborah Gordon, eds. Pp.104–130. Berkeley: University of California Press.

Baker, Lee. 1998. *From Savage to Negro: Anthropology and the Construction of Race, 1896–1954*. Berkeley: University of California Press.

Barnouw, Victor. 1969. Review of *Ojibwa Religion and the Midéwiwin* and *The Mystic Lake Sioux* in *Pacific Northwest Quarterly* 60(4). Photocopy.

———. 1980. Ruth Benedict. *American Scholar* 49 (autumn):504–507.

Barwick, Diane. 1971. Review of *The Prairie Potawatomi*. *Mankind* 8. Photocopy.

Bastide, Roger. 1978. *The African Religions of Brazil*. Helen Sebba, trans. Baltimore: Johns Hopkins University Press.

Bateson, Mary Catherine. 1984. *With a Daughter's Eye: A Memoir of Margaret Mead and Gregory Bateson*. New York: William Morrow.

———. 1989. *Composing a Life*. New York: Penguin.

Baum, Charlotte, Paula Hyman, and Sonya Michel. 1976. *The Jewish Woman in America*. New York: Dial.

Bee, Robert. 1970. Review of *The Prairie Potawatomi*. *American Anthropologist* 72(6):1492–1493.

Behar, Ruth, and Deborah Gordon, eds. 1995. *Women Writing Culture*. Berkeley: University of California Press.

Benedict, Ruth. 1923. *The Concept of the Guardian Spirit in North America.* Memoirs of the American Anthropological Association 29. Washington DC: American Anthropological Association.

———. 1930. Psychological Types in the Cultures of the Southwest. Proceedings of the Twenty-Third International Congress of Americanists, New York, September 17–22, 1928. Pp. 572–581. Lancaster PA: Science Press Printing.

———. 1934. *Patterns of Culture.* Boston: Houghton Mifflin.

———. 1940. *Race: Science and Politics.* New York: Modern Age.

———. 1948. Anthropology and the Humanities. *American Anthropologist* 45: 207–212.

———. 1966[1934]. Anthropology and the Abnormal. *Journal of General Psychology* 10(2):59–82. Reprinted in *An Anthropologist at Work: Writings of Ruth Benedict.* Margaret Mead, ed. Pp. 262–283. New York: Atherton Press.

Birman, Patricia. 1988. Fazer estilo criando gêneros: Estudo sobre a construção religiosa da possessão e da diferença de gêneros em terreiros da Baixada Fluminense. Ph.D. thesis, Universidade Federal de Rio de Janeiro.

Black-Rogers, Mary. 1989. Dan Raincloud: "Keeping Our Indian Way." In *Being and Becoming Indian: Biographical Studies of North American Frontiers.* James A Clifton, ed. Pp. 226–248. Chicago: Dorsey Press.

Blackwood, Evelyn. 1984. Sexuality and Gender in Certain Native American Tribes: The Case of Cross-Gender Females. *Signs* 10(1):27–42.

Boas, Franz. 1896. Limitations of the Comparative Method in Anthropology. *Science* 4:901–908.

———. 1928. *Anthropology and Modern Life.* New York: W. W. Norton.

———. 1940. *Race, Language and Culture.* New York: Macmillan.

Bordo, Susan, with Binnie Klein and Marilyn K. Silverman. 1997. Missing Kitchens. In *Twilight Zones: The Hidden Life of Cultural Images: From Plato to O.J.* By Susan Bordo. Pp. 214–241. Berkeley: University of California Press.

Brotz, Howard. 1964. *The Black Jews of Harlem.* New York: Free Press.

Brown, Diana. 1994. *Umbanda: Religion and Politics in Urban Brazil.* 2nd ed. New York: Columbia University Press.

Brown, Jennifer S. H. 1989. "A Place in Your Mind for Them All": Chief William Berens. In *Being and Becoming Indian: Biographical Studies of North American Frontiers.* James A Clifton, ed. Pp. 204–225. Chicago: Dorsey Press.

Brown, Jennifer S. H., in collaboration with Maureen Matthews. 1993.

Fair Wind: Medicine and Consolation on the Berens River. *Journal of the Canadian Historical Association* 4:55–74.

Buffalohead, Priscilla K. 1983. Farmer, Warriors, Traders: A Fresh Look at Ojibwa Women. *Minnesota History* 48:236–244.

Burstein, Janet. 1998. Translating Immigrant Women: Surfacing the Manifold Self. In *Talking Back: Images of Jewish Women in American Popular Culture*. Joyce Antler, ed. Pp. 15–29. Hanover NH: Brandeis University Press/University Press of New England.

Butler, Kim. 1998. *Freedoms Given, Freedoms Won: Afro-Brazilians in Post-Abolition São Paulo and Salvador*. New Brunswick NJ: Rutgers University Press.

Caffrey, Margaret. 1989. *Ruth Benedict: Stranger in This Land*. Austin: University of Texas Press.

Caine, Barbara. 1994. Feminist Biography and Feminist History. *Women's History Review* 3(2):247–261.

———. 1997. *English Feminism, 1780–1980*. Oxford: Oxford University Press.

Callender, Charles. 1969. Review of *The Mystic Lake Sioux*. *American Anthropologist* 71(4):739–740.

Callender, Charles, and Lee M. Kochems. 1983. The North American Berdache. *Current Anthropology* 24(4):443–470.

Cameron, Elspeth. 1997. The Wrong Time and the Wrong Place: Gwethalyn Graham, 1913–1965. In *Great Dames*. E. Cameron and J. Dickin, eds. Pp. 145–164. Toronto: University of Toronto Press.

Cameron, Elspeth, and Janice Dickin, eds. 1997. *Great Dames*. Toronto: University of Toronto Press.

Canning, Hazel. 1939. Magic Powers of Jungle Priestesses Who Rule 40,000 Men — Ruth Landes Brings Back Weird Tales of Brazilian Matriarchs. *Boston Sunday Post*, August 6. Photocopy.

Cannizzo, Jeanne. 1983. George Hunt and the Invention of Kwakiutl Culture. *Canadian Review of Sociology and Anthropology* 20(1):44–58.

Carneiro, Edison. 1940. The Structure of African Cults in Bahia. *Journal of American Folklore* 53:271–278.

———, ed. 1950. *Antologia do Negro Brasileiro*. Rio de Janeiro: Editora Globo.

———. 1964. Uma "Falseta" de Artur Ramos. In *Ladinos e Crioulos: Estudos sobre o Negro no Brasil*. E. Carneiro, ed. Pp. 223–227. Rio de Janeiro: Civilização Brasileira.

———. 1978. *Candomblés da Bahia*. 6th ed. Rio de Janeiro: Civilização Brasileira.

———. 1981[1936 and 1937]. *Religiões Negras* and *Negros Bantus*. 2nd. ed. (orig. published separately). Rio de Janeiro: Civilização Brasileira.

Carneiro, Edison, and Aydano do Couto Ferraz, eds. 1940. Congresso Afro-

Brasileiro da Bahia. In *O Negro no Brasil*. Biblioteca de Divulgação Scientifica. Rio de Janeiro: Civilização Brasileira S.A.

Chapin, Elsa. 1947. Folkways of Brazilian Negroes. Review of *The City of Women*. *Brooklyn Eagle*, December 14. Photocopy.

Clifford, James. 1988. On Ethnographic Authority. In *The Predicament of Culture*. Pp. 21–54. Cambridge: Harvard University Press.

Clifford, James, and George Marcus, eds. 1986. *Writing Culture: The Poetics and Politics of Ethnography*. Berkeley: University of California Press.

Clifton, James A. 1977. *The Prairie People: Continuity and Change in Potawatomi Indian Culture, 1665–1965*. Lawrence: Regents Press of Kansas.

Cole, Jean Murray. 1979. *Exile in the Wilderness*. Seattle: University of Washington Press.

Cole, Sally. 1991. *Women of the Praia: Work and Lives in a Portuguese Coastal Community*. Princeton NJ: Princeton University Press.

———. 1995a. Ruth Landes and the Early Ethnography of Race and Gender. In *Women Writing Culture*. Ruth Behar and Deborah Gordon, eds. Pp. 166–185. Berkeley: University of California Press.

———. 1995b. Women's Stories and Boasian Texts: The Ojibwa Ethnography of Ruth Landes and Maggie Wilson. *Anthropologica* 37:3–25.

———. 1997. Dear Ruth: This Is the Story of Maggie Wilson, Ojibwa Ethnologist. In *Great Dames*. Elspeth Cameron and Janice Dickin, eds. Pp. 75–96. Toronto: University of Toronto Press.

Cole, Sally, and Lynne Phillips, eds. 1995. *Ethnographic Feminisms: Essays in Anthropology*. Ottawa: Carleton University Press.

Constantinides, Pamela. 1982. Women's Spirit Possession and Urban Adaptation. In *Women United, Women Divided: Comparative Studies of Ten Contemporary Cultures*. P. Caplan and J. Bujra, eds. Pp. 185–205. Bloomington: Indiana University Press.

Copway, George (or Kahgegagahbowh). 1850. *The Traditional History and Characteristic Sketches of the Ojibway Nation*. London: Charles Gilpin.

Corrêa, Mariza. 1988. Traficantes do excêntrico: Os antropólogos no Brasil dos anos 30 aos anos 60. *Revista brasileira de ciencias sociais* 3(6):79–98.

———. 1997. Dona Heloisa e a pesquisa da campo. *Revista da antropologia*, São Paulo, USP 40:11–54.

———. 2000. O Mistério dos orixás e das bonecas: Raça e gênero na antropologia brasileira. *Etnográfica* 4(2):233–265.

———. 2002. Prefácio. Esboços no espelho. *A cidade das mulheres* de Ruth Landes. 2nd ed. Rio de Janeiro: Editora Universidade Federal de Rio de Janeiro.

Cott, Nancy. 1987. *The Grounding of Modern Feminism*. New Haven: Yale University Press.

Cruikshank, Julie, in collaboration with Angela Sidney, Kitty Smith, and Annie Ned. 1990. *Life Lived Like a Story: Life Stories of Three Yukon Native Elders*. Vancouver: University of British Columbia Press.

Cunha, Olívia Maria Gomes de. 1999. Sua alma em sua palma: Identificando a "raça" e inventando a nação. In *Repensando o Estado Novo*. Dulce Chaves Randolfi, org. Pp. 257–288. Rio de Janeiro: Editora FGV.

Darnell, Regna. 1976. The Sapir Years at the National Museum, Ottawa. In *The History of Canadian Anthropology*. James Freedman, ed. Pp. 98–121. Hamilton ON: Canadian Ethnology Society.

———. 1977. Hallowell's "Bear Ceremonialism" and the Emergence of Boasian Anthropology. *Ethos* 5(1):13–30.

———. 1990. *Edward Sapir*. Berkeley: University of California Press.

———. 1992. The Boasian Text Tradition and the History of Anthropology. *Culture* 12(1):39–47.

———. 2001. *Invisible Genealogies: A History of Americanist Anthropology*. Lincoln: University of Nebraska Press.

Deacon, Desley. 1997. *Elsie Clews Parsons: Inventing Modern Life*. Chicago: University of Chicago Press.

Densmore, Frances. 1979[1929]. *Chippewa Customs*. Bureau of American Ethnology Bulletin 86. Washington DC: Government Printing Office. Rpt., St. Paul: Minnesota Historical Society.

de Lauretis, Teresa. 1984. *Alice Doesn't: Feminism, Semiotics and Cinema*. Bloomington: Indiana University Press.

Devereux, George. 1937. Institutionalized Homosexuality of the Mohave Indians. *Human Biology* 9:498–527.

Douglas, Mary. 1966. *Purity and Danger*. London: Routledge and Kegan Paul.

Di Leonardo, Micaela. 1998. *Exotics at Home: Anthropologies, Others, and American Modernity*. Chicago: University of Chicago Press.

DuBois, Cora. 1944. *The People of Alor: A Social Psychological Study of an East-Indian Island*. Minneapolis: University of Minnesota Press.

Dunning, R. W. 1959. *Social and Economic Change among the Northern Ojibwa*. Toronto: University of Toronto Press.

———. 1968. Review of *Ojibwa Religion and the Midéwiwin*. *Nature*, October 19. Photocopy.

Echols, Alice. 1999. *Scars of Sweet Paradise: The Life and Times of Janis Joplin*. New York: Henry Holt.

Eco, Umberto. 1983. *Travels in Hyperreality*. William Weaver, trans. New York: Harcourt Brace Jovanovich.

Erikson, Erik. 1950. *Childhood and Society*. New York: W. W. Norton.

Etienne, M., and E. Leacock, eds. 1980. *Women and Colonization: Anthropological Perspectives*. New York: Praeger.

Fausto, Boris. 1999. *A Concise History of Brazil*. Arthur Brakel, trans. Cambridge: Cambridge University Press.

Finn, Janet. 1995. Ella Cara Deloria and Mourning Dove: Writing against the Grain. In *Women Writing Culture*. Ruth Behar and Deborah Gordon, eds. Pp. 131–147. Berkeley: University of California Press.

Franklin, John Hope. 1974. *From Slavery to Freedom: A History of Negro America*. 4th ed. New York: Knopf.

Frantz, C. 1985. Relevance: American Ethnology and the Wider Society, 1900–1940. In *Social Contexts of American Ethnology, 1840–1984*. June Helm, ed. Pp. 83–100. Washington DC: American Ethnological Society.

Fraser, Gertrude. 1991. Race, Class, and Difference in Hortense Powdermaker's *After Freedom: A Cultural Study of the Deep South*. "The Legacy of Hortense Powdermaker," special issue, *Journal of Anthropological Research* 47(4):403–415.

Freedman, Estelle. 1983. The New Woman: Changing Views of Women in the 1920s. In *Decades of Discontent: The Women's Movement, 1920–1940*. Lois Scharf and Joan Jensen, eds. Pp. 21–42. Westport CT: Greenwood Press.

Freyre, Gilberto. 1933. *Casa grande e senzala: Formação da família brasileira sob o regime da economia patriarcal*. Rio de Janeiro: Livraria José Olympia Editora S.A.

Friedl, Ernestine. 1951. An Attempt at Directed Culture Change: Leadership among the Chippewa, 1640–1948. Ph.D. dissertation, Columbia University.

———. 1956. Persistence in Chippewa Culture and Personality. *American Anthropologist* 58:814–825.

———. 1995. The Life of an Academic: A Personal Record of a Teacher, Administrator, and Anthropologist. *Annual Reviews in Anthropology* 24:1–19.

Frisbie, Charlotte. 1989. Frances Theresa Densmore. In *Women Anthropologists: Selected Biographies*. Ute Gacs et al., eds. Pp. 51–58. Urbana: University of Illinois Press.

Fry, Peter. 1995[1974]. Male Homosexuality and Afro-Brazilian Possession Cults. In *Latin American Male Homosexualities*. Stephen O. Murray, ed. Pp. 193–220. Albuquerque: University of New Mexico Press.

———. 2002. Introduction. *A cidade das mulheres* de Ruth Landes. 2nd ed. Rio de Janeiro: Editora Universidade Federal de Rio de Janeiro.

Galembo, Phyllis. 1993. *Divine Inspiration*. Albuquerque: University of New Mexico Press.

Gannett, Lewis. N.d. Review of *The City of Women*. Books and Things. Photocopy.

Glenn, Susan A. 1990. *Daughters of the Shtetl: Life and Labor in the Immigrant Generation.* Ithaca: Cornell University Press.

Goldfrank, Esther. 1978. *Notes on an Undirected Life as One Anthropologist Tells It.* Publications in Anthropology no. 3. Flushing NY: Queens College.

Gordon, Deborah. 1993. Among Women: Gender and Ethnographic Authority of the Southwest, 1930–1980. In *Hidden Scholars.* Nancy Parezo, ed. Pp. 129–145. Albuquerque: University of New Mexico Press.

Goulet, Jean-Guy. 1997. The Northern Athapaskan "Berdache" Reconsidered: On Reading More Than There Is in the Ethnographic Record. In *Two-Spirit People: Native American Gender Identity, Sexuality and Spirituality.* Sue-Ellen Jacobs, Wesley Thomas, and Sabine Long, eds. Pp. 45–68. Urbana: University of Illinois Press.

Green, Rayna. 1980. Review Essay: Native American Women. *Signs* 6:248–267.

Greenberg, David. 1986. Why Was the Berdache Ridiculed? In *The Many Faces of Homosexuality.* Evelyn Blackwood, ed. Pp. 179–190. New York: Harrington Park Press.

Hallowell, A. Irving. 1928. Was Cross-Cousin Marriage Practiced by the North-Central Algonkian? In *Proceedings, Twenty-third International Congress of Americanists.* Pp. 519–544. New York: International Congress of Americanists.

———. 1936. The Passing of the Midewiwin in the Lake Winnipeg Region. *American Anthropologist* 38:32–51.

———. 1938. Review of *Ojibwa Sociology* and *The Ojibwa Women. American Sociological Review* 3:892–893.

———. 1942. The Role of Conjuring in Saulteaux Society. Publications of the Philadelphia Anthropological Society no. 2. Philadelphia: Philadelphia Anthropological Society.

———. 1953. Culture, personality, and society. In *Anthropology Today: An Encyclopedic Inventory.* A. L. Kroeber, ed. Pp. 597–620. Chicago: University of Chicago Press.

———. 1955. *Culture and Experience.* Philadelphia: University of Pennsylvania Press.

———. 1981. Ojibway Ontology, Behaviour and World View. In *Culture in History: Essays in Honor of Paul Radin.* Stanley Diamond, ed. Pp. 20–43. New York: Octagon Books.

———. 1992. *The Ojibwa of Berens River, Manitoba: Ethnography into History.* Jennifer Brown, ed. New York: Harcourt Brace Jovanovich.

Handler, Richard. 1990. Ruth Benedict and the Modernist Sensibility. In *Modernist Anthropology: From Fieldwork to Text.* Marc Manganaro, ed. Pp. 163–180. Princeton NJ: Princeton University Press.

Haraway, Donna. 1989. *Primate Visions: Gender, Race, and Nature in the World of Modern Science.* New York: Routledge.

Harris, Marvin. 1968. *The Rise of Anthropological Theory.* New York: Columbia University Press.

Healey, Mark. 1996. Os descontros da tradição em A cidade das mulheres: Raça e gênero na etnografia de Ruth Landes. *Cadernos pagu* 6/7:153–199.

Heilbrun, Carolyn. 1988. *Writing a Woman's Life.* New York: W. W. Norton.

———. 1995. *The Education of a Woman: The Life of Gloria Steinem.* New York: Ballantine Books.

Henry, Jules. 1941. *Jungle People: A Kaingáng Tribe of the Highlands of Brazil.* New York: J. J. Augustin.

Hernandez, Graciela. 1995. Multiple Subjectivities and Strategic Positionality: Zora Neale Hurston's Experimental Ethnographies. In *Women Writing Culture.* Ruth Behar and Deborah Gordon, eds. Pp. 148–165. Berkeley: University of California Press.

Herskovits, Melville. 1937. African Gods and Catholic Saints in New World Negro Belief. *American Anthropologist* 39:635–643.

———. 1943. The Negroes of Brazil. *Yale Review* 32:263–279.

———. 1948. Review of *The City of Women. American Anthropologist* 50:123–125.

———. 1966. *The New World Negro.* Frances Herskovits, ed. Bloomington: Indiana University Press.

———. 1990[1941]. *The Myth of the Negro Past.* Boston: Beacon Press.

Hickerson, Harold. 1967. Some Implications of the Theory of Particularity, or "Atomism," of Northern Algonkians. *Current Anthropology* 8:313–343.

Hobsbawm, E. J. 1959. *Primitive Rebels: Studies in Archaic Forms of Social Movements in the 19th and 20th Centuries.* New York: W. W. Norton.

Hoffman, Walter J. 1891. The Midéwiwin or "Grand Medicine Society" of the Ojibwa. Seventh Annual Report of the Bureau of American Ethnology, 1885–86. Washington DC.

Honig, Nat. 1970. Review of *The Prairie Potawatomi. Independent Press Telegram* (Long Beach CA), February 12. Photocopy.

Honigman, John. 1947. Review of *The City of Women. Social Forces* 26:227.

hooks, bell. 1990. *Yearning: Race, Gender and Cultural Politics.* Toronto: Between-the-Lines.

Huggins, Nathan Irvin. 1971. *Harlem Renaissance.* New York: Oxford.

Hughes, Pollyanna. 1947. How Negroes Live in Bahia and USA. Review of *The City of Women. Daily Times-Herald,* June 1. Photocopy.

Hurston, Zora Neale. 1935. *Mules and Men.* Philadelphia: J. B. Lippincott.

Hyman, Paula. 1998. Gender and the Immigrant Jewish Experience in the

United States. In *Jewish Women in Historical Perspective*. Judith Baskin, ed. Pp. 312–336. Detroit: Wayne State University Press.

Jackson, Walter. 1986. Melville Herskovits and the Search for Afro-American Culture. In *Malinowski, Rivers, Benedict and Others: Essays on Culture and Personality*. George Stocking, ed. History of Anthropology, vol. 4. Pp. 95–126. Madison: University of Wisconsin Press.

——. 1990. *Gunnar Myrdal and America's Conscience: Social Engineering and Racial Liberalism, 1938–1987*. Chapel Hill: University of North Carolina Press.

Jenness, Diamond. 1935. *The Ojibwa Indians of Parry Island, Their Social and Religious Life*. Bulletin no. 78. Anthropological series no. 17. Ottawa: National Museum of Canada.

Jensen, Joan M., and Lois Scharf. 1983. Introduction. In *Decades of Discontent: The Women's Movement, 1920–1940*. Lois Scharf and Joan Jensen, eds. Pp. 3–18. Westport CT: Greenwood Press.

Johnson, James Weldon. 1968[1930]. *Black Manhattan*. New York: Arno Press.

Johnston, Basil. 1982. *Ojibwa Ceremonies*. Toronto: McClelland and Stewart.

Jones, Peter. 1861. *History of the Ojibway Indians*. London: A. W. Bennett.

Kaberry, Phyllis. 1939. *Aboriginal Woman: Sacred and Profane*. London: Routledge.

——. 1952. *Women of the Grassfields*. London: Her Majesty's Stationery Office.

Kardiner, Abram, ed. 1939. *The Individual and His Society*. New York: Columbia University Press.

Kehoe, Alice Beck. 1996. Transcribing Insima, a Blackfoot "Old Lady." In *Reading beyond Words: Contexts for Native History*. Jennifer Brown and Elizabeth Vibert, eds. Pp. 381–402. Peterborough ON: Broadview Press.

Kendall, Laurel. 1985. *Shamans, Housewives, and Other Restless Spirits: Women in Korean Ritual Life*. Honolulu: University of Hawaii Press.

Kohl, Johann. 1985[1860]. *Kitchi-Gami: Life among the Lake Superior Ojibway*. St. Paul: Minnesota Historical Society.

Krogman, Walter. 1947. Study of Cult of Brazilian City of Women. Review of *The City of Women*. *Chicago Sunday Tribune*, May 25. Photocopy.

Kulick, D. 1997. The Gender of Brazilian Transgendered Prostitutes. *American Anthropologist* 99(3):574–585.

Lamphere, Louise. 1993. Gladys Reichard among the Navajo. In *Hidden Scholars: Women Anthropologists and the Native American Southwest*. Nancy Parezo, ed. Pp. 157–188. Albuquerque: University of New Mexico Press.

——. 1995. Feminist Anthropology: The Legacy of Elsie Clews Parsons.

In *Women Writing Culture*. Ruth Behar and Deborah Gordon, eds. Pp. 85–103. Berkeley: University of California Press.

Lang, Sabine. 1997. There Is More Than Just Men and Women: Gender Variance in North America. In *Gender Reversals and Gender Culture*. Sabrina Petra Ramet, ed. Pp. 183–196. London: Routledge.

———. 1998. *Men as Women, Women as Men: Changing Gender in Native American Cultures*. John L. Vantine, trans. Austin: University of Texas Press.

Lapsley, Hilary. 1999. *Margaret Mead and Ruth Benedict: The Kinship of Women*. Amherst: University of Massachusetts Press.

Laslett, Barbara. 1991. Biography as Historical Sociology: The Case of William Fielding Ogburn. *Theory and Society* 20:511–38.

Leacock, Eleanor. 1954. The Montagnais "Hunting Territory" and the Fur Trade. *American Anthropologist* 56(5):50–59. Memoir 78. Washington DC: American Anthropological Association.

———. 1978. Women's Status in Egalitarian Society: Implications for Social Evolution. *Current Anthropology* 19(2):247–275.

Leacock, Seth, and Ruth Leacock. 1975. *Spirits of the Deep: A Study of an Afro-Brazilian Cult*. New York: Anchor Books.

Lee, Hermione. 1997. *Virginia Woolf*. London: Vintage.

Long, John. 1974[1791]. *Voyages and Travels of an Indian Interpreter and Trader*. Toronto: Coles.

Lowie, Robert. 1937. *History of Ethnological Theory*. New York: Farrar and Rinehart.

Lurie, Nancy. 1966. Women in Early American Anthropology. In *Pioneers of American Anthropology: The Uses of Biography*. June Helm, ed. Pp. 29–81. Seattle: University of Washington Press.

Lutz, Catherine. 1995. The Gender of Theory. In *Women Writing Culture*. Ruth Behar and Deborah Gordon, eds. Pp. 249–266. Berkeley: University of California Press.

Mageo, Jeanette Marie. 1996. Spirit Girls and Marines: Possession and Ethnopsychiatry as Historical Discourse in Samoa. *American Ethnologist* 23(1):61–82.

Malcolm, Janet. 2001. Justice to J. D. Salinger. *New York Review of Books* 48(10):16–22.

Marcus, Jane. 1988. *Art and Anger: Reading Like a Woman*. Columbus: Ohio State University Press.

Mark, Joan. 1988. *A Stranger in Her Native Land: Alice Fletcher and the American Indians*. Lincoln: University of Nebraska Press.

Martin, Biddy. 1988. Lesbian Identity and Autobiographical Difference[s]. In *Life/Lines: Theorizing Women's Autobiography*. Bella Brodzki and Celeste Schenck, eds. Pp. 77–108. Ithaca: Cornell University Press.

Matthews, Maureen, and Roger Roulette. 1996. Fair Wind's Dream: Naami-wan Obawaajigewin. In Reading beyond Words: Contexts for Native History. Jennifer Brown and Elizabeth Vibert, eds. Pp. 330–359. Peterborough ON: Broadview Press.

McCarthy Brown, Karen. 1991. Mama Lola: A Vodou Priestess in Brooklyn. Berkeley: University of California Press.

McMillan, Robert. 1986. The Study of Anthropology, 1931 to 1937, at Columbia University and the University of Chicago. Ph.D. dissertation. York University, North York ON.

Mead, Margaret. 1937. Introduction. Cooperation and Competition among Primitive Peoples. New York: McGraw Hill.

———. 1952. Foreword. Life Is with People: The Culture of the Shtetl. By Mark Zborowski and Elizabeth Herzog. Pp. 11–21. New York: Schocken Books.

———. 1959. An Anthropologist at Work: Writings of Ruth Benedict. Boston: Houghton Mifflin.

Medicine, Beatrice. 1983. "Warrior Women" — Sex Role Alternatives for Plain Indian Women. In The Hidden Half: Studies of Plains Indian Women. Patricia Albers and Beatrice Medicine, eds. Pp. 267–280. New York: University Press of America.

Merriam, Alan. 1964. Obituary. Melville J. Herskovits, 1895–1963. American Anthropologist 66: 3–109.

Meyer, Roy. 1969. Review of The Mystic Lake Sioux in Minnesota History. Summer. Photocopy.

Mintz, Sidney. 1981. Ruth Benedict. In Totems and Teachers: Perspectives on the History of Anthropology. S. Silverman, ed. Pp. 141–168. New York: Columbia University Press.

———. 1990[1941]. Introduction. The Myth of the Negro Past. By Melville Herskovits. 2nd ed. Boston: Beacon Press.

Mishnun, Virginia. 1947. Review of The City of Women. Nation 165 (August 2): 128. Photocopy.

Modell, Judith. 1983. Ruth Benedict: Patterns of a Life. Philadelphia: University of Pennsylvania Press.

Moore, Henrietta. 1988. Feminism and Anthropology. Minneapolis: University of Minnesota Press.

Murray, Stephen O. 1981. The Canadian "Winter" of Edward Sapir. Historiographia Linguistica 6: 63–68.

———. 1997. Explaining Away Same-Sex Sexuality When It Obtrudes on Anthropologists' Attention. Anthropology Today 13(3):2–5.

———. 2000. Homosexualities. Chicago: University of Chicago Press.

Myrdal, Gunnar. 1962[1944]. An American Dilemma: The Negro Problem and Modern Democracy. 2 vols. New York: Harper.

Nina Rodrigues, Raymundo. 1935. *O animismo fetichista dos negros bahianos.* Rio de Janeiro: Civilização Brasileira.

——. 1976[1932]. *Os africanos no Brasil.* 4th ed. São Paulo: Companhia Editora Nacional.

Oliveira, Waldir Freitas, and Vivaldo da Costa Lima. 1987. *Cartas de Edison Carneiro a Artur Ramos.* São Paulo: Editora Corrupio.

Parezo, Nancy, ed. 1993. *Hidden Scholars: Women Anthropologists and the Native American Southwest.* Albuquerque: University of New Mexico Press.

Passerini, Luisa. 1989. Women's Personal Narratives: Myths, Experiences, and Emotions. In *Interpreting Women's Lives: Feminist Theory and Personal Narratives.* Personal Narratives Group, ed. Pp. 189–197. Bloomington: Indiana University Press.

Pierson, Donald. 1942. *Negroes in Brazil: A Study of Race Contact in Bahia.* Chicago: University of Chicago Press.

Pollnac, Richard. 1971. Review of *The Prairie Potawatomi. Plains Anthropologist* 16(52). Photocopy.

Potash, Betty. 1989. Gender Relations in Sub-Saharan Africa. In *Gender and Anthropology: Critical Reviews for Teaching.* Sandra Morgen, ed. Pp. 189–227. Washington DC: American Anthropological Association.

Poznanski, Gitel. 1947. Review of *The City of Women. New York Times,* August 3:22. Photocopy.

Prell, Riv-Ellen. 1999. *Fighting to Become American: Jews, Gender and the Anxiety of Assimilation.* Boston: Beacon Press.

Ramos, Arthur (Artur). 1934. *O negro brasileiro—etnografia religiosa e psicanálise.* Rio de Janeiro: Civilização Brasileira.

——. 1935. *O folk-lore negro do Brasil.* Rio de Janeiro: Civilização Brasileira.

——. 1940. Report to the Myrdal Commission. Unpublished.

——. 1942. *A Aculturação negra no Brasil.* São Paulo: Companhia Editora Nacional.

Reichard, Gladys. 1939. *Dezba, Woman of the Desert.* New York: J. J. Augustin.

Reichmann, R., ed. 1999. *Race in Contemporary Brazil.* University Park: Pennsylvania State University Press.

Rogers, Edward. 1962. *The Round Lake Ojibwa.* Toronto: Ontario Department of Lands and Forests.

——. 1969. Review of *Ojibwa Religion and the Midéwiwin. American Anthropologist* 71(3):530–532.

Roscoe, Will. 1991. *The Zuni Man-Woman.* Albuquerque: University of New Mexico Press.

——. 1998. *Changing Ones: Third and Fourth Genders in Native North America.* London: Macmillan.

Rossiter, Margaret. 1982. *Women Scientists in America: Struggles and Strategies to 1940*. Baltimore: Johns Hopkins University Press.

Ryan, Mary. 1983. The Projection of a New Womanhood: The Movie Moderns in the 1920's. In *Decades of Discontent: The Women's Movement, 1920–1940*. Lois Scharf and Joan Jensen, eds. Pp. 113–130. Westport CT: Greenwood Press.

Santee, J. F. 1948. Review of *The City of Women. Social Studies*, January. Photocopy.

Sapir, Edward. 1924. Culture, Genuine and Spurious. *American Journal of Sociology* 29:401–29.

Schackelford, Nigel. 1947. Negroes Living sans Racialism. Review of *The City of Women. Lexington Herald-Leader*, July 13. Photocopy.

Scharf, Lois, and Joan Jensen, eds. 1983. Introduction. *Decades of Discontent: The Women's Movement, 1920–1940*. Pp. 3–18. Westport CT: Greenwood Press.

Schuyler, Josephine. 1947. Women in Brazil's Black City. Review of *The City of Women. Pittsburgh Courier*, November 22. Photocopy.

Sharp, Henry S. 1994. Asymmetric Equals: Women and Men among the Chipewyan. In *Women and Power in Native North America*. Laura F. Klein and Lillian A. Ackerman, eds. Pp. 46–74. Norman: University of Oklahoma Press.

Silverman, Sydel. 1981. Introduction. In *Totems and Teachers: Perspectives on the History of Anthropology*. Pp. ix–xv. New York: Columbia University Press.

Silverstein, Leni. 1994. Candomblé Authenticity Struggles and the Brazilian National Project: Gender, Race, Religion, and Power in Brazil. Ph.D. dissertation, New School for Social Research.

Smith-Rosenberg, Carroll. 1985. *Disorderly Conduct: Visions of Gender in Victorian America*. New York: Alfred A. Knopf.

———. 1989. The Body Politic. In *Coming to Terms: Feminism, Theory and Politics*. Elizabeth Weed, ed. Pp. 101–121. London: Routledge.

Speck, Frank. 1915. The Family Hunting Band as the Basis of Algonkian Social Organization. *American Anthropologist* 17:289–305.

Spencer, Jonathan. 1989. Anthropology as a Kind of Writing. *Man* 24:145–164.

Stack, Carol B. 1974. *All Our Kin: Strategies for Survival in a Black Community*. New York: Harper and Row.

Steward, Julian. 1936. The Economic and Social Basis of Primitive Bands. In *Essays in Honor of A. L. Kroeber*. Robert H. Lowie, ed. Pp. 331–350. Berkeley: University of California Press.

Stocking, George W., Jr., ed. 1974. *The Shaping of American Anthropology, 1883–1911: A Franz Boas Reader*. New York: Basic Books.

———. 1992. *The Ethnographer's Magic and Other Essays in the History of Anthropology*. Madison: University of Wisconsin Press.

Stolcke, Verena. 1998. Brasil: Una nación vista a través del cristal de la "raza." *Revista de Cultura Brasileña* 1 (March):51–66.

Strachey, Lytton. 1988[1918]. *Eminent Victorians*. Illus. ed. London: Bloomsbury.

Tedlock, Barbara. 1995. Works and Wives: On the Sexual Division of Textual Labor. In *Women Writing Culture*. Ruth Behar and Deborah Gordon, eds. Pp. 267–286. Berkeley: University of California Press.

Thompson, Robert Faris. 1993. *Face of the Gods: Art and Altars of Africa and the African Americas*. New York: Museum for African Art.

Todd, Ellen Wiley. 1993. *The "New Woman" Revised: Painting and Gender Politics on Fourteenth Street*. Berkeley: University of California Press.

Van Kirk, Sylvia. 1980. *"Many Tender Ties": Women in Fur Trade Society, 1670–1870*. Winnipeg: Watson and Dyer.

Vennum, Thomas, Jr. 1982. *The Ojibwa Dream Dance Drum: Its History and Construction*. Washington DC: Smithsonian Institution.

Vincent, Joan. 1991. Engaging Historicism. In *Recapturing Anthropology: Working in the Present*. Richard G. Fox, ed. Pp. 45–58. Santa Fe: School of American Research Press.

Wafer, Jim. 1991. *The Taste of Blood: Spirit Possession in Brazilian Candomblé*. Philadelphia: University of Pennsylvania Press.

Wagley, Charles. 1952. *Race and Class in Rural Brazil*. New York: Russell and Russell.

———. 1977. *Welcome of Tears: The Tapirapé Indians of Central Brazil*. Prospect Heights IL: Waveland Press.

———. 1979. Anthropology and Brazilian National Identity. In *Brazil: Anthropological Perspectives. Essays in Honor of Charles Wagley*. Maxine Margolis and William Carter, eds. New York: Columbia University Press.

Waisberg, Leo G., and Tim E. Holzkamm. 1993. "A Tendency to Discourage Them from Cultivating": Ojibwa Agriculture and Indian Affairs Administration in Northwestern Ontario. *Ethnohistory* 40(2):175–211.

Wallace, Anthony. 1956. Revitalization Movements: Some Theoretical Considerations for Their Comparative Study. *American Anthropologist* 58:264–281.

Ware, Susan. 1992. Unlocking the Porter-Dewson Friendship: A Challenge for a Feminist Biographer. In *The Challenge of Feminist Biography: Writing the Lives of Modern American Women*. Sara Alpern et al., eds. Pp. 51–64. Urbana: University of Illinois Press.

——. 1993. *Still Missing: Amelia Earhart and the Search for Modern Feminism.* New York: W. W. Norton.

Weinberg, Sidney. 1988. *The World of Our Mothers: The Lives of Jewish Immigrant Women.* Chapel Hill: University of North Carolina Press.

Wexler, Alice. 1992. Emma Goldman and the Anxiety of Biography. In *The Challenge of Feminist Biography: Writing the Lives of Modern American Women.* Sara Alpern, ed. Pp. 34–50. Urbana: University of Illinois Press.

White, Leslie. 1949. *The Science of Culture.* New York: Grove Press.

——. 1959. *The Evolution of Culture.* New York: McGraw Hill.

Whitehead, Harriet. 1981. The Bow and the Burden Strap: A New Look at Institutionalized Homosexuality in Native North America. In *Sexual Meanings: The Cultural Construction of Gender and Sexuality.* Sherry Ortner and Harriet Whitehead, eds. Pp. 80–115. Cambridge: Cambridge University Press.

Williams, Walter L. 1992. *The Spirit and the Flesh: Sexual Diversity in American Indian Culture.* 2nd. ed. Boston: Beacon Press.

Wilson, Bryan. 1973. *Magic and the Millennium: A Sociological Study of Religious Movements of Protest among Tribal and Third-World Peoples.* New York: Harper and Row.

Wolfe, Bertram. 1947. Candomblé. Review of *The City of Women. New York Herald Tribune,* August 24. Photocopy.

Worsley, Peter. 1968[1957]. *The Trumpet Shall Sound: A Study of "Cargo" Cults in Melanesia.* 2nd ed. New York: Schocken Books.

Index

African American culture, 44–45, 181–182, 186, 193, 196, 197, 223

Afro-Brazilian culture, 157–158; as African survival, 152, 162; and Brazilian national culture, 156–159, 205, 217; candomblé, 149, 162–166, 193–195; matriarchy, 149; and women, 149, 151, 193–194, 215. *See also* candomblé

Afro-Brazilian studies, 151, 156, 162, 164, 169–170

Alexander, Herbert, 104–105

Amado, Jorge, 156

The Amalgamated Clothing Workers of America, 24–27; and education, 25–26; and women, 25–28. *See also* Schlossberg, Joseph

An American Dilemma, 180–182. *See also* Myrdal, Gunnar

anthropology, 12; and the "abnormal," 58–61; canon-building, 6–7, 152, 224; at Columbia, 52–53, 259 n.5; feminist, 4–5; feminist history of, 5–6; fieldwork, 51, 105; and gender, 4–5; graduate training, 259 n.6; history of, 5–8, 13, 224, 248; patron-client relations in, 7, 12, 152, 198, 263 n.13; women in, 5–6, 9, 54–56, 91, 231, 245, 260 n.7

autobiography, 108

Babcock, Barbara, 5–6, 55

Bachofen, Johann, 149

Bahia, 149, 151, 156, 160–169, 198

Baker, Lee, 180–182

Baldus, Herbert, 270 n.6

Barnouw, Victor, 121, 129

Bateson, Gregory, 184, 187

Bee, Robert, 137, 139–140

Benedict, Ruth: and the "abnormal," 58–61; and anthropology, 262 n.11; and culture and personality, 260 n.8; culture theory of, 51, 52, 57–59, 247; death of, 230; on life history method, 60; and Margaret Mead, 8–9, 14, 32, 187–188, 200–202, 255 n.3; as mentor, 54, 58; as patron, 109, 112, 121; and teaching, 56–58, 261 n.9; as thesis supervisor, 61. *See also* Landes, Ruth; Mead, Margaret

Ben-Gurion, David, 24, 254 n.6

berdache, 141–145, 164, 194, 267 n.4, 268 n.5

biography, 8–9; feminist, 8; as historical anthropology, 7

Boas, Franz, 14, 19, 42–44, 50, 125, 155, 157, 204; anthropology of, 49–54, 191; and Columbia University, 259 n.5; and Gilberto Freyre, 155; on women and marriage, 258 n.1

Bonfim, Martiniano do, 151, 213–214

Brazil: anthropology in, 157, 170, 177–178, 197; Estado Novo, 158, 209; as racial democracy, 155, 209. *See also* Afro-Brazilian culture; Afro-Brazilian studies; Bahia; candomblé

Bunche, Ralph, 182, 271 n.2 n.3

Bunzel, Ruth, 134, 167, 260 n.8

caboclo, 56, 166, 200, 213–215
Caffrey, Margaret, 58
Callender, Charles, 132
Cameron, Elspeth, 9–10
candomblé, 12, 15, 162–166, 186, 200, 209, 212, 215, 223; history of, 269 n.4; as mutual aid associations, 149, 165, 216; and women, 149, 151, 193–194, 198–199, 206, 212, 222
canon-making, 6–7, 224, 248
capoeira, 166, 185
The Carnegie Foundation, 174, 180, 182
Carneiro, Edison, 151, 156, 164, 166, 168–169, 176–179, 190, 195, 196, 204, 206, 208, 210, 213–217, 224; later career of, 269 n.5; on meeting Landes, 166; and Portuguese translation of The City of Women, 242; and Second Afro-Brazilian Congress, 151, 156. See also Landes, Ruth
Chilvers, Sally, 234–235
The City of Women, 15, 152, 203–205, 207, 211, 221–225, 248; second edition of, 251; Portuguese translation of, 242, 251; publication of, 227, 230–231
Clifton, James, 140, 152
Columbia University, 32, 50, 52–54, 109, 121, 145, 155, 170, 173
companionate marriage, 39–41
Cooper, Father John, 62
Corrêa, Mariza, 152–153, 169
Cott, Nancy, 39, 41
cross-cousins, 72–73, 116, 131, 144
Cruikshank, Julie, 98
cultural relativism, 50–51, 250
culture: patterns, 108; and personality, 51–52, 187–188; and race, 155; theory of, 51–53. See also Benedict, Ruth; Landes, Ruth

Deloria, Ella, 54
Densmore, Frances, 71, 122–129, 170,

265 n.6; and the Bureau of American Ethnology, 123; and Alice Cunningham Fletcher, 123
Drum Dance, 135–139
Du Bois, Cora, 260–261 n.8
DuBois, W. E. B., 155, 256–257 n.6, 271 n.2
Dunning, William, 102, 120

Estado Novo (New State). See Brazil
ethnography, 4–6, 89–90, 108, 224–225, 248; feminist, 4–5
eugenics, 156, 159

feminism, 37, 39, 41–42, 255 n.2 n.4; and anthropology, 4–6, 56; and biography, 8
Firth, Raymond, 235
Fisk University, 145, 150–151, 191, 222, 268 n.1
Fletcher, Alice Cunningham, 54, 123
Ford, Arnold J., 43–45, 257 n.8
Fortune, Reo, 112
Frazier, E. Franklin, 181–182, 186
Freyre, Gilberto, 155–156, 196; and First Afro-Brazilian Congress, 156
Friedl, Ernestine, 263–264 n.2

Garvey, Marcus, 45, 256 n.6
gender, 12–14, 161, 204, 217, 224–225; in anthropology, 4–5, 96, 102; and diversity, 141–145, 267 n.4, 268 n.5; theories of, 77, 96–101; and social change, 84–85, 144–145
Goldenweiser, Alexander, 43
Goldfrank, Esther, 253 n.2
Goldman, Emma, 32, 241
Gordon, Deborah, 91
Grossman, Anna, 19–22, 28–35
guardian spirit concept, 61, 110, 117

Hallowell, A. Irving, 61–62, 71–73, 101–102, 263–264 n.2
Handler, Richard, 49

Haraway, Donna, 108
Harlem, 42–46; Black Jews in, 42–46, 256 n.5, 257 n.7 n.8
Harlem Renaissance, 42, 44, 45, 150, 256–257 n.6
Heilbrun, Carolyn, 10–11
Henry, Jules, 113, 134, 177, 238, 267 n.2
Herskovits, Frances, 54
Herskovits, Melville, 152, 156–157, 162, 177, 179, 182, 184, 187–193, 196–198, 202, 221–224, 272 n.8; and African survival, 182, 190, 196, 247; and *The City of Women*, 192, 222–224; *Life in a Haitian Village*, 189; *The Myth of the Negro Past*, 196; and Arthur Ramos, 152, 157, 197–198. *See also* Landes, Ruth; Ramos, Arthur
homosexuality, 40–41, 185, 198–200; and feminism, 42. *See also* Landes, Ruth
Hurston, Zora Neale, 54, 149, 221

Imes, Elmer, 150–151, 179, 269 n.5
Indian Reorganization Act of 1934, 136

Jackson, Walter, 181, 183
Jenness, Diamond, 61–62, 262–263 n.13
Johnson, Charles, 150, 182, 193, 231
Johnson, Guy, 182–184, 186–188, 192
Johnson, James Weldon, 44–45

Kaberry, Phyllis, 14, 234
kinship, 72–73, 113
Klineberg, Otto, 182, 187
Kroeber, A. L., 52

labor movement, 24–27; and women, 25–28. *See also The Amalgamated Clothing Workers of America*; Schlossberg, Joseph

Landes, Ruth: and acculturation, 15, 42, 44, 46, 53, 61, 85, 110–113, 127, 133, 139, 140, 144, 151, 162, 204, 212, 224–225, 247; and the American Jewish Congress, 32, 229–230; and anti-semitism, 173–174; autobiographical writing of, 46–48, 106, 108, 236; awards received, 244–245; and Ruth Benedict, 12, 19, 49, 103, 107, 167–168, 171, 174–175, 187, 200–202, 227–229, 231–233 (*see also* Benedict, Ruth); on bilingualism, 243; and Franz Boas, 44, 49; on the body, 218–220; in Brazil, 151, 156, 159–176, 205–211, 217, 241–242; in California, 229, 236; in Canada, 19, 71–72, 239–241, 243; and Carnegie Foundation Myrdal Commission, 179–180, 183–187, 196; and Edison Carneiro, 166, 169, 176–179, 190, 204, 206, 208, 210–211, 214–217 (*see also* Carneiro, Edison); and communism, 168; and cultural analysis, 152; death of, 246; divorce of, 48; education of, 12, 28, 38; in England, 234–235; and ethnography, 13, 59, 89, 97, 132, 137, 152, 205, 225, 247–249; and Fair Employment Practices Commission, 228; and feminism, 39, 41–42, 87, 103, 248; and fieldwork, 105, 185–186, 194–195, 207–209, 223–224, 247, 249–250; as fieldworker, 58, 72–73, 103, 109, 112, 159, 207–208, 223–224; and finding anthropology, 10, 14, 19, 31, 42–44, 48, 50; at Fisk, 145, 150, 244, 247; and Fulbright fellowship, 231–235; and gender, 13–14, 96–101, 103–104, 144, 151, 204, 224–225, 247; in Harlem, 43–46; and Melville Herskovits, 188–193, 197–198 (*see also* Herskovits, Melville); on homosexuality, 40,

Landes, Ruth (*continued*)
42, 144, 149–150, 152, 159, 164, 169, 185, 189–190, 193–196, 197, 198–202, 222; as immigrant daughter, 12, 14, 20, 27–28, 31–32, 34, 38, 43, 91–92; and individual agency, 75, 107, 136, 140; and individualism, 7, 11–12, 39, 74–77, 97; on Jewish immigrant family life, 32–34; on Jews, 230; in Kansas, 109, 134–146; and life history method, 96–97; in Los Angeles, 229–230, 236; at McMaster University, 238–246; at Manitou Rapids, 71–72, 83; marginality of, 5–8, 15, 19, 61, 91, 149, 246–248; and marriage, 11, 12, 28, 31, 34, 38–41, 46–48, 92, 99–101, 102, 180, 218, 227–229, 233–234, 235; on matriarchy, 149–150, 152, 169, 174, 189–190, 193–195, 197, 198–199, 218; and Margaret Mead, 13, 75–76, 179–180, 187–188, 200–202, 230–234, 236–238, 244 (*see also* Mead, Margaret); in Nashville, 150–151; as New Woman, 14, 39–42, 100; and patron-client relations, 7, 12–13, 152, 198; at Prairie Island, 125–133; on race, 151, 204–212, 214–215, 217, 224, 245, 247; and Arthur Ramos, 152, 156, 161, 169, 178, 186, 190–198 (*see also* Ramos, Arthur); at Red Lake, 109–117; in Red Wing, 109, 124–129; and religion, 46, 85, 151, 209; and retirement, 243–244; and Will Rogers, 114–117, 122, 141; seeking employment, 9, 32, 35, 58, 107, 109, 114, 167–168, 172, 174–175, 203, 227, 229, 231–232, 234, 236–237; and Seminar on Cooperation and Competition among Primitive Peoples, 76–77; and science, 104, 204–209, 225; on social class, 26–27, 160–161, 186, 205, 207, 209–211,

247; and social work, 42–44; and syncretism, 135, 137, 139, 140, 151; theory of culture of, 7, 14–15, 53, 59, 75, 108, 127, 131, 137, 139, 152, 170, 191, 204, 212, 215, 224, 245, 247, 250; as urban anthropologist, 46, 151; in Washington, 228; and Maggie Wilson, 14, 71–72, 75, 89–92, 122 (*see also* Wilson, Maggie); on women in anthropology, 56, 105, 245; as writer, 77, 106–108, 111, 174, 203, 212, 228, 231; and writing women's lives, 11, 31, 75
— Works: *The City of Women* (see *The City of Women*); "A Cult Matriarchate and Male Homosexuality," 152, 169, 198–200; *Culture in American Education*, 236; "The Ethos of the Negro in the New World," 184–188, 192–194; "Hypotheses Concerning the Eastern European Jewish Family," 32–34, 230; *The Mystic Lake Sioux*, 127, 129–133, 242–243, 248; "Negro Jews in Harlem," 42–46, 256 n.5; "The Ojibwa of Canada," 75–77; *Ojibwa Religion and the Midéwiwin*, 110, 117–123, 242–243, 248; *Ojibwa Sociology*, 73–75; *The Ojibwa Woman* (see *The Ojibwa Woman*); *The Prairie Potawatomi*, 135, 139–140, 150, 242–243, 248; "Tongues That Defy the State," 243–244
Landes, Victor, 28
Leach, Edmund, 234
Leacock, Eleanor, 103–104
Lesser, Alexander, 161, 171–172, 270 n.7
Levi-Strauss, Claude, 177
life histories, 4–5, 7, 60, 96–101, 107, 142
life writing, 8, 10–11, 31
Linton, Ralph, 187–188, 258 n.3, 260 n.8, 263–264 n.2

Lipkind, Walter, 151, 167, 171–173
Little, Kenneth, 231, 235
Lopez, Ignacio Lutero, 230, 235–236
Lowie, Robert, 52, 54
Lurie, Nancy, 56

Mageo, Jeannette, 212, 222
Malinowski, Bronislaw, 12, 172
marginality, 6, 15, 58–61. *See also*
    Landes, Ruth
marriage: companionate, 39–
    41; cross-cousin, 72–73; rates
    of, 38; romantic, 40. *See also*
    Landes, Ruth
Masquat, Joe, 138–139, 205
matriarchy. *See* Landes, Ruth
McMaster University, 237–246
Mead, Margaret, 13, 14, 51, 54, 179;
    and Ruth Benedict, 8–9, 200–202,
    255 n.3; and culture and per-
    sonality, 187–188, 260 n.8; death
    of, 244; Raymond Firth on, 235;
    and the Omaha, 112–113; and Re-
    search in Contemporary Cultures
    Project, 32, 230; and Seminar on
    Cooperation and Competition
    among Primitive Peoples, 76–
    77; and women in anthropology,
    201, 231. *See also* Benedict, Ruth;
    Landes, Ruth
Menininha, 210, 216, 219–220
mide (shamans), 71, 115–118
midéwiwin, 61, 110, 114–121, 138.
    *See also Ojibwa Religion and the
    Midéwiwin*
Mintz, Sidney, 61, 261 n.9
Morgan, Lewis Henry, 149
Myrdal, Gunnar, 174, 179–184, 196,
    271 n.2; on Melville Herskovits,
    272 n.8
The Mystic Lake Sioux, 110, 127, 129–
    133, 242–243, 248

narrative, 98

Ojibwa: culture of, 73–77, 83, 96;
    gender relations among, 97–101,
    104, 107; and kinship, 72–74; and
    marriage, 74, 84, 98–102; and
    notions of property, 74, 84; and
    religion, 71, 110, 117–123, 138; and
    teaching, 90
Ojibwa Religion and the Midéwiwin, 10,
    117–123, 242–243, 248
Ojibwa Sociology, 73–75
The Ojibwa Woman, 14, 88, 245, 247–
    248, 266–267 n.13; gender theory
    in, 96–101; publication of, 107–
    108, 150; reception of, in the
    discipline, 101–105, 245; sec-
    ond edition, 89, 102–104; third
    edition, 105, 251
oral tradition, 119

Parezo, Nancy, 54–56
Park, Robert, 150–151, 181, 191
Parsons, Elsie Clews, 54
Pierson, Donald, 150–152, 156, 162,
    164, 177, 191, 196
Pinski, David, 20–22
Potawatomi, 121, 129, 134–146. *See also*
    Landes
Pourchet, Maria Julia, 169, 242
The Prairie Potawatomi, 110, 135, 139–
    140, 150, 242–243, 248
Prell, Riv-Ellen, 40

Quain, Buell, 76, 151, 167, 171–173,
    175, 177, 270 n.7

race relations, 15, 151–152, 155, 161,
    180–184, 205–206, 209, 211
racial democracy. *See* Brazil
Radcliffe-Brown, Alfred Reginald,
    113–114
Radin, Paul, 52
Ramos, Arthur, 151–152, 156–162, 164,
    166, 169, 176–179, 186, 187, 190–
    198, 202, 222, 224, 268 n.1; and

Ramos, Arthur (continued)
    Melville Herskovits, 152, 157, 197–
    198, 271 n.5. See also Herskovits,
    Melville; Landes, Ruth
Reichard, Gladys, 14, 91
religion: Afro-Brazilian, 149, 151,
    157, 162–166, 196, 215, 223; Chip-
    pewa, 114; Ojibwa, 71, 110, 117–123,
    138; Potawatomi, 135–140. See
    also candomblé; Landes, Ruth;
    midéwiwin
revitalization movements, 46, 71,
    135, 137, 139
Rodrigues, Raymundo Nina, 151,
    157, 162, 164, 193, 213, 216
Rogers, Edward, 120
Rogers, Will, 114–117, 122–123, 141,
    205; and the midéwiwin, 117–123.
    See also Landes, Ruth
romantic primitivism, 211–212,
    214, 225
Rouillard, Grace, 125–126, 129–133

Salvador, 161–169 (see also Bahia)
Santee Sioux, 125–133
Santos, Eugenia Anna dos Santos
    (Anninha), 151
Sapir, Edward, 51, 61, 201, 247, 260
    n.8
Schlossberg, Joseph, 22–32, 35,
    254 n.6; and the Amalgamated
    Clothing Workers of America, 24–
    27; and David Ben-Gurion, 24;
    and Labor Zionism, 24; in Red
    Wing, 128
shamanism, 107, 115–118
Silverman, Sydel, 7
Sioux, 125–133; gender relations
    among, 141, 143–144; and Ojibwa,
    126, 129–130; social organization,
    127, 130–132
Slobodin, Richard, 11, 218, 237, 240
Smith, Stevie, 234

Smith-Rosenberg, Carroll, 12, 41
Speck, Frank, 74
Stack, Carol, 132
Steinem, Gloria, 10
Steward, Julian, 52, 149–150
Stocking, George, 7
syncretism, 135, 137, 139, 151

Tax, Sol, 113–114
Topash, Tom, 134, 136, 137–138, 205
Torres, Heloisa Alberto, 156, 169–176
trait distribution studies, 51–53,
    184–188
transvestism, 141–145, 164, 185, 189–
    190, 194–197, 201, 213, 216

Vargas, Getúlio, 157–158, 209, 269 n.2
Vincent, Joan, 6

Wagley, Charles, 151, 161, 167, 170–
    173, 270 n.6
Washington, Booker T., 155, 257 n.7
whitening, 159, 210, 213
Wilson, Maggie, 71–72, 205; and
    acculturation, 81, 85; as biogra-
    pher, 89; childhood of, 77–81; as
    craftswoman, 90–91; and Frances
    Densmore, 123; as ethnologist,
    89; as interpreter, 62; at Manitou
    Rapids, 81–85; marginality of,
    91–92; on marriage, 84–85, 99–
    101; as matriarch, 89; and Ojibwa
    religion, 118–121; as storyteller, 89,
    92–96, 97–101, 106; as teacher, 11,
    75, 90, 97; as visionary, 85–88, 90.
    See also Landes, Ruth
women: Afro-Brazilian, 149, 159,
    164–165, 193, 212; and the Ameri-
    can labor movement, 25–28;
    anthropologists and Native
    American women, 91; in anthro-
    pology, 5–6, 54–56, 170, 231, 245,
    259 n.6, 260 n.7; and education,

38; in hunter-gatherer studies, 102; Jewish immigrant, 25–28, 38; and marriage in the 1920s, 38–42; The New Woman, 39, 41, 254 n.1, 255 n.2; in Ojibwa culture, 97–

102; in "primitive society," 105, 108; in universities, 259 n.6

Woolf, Virginia, 10

Zborowski, Mark, 32–33, 230

In the Critical Studies in the History of Anthropology series

Invisible Genealogies: A History of Americanist Anthropology by Regna Darnell

The Shaping of American Ethnography: The Wilkes Exploring Expedition, 1838–1842 by Barry Alan Joyce

Ruth Landes: A Life in Anthropology by Sally Cole